THE CHARLETON LINE:

AWCO's Decorations on Fenton, Cambridge, Consolidated, Westmoreland, Duncan & Miller, Heisey, Imperial, Limoges, and Others.

Michael and Lori Palmer

Dedication

This book is respectfully dedicated to the late William Heacock. He was a modest man, meticulous in his methods, and was never above pointing out his errors in any of his previous publications. Although never seeking accolades from the world, he has received the highest praise of all, the universal respect and admiration of his peers. His thirst for knowledge was insatiable and his acquired expertise he shared selflessly. His works have become and will remain the standard to which all others are judged. Through his tireless efforts he enabled collectors to understand and more fully appreciate the inherent beauty of art glass. In his books, his vivid descriptions of patterns, history, and production methods added new and meaningful depths of understanding for glass enthusiasts everywhere.

Copyright © 2002 by Michael & Lori Palmer
Library of Congress Control Number: 2002104224

All rights reserved. No part of this work may be reproduced or used in any form or by any means—graphic, electronic, or mechanical, including photocopying or information storage and retrieval systems—without written permission from the copyright holder.
"Schiffer," "Schiffer Publishing Ltd. & Design," and the "Design of pen and ink well" are registered trademarks of Schiffer Publishing Ltd.

Designed by John P. Cheek
Cover design by Bruce M. Waters
Type set in Embassy BT/Korinna BT

ISBN: 0-7643-1645-1
Printed in China
1 2 3 4

Published by Schiffer Publishing Ltd.
4880 Lower Valley Road
Atglen, PA 19310
Phone: (610) 593-1777; Fax: (610) 593-2002
E-mail: Schifferbk@aol.com
Please visit our web site catalog at
www.schifferbooks.com
We are always looking for people to write books on new and related subjects. If you have an idea for a book please contact us at the above address.

This book may be purchased from the publisher.
Include $3.95 for shipping.
Please try your bookstore first.
You may write for a free catalog.

In Europe, Schiffer books are distributed by
Bushwood Books
6 Marksbury Ave.
Kew Gardens
Surrey TW9 4JF England
Phone: 44 (0)20-8392-8585
Fax: 44 (0)20-8392-9876
E-mail: Bushwd@aol.com
Free postage in the UK. Europe: air mail at cost

Contents

Acknowledgments 4
Introduction 5
Chapter 1. History of Abels, Wasserberg, & Co. (AWCO) 7
Chapter 2. Fenton 26
Chapter 3. Cambridge 83
Chapter 4. Consolidated 107
Chapter 5. Westmoreland 121
Chapter 6. AWCO Decorations on Items by
 Unknown Manufacturers 131
Chapter 7. All Other Known Manufacturers 148
Chapter 8. Unknown Decorations on Items by
 Unknown Manufacturers 163
Chapter 9. Similarities and Identification 166
Chapter 10. Advertisements 168
Endnotes 183
Selected Bibliography 184

Acknowledgments

This book, like so many before, was made possible through the hard work of previous authors and researchers. My fading memory puts me at the risk of leaving out someone's name, and if I do so in error, it certainly does not mean that their help was not sincerely appreciated.

A very special thanks to Mr. Frank M. Fenton, retired Chairman of the Board of the Fenton Art Glass Company and current company historian. Frank gave us total access to Fenton's archives of glass and business records, which allowed the detailed history of their association with Abels, Wasserberg & Company possible. Anytime we called he was more than considerate with his time and insights and we were constantly amazed with his sharp intellect and memory. His dry humor and sparkle in his eye made us want to extend our stay for as long as possible.

All of the staff at Fenton made us very welcome and by the end of our visit we felt like family. Their warmth and generosity will never be forgotten. The Museum staff, tour guides, and administrative staff were very professional and were never to busy to answer questions or guide us in our wanderings inside the plant.

Our gratitude also is extended to Mr. John Walk, author of *The Big Book of Fenton Glass* and other Fenton books. John was very generous with his time and expertise, and was always of great encouragement throughout this project. He invited us to his home and studio, where we photographed several new Charleton items. His parents graciously fed us supper and entertained us with hilarious stories of John's childhood.

We appreciate so much the assistance of Lorraine Kovar, the leading expert and author whose detailed Westmoreland Glass books were an inexhaustible supply of new and corroborating information. Lorraine proofread the Westmoreland section and also supplied us with leads on new patterns and decorations.

Helen Klemko has authored the most accurate and comprehensive article on the history of the Abels, Wasserberg & Company (AWCO) to date. She and her husband, Steve, were always willing to accommodate our requests for help on identification and generously offered their extraordinary Charleton on Cambridge collection for documentation.

Rich and Laurie Karman, editors of The Fenton Flyer as well as avid Fenton and Charleton collectors, generously opened their home and collection to us for research. Many of the beautiful Charleton on Fenton items pictured here reside in their collection. We ate a delicious lunch there, prepared and served by Laurie on Fenton Silver Crest! It is people like Rich and Laurie that provide us with a much deeper satisfaction about being involved with a project such as this.

Charles and Mary Upton provided us with access to their fabulous Charleton "Milk" Cambridge collection as well as allowing us to document pieces in the Cambridge Glass Museum.

Mike and Cindy Arent of Cambridge Ohio graciously allowed us to use their home to document a number of their extraordinary Charleton on Cambridge items. During our visit they also invited their friends Shirley Beynon and Mike and Lisa Nielson to bring over several one of a kind Charleton/Cambridge items which are pictured in this volume.

Dean Six, glass author and researcher was most kind in allowing us to comb through the research archives at Replacements, Ltd. (1-800-REPLACE) in Greensboro, N.C. It was through his assistance that we were able to provide all of the full page Charleton advertisements found in this book.

We are also very grateful to Mr. Michael Hardy, Serials Technician, American History Branch, Smithsonian Institution, Washington D.C. Mr. Hardy allowed us full access to their periodical archives which among other items provided us with the beginning date of Abels, Wasserberg & Company.

A special thanks to Mr. Art Haney, Associate Dean of East Carolina University's Department of Fine Arts for his expertise on the various methods utilized to decorate Charleton wares.

Mr. Clay Carter, an expert horticulturalist of Greenville, NC, was instrumental in educating us in identifying the numerous types of flowers so beautifully portrayed by AWCO.

Our dear friend and co-conspirator, Mark Harrington, generously provided the camera equipment and patient guidance necessary for all of the photographs.

The Rakow Library at the Corning Museum of Glass, and more directly, Mrs. Gail Bardhan, was so helpful in providing the records archived in their collection.

We would like to offer a special thanks to Peter B. Schiffer, CEO of Schiffer Publishing Ltd. for publishing this book, and to our editor, Jeff Snyder for his enduring patience throughout this project.

As you can see, this work was aided by more than a few giants in the field of art glass. But the lesser known collectors and enthusiasts aided this work as well. After mentioning the work in progress we were assisted time and again by our friends who faithfully supplied us with information that allowed us to acquire some of the most beautiful items in our collection. I do not have room here to name them all but we would feel remiss without publicly thanking the following:

John Gager, creator and webmaster of the invaluable "Fenton Fanatics" website, (*http://www.fentonfan.com/*).

Frank Sereno, creator and moderator of the "Fenton Glass e-Group", (*http://www.egroups.com/group/fenton-glass/*).

Dan Robertson of Dapper Dan's Antiques.

Lee Modlin of Johnson's Antiques.

Ronnie and Becky Jenkins of Jenkins Antiques.

Richard and Ann Kruse of Remember When Antiques.

Valerie Sedlack and **Susan Howell**, Charleton eBay Charleton extraordinaires.

Finally, we are always interested in exchanging new information on Charleton. We may be contacted by e-mail at this address: mlpalmer@glasshousenc.com or you may write us at:

Michael & Lori Palmer
1807 Flemming School Road
Greenville, NC 27834

Introduction

When my wife and I reflect back upon what started us upon this path of glass collecting we both agree it all began with a relatively modest, yet delightful, Fenton Dusty Rose art glass basket, the first and only piece that my wife acquired before we met. It sat delicately upon an end table in our first apartment, until the birth and growing inquisitiveness of our twin boys necessitated its removal to a safer place.

This little basket, with its unassuming grace and charm, was the seed of what has become an almost overwhelming jungle of research, collecting, documenting, photographing, and writing about art glass. Not the least of this is also the appreciation we share for the joy and reflection of the beauty that Art Glass can bring into what in many respects can be a harried, hurried, and humdrum world.

Our mutual interest in art and history motivated us early on in our marriage to seek out and visit those museums and historical sites of interest in our surrounding area of the southeastern United States. We soon came to find that the places we visited were more often than not sprinkled with antique shops. Visiting most antique stores is much akin to visiting a history museum, and if the keepers are knowledgeable it can be a double treat.

There is an aroma unique to antique shops that you will find nowhere else. It defies description, yet each time you cross the threshold it descends upon you like a warm blanket, and ushers in the tingling anticipation of discovering hidden treasures. We wandered through the aisles, marveling at the craftsmanship employed by the past generations, and stumbling upon strange objects that piqued our interest.

As the world of antiques unfolded to our catlike curiosity, we began to explore the fledgling electronic aisles of eBay, the phenomenon that has revolutionized the world of collecting. Our interests in this area always seemed to be focused on art glass, especially from the turn of the twentieth century when the U.S. glass industry was in the height of tremendous growth through the vision and sweat of people such as Harry Northwood, John and Frank L. Fenton, John L. Hobbs, William Leighton, and others.

As we began to buy a piece every now and then, we also began building a small library of glass guide books, a library that now threatens to spill out of the study into our "normal" living area. Through countless hours of study and fieldwork we slowly educated ourselves enough to really be dangerous in our assumptions. After several years some of the rough corners have become smoother, but we try not to let a day pass without learning some new aspect of our hobby.

The direction that our interest followed has now lead to the publishing of this book. Early on in our "Fenton" addiction, we began to occasionally find pieces that were hand painted. Remembering that author William Heacock had briefly documented the association of Fenton with the decorating firm of Abels, Wasserberg, & Co. (AWCO), we began to learn how to distinguish between the glass Fenton decorated and the items that were done outside the factory. We later discovered that other firms besides AWCO utilized Fenton glass blanks to decorate as well, and sometimes the similarities between AWCO and the other decorators was very confusing.

In our efforts to become more knowledgeable about this decorated glassware, we found there was a dearth of published information. What little information we did uncover was often vague, and the pictures consisted of small, grainy advertisements, and the information was sometimes contradictory of other sources. As we dealt with more and more Fenton/Charleton items, we found ourselves hoping that someone would publish a definitive work on this subject to aid us with our collection. We observed that other collectors desired such a work as well and found ourselves spending more time sharing accumulated knowledge with other people with similar interests.

After a period of time we were finding many new items not seen before and we realized the scope of Charleton decorated items extended far beyond the items found on Fenton glassware. Charleton labeled items from Consolidated, Cambridge, Westmoreland, and other elegant glassware companies began to surface with regularity.

While the best known and most easily identified Charleton decorations depict hand painted roses of various types, sizes, and hues with gold accents and sometimes bows, AWCO's Charleton line was extensive and many very surprising and atypical examples have been found. From depictions of various fruit to pastoral scenes to modern geometric designs to Oriental inspired themes, all can be found in Charleton decorations.

Through further concentrated effort and study we have been able to document an astounding variety of objects decorated by AWCO. This book could be entitled, "The World of Charleton," as Charleton decorations are found on items from manufacturers all over the world.

Because of the wide range of media, varied techniques, and different blanks, some of these items would never have been linked as Charleton. It is only because AWCO utilized a very durable foil label that some of this "family" of beautifully rendered art designs is now being reunited and documented.

Enamel and china paints were employed by Charleton artists in a variety of techniques to create the beautiful decorations. Masking and spraying, syringe art, acid etching, as well as the tried and true paint brush are among the many techniques used for decorating. While most decorating companies of the era used transfers or stencils to some degree, Charleton decorations were entirely hand painted. The gold highlights and edge treatments were applied last and by a different artist in a separate area probably known as the "gold room." Since inhaled gold particles are known to be toxic (and only real gold was used in Charleton decorations), safety precautions would require proper ventilation and the wearing of masks by those decorating with gold. All of this is discussed in more detail later in the sections entitled "The Decorators" and "The Decorations."

Although the Fenton/Charleton book we originally hoped someone else would publish never materialized, we now realize that if it had, it would have only provided a portion of the information we now desire. We suspect there are only a few that share the enthusiasm we have in collecting as many different types of Charleton items as can be found. But, due to the wide spectrum of AWCO art objects, there is an excellent chance that in this book there will be something of interest to be found for even the more focused collector.

We hope that the information and the photographs of the beautiful pieces found herein will not only enlighten, but also inspire and foster the desire to acquire, preserve, appreciate, and share with others the beauty of the world of Charleton.

A Note Concerning the Prices

The prices shown are intended to be only a guide and are for pieces in mint condition. Those with chips, cracks, repairs, or excessive wear will be worth considerably less. Prices shown are based on rarity and generally reflect dealer pricing or what collectors have said they would pay for rarer pieces. Some pieces are so rare that a value cannot be established.

Charleton is virtually a new, uncharted territory, so some items believed to be rare may prove to be otherwise. In such cases, the value would decrease proportionally with the increase in availability.

It is not the intention of the authors to set or establish prices. Neither the authors nor the publisher can be held liable for any losses incurred when using the prices set forth in this book as a basis for any transaction.

In the end, the true value of any collectible is determined by the individual collector and varies considerably. Never pay more than you feel comfortable with just because of a value in a price guide.

In this volume we only list prices for Charleton decorated items. Throughout the various items pictured there are pieces that are either decorated by a known firm other than AWCO or whose decorating company is undetermined. There are no values listed for these items.

Chapter 1
Abels, Wasserberg & Company

The History

Abels, Wasserberg & Company (AWCO) was a premier interior design and lighting company, renowned for the hand painted decorations of their "Charleton" line. The company was owned and operated by Walter J. Abels and Harry Wasserberg. Their offices were located at 23 East 26th Street, New York City, and they later established a decorating studio in the city at 63 Greene Street.

Walter Jerome Abels was born on November 7th, 1893. His wife, nee Elizabeth Mackenzie Arden, was born May 25th, 1899. Elizabeth and Walter had two children, William Henry Abels born in 1924, and Ann Jane Arden Abels, born in 1930. Sadly, both of Walter and Elizabeth's children passed away in the early months of 2001.

Walter Jerome Abels, date unknown. *Photograph courtesy of Janet Eshbaugh.*

William Abels married Ann Staudinger and they have a total of five children.

Ann Jane (or simply Jane as she liked to be called) Abels married William Hall Eshbaugh and they had one child, Geoffrey Arden Eshbaugh, who later married Janet Elizabeth Russo. We will hear more of Janet Eshbaugh shortly.

Very little information has surfaced with which to cast light on Walter Abel's partner, Harry Wasserberg. Coming to the close of our research on the company we uncovered a "benevolent caricature" of Harry Wasserberg in a trade journal. Wasserberg is quoted in a couple paragraphs in some of these trade journals and then no further mention is made. In further research, we could only find one person named Harry Wasserberg in the Social Security Death Index. The birth date and location appear to be in the right range for him to be the Harry Wasserberg of AWCO. If so, Mr. Wasserberg died in March of 1964.

This is the only picture of Harry Wasserberg we were able to locate. From the September 1947 issue of *China, Glass and Decorative Accessories.*

The following is a reconstruction of the company that was made by detailing all the information we have been able to compile. This is only a small part of the story that we hope to one day tell in much fuller detail.

After three years of research, we finally found the starting date of the company. While examining records at the Smithsonian Institute in Washington, DC, the following small paragraph, from the June 1956 issue of *The Gift and Art Buyer*, under the heading "Quarter Century Club" (a series of short sketches of notable people in the giftware industry) was found:

"Walter Abels, president of Abels Wasserberg & Co., 23 E 26th St., New York, manufacturer, entered the industry in 1921 as New York salesman for Guthman-Solomon[1]. In 1926 he formed his own business, which specializes in lamps and shades. During World War II, Mr. Abels reports, the firm opened a decorating plant which is still one of the main features of the company."

Pinpointing the actual starting date of AWCO was a major finding and helped us to guide and focus our research. This information also lends support to material found in the late J. Stanley Brothers research collection.

A clipping that was hand dated "1967" in pencil by J. Stanley Brothers states that AWCO has been connected with interior design and lighting for the past forty years. By the tense of the word "has," we surmised this to mean they were still in business when this was published. The paragraph text also begins with "1927" which buttresses the handwritten date. Unfortunately, Mr. Brothers did not identify the publication from which the information was taken, although we suspect it was from *Retailing* due to its placement in his records.

Other than those in Mr. Brothers' collection, we have been unable to find copies of a periodical from that era that was known as *Retailing*. There are several different contemporary periodicals that use that name in one form or another, but none that appear to date back far enough to be of research interest. Therefore, we were not able to independently confirm this information.

The next evidence we found of the early existence of the company was derived from a listing of firms exhibiting wares at the Merchandise Mart Gift Show in Chicago. Abels, Wasserberg & Co., Inc. heads up the wholesaler list that was printed in the January 1935 edition of *The Gift and Art Buyer*.

According to Walter Abels, AWCO relied exclusively on imports during the early years of the company. These wares were much cheaper than domestic goods as they were being produced in "countries of low living standards, such as Japan, Czechoslovakia, Italy, etc." Since they did not have their own decorating studio at this time, any imported items they sold that were decorated had most likely been decorated prior to their importation.

Abels, Wasserberg & Company specialized in imported lamps and lamp parts. AWCO held the distinction of being one of the largest distributors of lamps in America during the 1940s and 1950s. Although the firm also offered a large selection of imported and domestic decorated giftware made from porcelain and glass, they were still primarily known as a lamp company, at least in the early years.

Returning to information from the Brothers' collection, Mr. Brothers included a pictorial advertisement from a Reitz Catalog, hand dated 1937, which depicts a decorated bathroom set. Although there is nothing shown in the advertisement that mentions Charleton or AWCO, Mr. Brothers has penciled above the picture "Abels, Wasserberg & Co." The decoration on this set is of a flying duck over a background of grain. The designs on these items do not appear to be a transfer as each scene differs slightly, although that is not conclusive evidence of it being hand decorated. Not typical of AWCO's 1940s American hand painted work, this set, if from 1937, precedes AWCO's own decorating department and was most likely decorated prior to importation.

We realize these penciled in remarks cannot be considered absolute proof for dating or attribution until a copy of *Retailing* can be located and studied; yet, there is no evidence to challenge the identification. Since other penciled in remarks made by Mr. Brothers have been verified by comparing them with the original trade journals, there is every reason to believe that this information is also accurate.

According to the late William Heacock, who was a noted glass expert and author, Mr. Brothers intended to publish information gleaned from these sources, but died before the project was completed. After his death, the collection was sold and parceled out to individual researchers as well as the Corning Museum of Glass in New York. Until recently, the J. Stanley Brothers collection was basically the only means that researchers had at their disposal to positively identify and date Charleton items with no label.

Fortunately, we were able to find other important trade journal articles independent of Mr. Brothers' collection, and much of this new information is being republished here for the first time. These records were crucial in adding to AWCO's sparse history.

As far as we know, Helen Klemko wrote the first detailed article on the history of AWCO, published in the August 1996 edition of *Glass Digest*. This overall accurate article was written with an emphasis on AWCO's decoration of Cambridge glassware. She and her husband Steve are avid collectors of both plain and decorated Cambridge, and many of the stunning pieces shown in this book reside in their collection. Like us, Helen also partially relied on the research material gleaned from the J. Stanley Brothers collection in detailing AWCO's history. For those who do not have access to Helen Klemko's article, we have echoed some of the same details she wrote about in order to benefit our readers.

The earliest known Charleton labeled piece in a collection that we are aware of is a Limoges porcelain vase that was designed and produced by the firm of Jean Pouyat, later owned by the Limoges firm of Bawo-Dotter (see page 160). The company that produced this white ware vase closed permanently in 1932. More detail on this piece is included in Chapter Seven, entitled "All Other Known Manufacturers."

An advertisement from the Brothers collection, with the hand written date of "July, 1943," was identified as being taken from *The Gift and Art Buyer* and showed Charleton decorated Cambridge Crown Tuscan items. This could possibly be the earliest advertisement showing items with AWCO's own decorations, as well as the first association of the word "Charleton" with the company. Again, the penciled date next to the advertisement is unconfirmed, but highly credible.

The first Charleton material that includes a confirmed, printed date is found in the October 1943 issue of the trade journal, *China and Glass*. This is the earliest established date we have found where the word "Charleton" appears in an AWCO advertisement. It portrays a wonderful full page Charleton advertisement picturing seventeen different items. This same issue also contains a reproduction of AWCO's business card and a well-written article by Walter Abels.

The impact of World War II drastically diminished AWCO's supply of imports from Europe and caused them not only to quickly turn to domestic suppliers for goods, but to also open their own decorating department in New York City. In the February 9, 1942 issue of *Retailing*, the following article appeared:

"Lamp Firm to Do Decorating and Firing"
Abels, Wasserberg & Co., Inc. has moved its factory in New York to a new location at 63 Greene Street. The space is about 1,200 square feet and the firm will now do its own decorating and firing there, shops having been installed. At its showroom address about 150 square feet have been added to form a showroom for a greatly extended giftware line. The color scheme is primarily yellow and gray.

Although no information has been found regarding AWCO's workshop location prior to the move to Greene Street, it was most likely a warehouse with an assembly area for their lamps. This previous facility was evidently located in New York, but the address is unknown. It was probably a great deal smaller as there was no room needed for firing kilns or a decorating studio.

As far as we know, AWCO's business office and main showroom was always located at 23 East 26th Street. Around the same time as the opening of their decorating department, AWCO affiliated themselves with other showrooms in Chicago and Los Angeles. A final showroom in Grand Rapids, Michigan, was added shortly thereafter. These showrooms were maintained by independent sales representatives and would have included wares from many companies besides AWCO.

AWCO's expansion blossomed during the war years and the firm established itself as a major player in the decorative gift and accessory market. One extraordinary document that noted glass researcher J. Stanley Brothers preserved was a form letter that AWCO sent to prospective distributors.

This letter reveals many fascinating facts about the company's offerings. The imagery this letter invokes should surely whet the collecting appetites of all Charleton enthusiasts. Although some information has been previously reported from this document by other authors, this is the first time the letter has been reprinted in its entirety. Dated December 21, 1943, the letter was written to the "Michigan Shop"[2] in Kalamazoo, Michigan.

> Gentlemen:
> We thank you very much for your inquiry asking for a catalog. We regret to advise that our line is so varied and of such proportions that it has been impractical to publish a catalog.
> We have in our current line of table and boudoir lamps over 375 styles each distinctively different and suitable for every type of interior decoration. The bases are made of Charleton porcelain, crystal, opal glass, cased glass, marble, metal, etc. Much of the crystal is hand cut and most of the porcelain and opal glass is hand decorated. Shades are individually designed for each lamp and all hand sewn.
> Our line of decorative gift accessories is made of Charleton Porcelain, crystal and opal glass. All are beautifully decorated by hand and are equal to the finest pieces that used to be obtained in Europe. Included are toilet sets, bottles, powder boxes, trays, desk sets, cache pots, flower pots, figurines, book ends, bath room sets, decorative plates and placques, ash trays, cigarette boxes, candy boxes, nut trays, and many other items.
> Showrooms are at 23 East 26 Street, New York, N.Y., Merchandise Mart, Room 1548, Chicago, Ill, and at the J. Marsh, 1037 No. Alvarado, Los Angeles, Cal. We hope you can visit us.
> (signed) W. Abels
> P.S. Orders are accepted only for shipment in Fall, 1944

What a wealth of information this letter provides! If only we could go back in time and walk through the showroom and see all of the marvelous items on display. Evidently business was so good that there was a one-year delay on orders, at least for new customers. Although they offered no catalog at this time, we do know they were available in later years.

This letter is also the first written account that makes mention of AWCO's marketing of "Charleton Porcelain." Although not made *by* AWCO, it is certainly possible that the porcelain was made exclusively *for* them. In later advertisements, we see this type of marketing again evidenced by references to "Charleton Limoges."

All indications point to the fact that AWCO was strictly a wholesale company that distributed their products through their own sales staff and independent representatives. Industry news reports contained very little information concerning AWCO's employees. There was also no photographic record in these trade journals of either of the owners or their associates. It could be that we just experienced bad luck in not finding the right trade journal issues, but, in the hundreds we have examined, we came away empty-handed.

Although no company records have been found for Abels, Wasserberg & Company, we have had the great fortune to establish contact with several people who supplied us with inside knowledge of the company. Each contact was "happenstance" and provided just the incentive we needed to forge ahead.

In an effort to contact anyone who might be able to provide leads to either the Abels or Wasserberg family, we posted a message on a genealogy bulletin board on the Internet expressing a desire to contact any family members. After a few months, having received no contacts, this avenue of research was forgotten.

While doing a whirlwind trip to the Fenton factory conducting research for the book, my wife lovingly stayed at home with our then two year old twins. It was she who received an e-mail from Janet Eshbaugh, a granddaughter-in-law of Walter Abels! Mrs. Eshbaugh had read our posting on the Internet and was very interested in the book we were writing. You can imagine my excitement when I called home that evening to check on my family and received this wonderful news. At last we had a lead that might provide personal insights into AWCO.

Through Mrs. Eshbaugh, we also established communications with Arden King, a granddaughter of Walter Abels. Mrs. King, like Mrs. Eshbaugh, has proved to be extremely helpful. Mrs. Eshbaugh provided us photographs and excerpts of some personal letters from Walter Abels to his wife, Elizabeth, which contained information concerning the company.

These accounts were written while Abels was on buying trips throughout Europe, which was then experiencing a time of great turmoil. These letters were instrumental in providing us with new documentation and intimate details about AWCO's dealings with other countries. Mrs. Eshbaugh also provided us with information and photographs that let us peek into some of the more personal aspects of the Abels family life as well. For this information, we are truly grateful. It provided a much-needed deeper look into the workings of the company on a daily basis.

Unfortunately, there are no living relatives that have in-depth knowledge of AWCO. Walter was, for some reason, reluctant to discuss the company with his children. In fact, the word "Charleton" had no meaning to the family when we first communicated! This is not meant to convey anything amiss in the family relationship, as ofttimes people will compartment their business life from their home life as much as possible.

The following, taken from one side of a letter written by Abels to his wife, also quotes from the other side of the letter which was to the "boys" at the firm. The "boys" in this instance do not refer to Abel's family members, but to his business associates.

Keep in mind that the part of Europe he was traveling in was very unstable and this trip was probably undertaken with some risk to Walter's safety. This insightful excerpt is dated March 28, 1939, and is recorded here as follows:

. . . The other side is a copy of a letter written to the office which tells the story of our purchases in Poland. I am very pleased with what I did and I hope everything comes thru alright . . . if they do not understand anything about cabling the letter of credit to the forwarder in Warsaw, they should get in touch with Mr. Taubenfeldt at the Polish consulate. He is there to help Polish exports.

Janet wrote to me that the letter continues with Walter's thoughts that he was ". . . positive that the Poles will fight Germany".

The other side of the letter now follows:

Dear Boys,

I finished up yesterday at Zawiercie, and I have great hopes of getting a lot of stuff from them which will equal what I used to get from Checko. Prices on cut stuff are a little higher – on pastel glass about the same. It has been a job teaching these factories what to do. They never made or heard of a glass lamp stand in their lives. I bought from them about $3000 and wanted many more items, but they would not make anymore. Very fine people and I have much confidence they will do the work alright . You must realize that I only saw about 3 items finished – the rest I am buying from our sketches.

In addition to the above, I bought $700 from Hortensja (sp??) at Piotrkow (sp??). Some job for me there as they do not speak a word of English – it was all done in my lousy German. This is not as good a factory for us as the other one but there are many things to consider and I thot (sic) I better have another country to count on. Their prices are higher but we can still make out. I believe [Sol] Horn and ourself (sic) will be the only ones with a glass line of lamps not marked Germany, so we should make some money from this stuff.

It has been very expensive for me here as I have had to travel by train each day to the factories and back at night to Katource, and after finishing at the factories yesterday, I decided to go back to Warsaw and make arrangement for shipments and credits as I did not want any hold up on these orders. The factory Hortensja will do no work even on samples until a letter of credit is established. **So you must take care of this at once.** It is so important that I will send a duplicate of this letter in case this is lost. Enclosed is the contract with the forwarding written in German which you must have translated. They are forwarding a translation to me in Italy, but I want this to go on the Queen Mary so it must be mailed at once. Read conditions in letter, but you must go to Chase bank and have them cable irrevocable letter of credit for $2000 in the name of Nordische Transport and Speditions – Gesellschaft – Warszawa –Widokstrig. This is for about 1/2 of orders for 6/1 shipments. On 6/15 I will send one addition . . . credit. YOU MUST HAVE THIS CABLED AT ONCE. Tell the bank the money will be drawn upon by the forwarder to pay consular invoices presented by factories S. Reich Zawiercie and Emile Haebler – Poitrkow both in Poland. The order for Reich is about 3000 and the other about 750. The forwarder has copies of orders and all terms and will see that all conditions are met. The irrevocable letter of credit must be to them to use to pay these invoices. Hope I have made it clear. Get Chase bank to cable this at once.

We're damn lucky to get this break here and we should make some real money on this stuff and this resource. Hope I can tye (sic) them up by keeping them busy on reorders.

I am on the run now to Italy – 26 hour ride. Haven't heard a word from Burlamacchi and hope he meets me in Venice. Sol Horn sails on the Paris, Friday, so if you want any further information about the letter of credit, he can tell you if you call him.
Best,
Walter

This is just a wonderful peek into the daily transactions that Walter Abels experienced on his extended overseas buying trips. The letter also documents for the first time that AWCO offered glassware made in Poland, none of which has been identified to date. That said, however, it is highly unlikely that any of the orders from this trip to Poland were ever shipped to America. It takes a considerable amount of time for the production of goods based on the drawings and sketches Mr. Abels would have given them, and the war was soon in full swing.

Although completing this trip safely, Abels' trip just barely preceded Hitler's onslaught of Poland and the ensuing invasion of other European countries. In retrospect, this journey had many inherent dangers to Abels' personal safety brought about by the instability of the area due to German aggression.

The devastation in Europe from World War II was horrendous and its impact affected the American market in many ways. Imported goods from Europe were interrupted and many factors contributed to the dwindling supplies from overseas. These include the holocaust, the mass exodus of refugees, factory workers being conscripted into the military, factories being nationalized, and others being destroyed. Even if the wares were available, it would have been difficult and costly to have them shipped to the United States. German submarine wolf packs roamed the shipping lanes and their early success led to hundreds of sunken freighters. Most of the limited shipments coming into the U.S. during this period were bearing freight dedicated for the war.

Despite the country being at war, retail sales at home for giftware were very strong. Servicemen would send most of their paycheck back home to their families to provide for them. Also, thousands of women earned their first paycheck by staffing positions formerly held by men who were off to fight in the war. Many durable goods were rationed or impossible to get so the options on what to spend money on were somewhat limited. Decorating and home improvement magazines were very popular and the advertisements in them were very alluring. In those trying times, it is not surprising that housewives and mothers would try to cheer things up by brightening their homes with the latest in furnishings.

American firms that had depended on Europe for wares prior to the war had to scramble to survive by trying to find domestic suppliers to fill their inventories. This led to AWCO's beginning association with many U.S. glass companies such as Fenton, Cambridge, and Consolidated. The industry still faced problems here at home, such as disrupted freight schedules and, especially, the shortage of raw materials for coloring glass.

After the war, some of these conditions improved, but the ripple effect of the damage that had been inflicted was still reverberating. Walter wrote two excellent articles concerning this subject, both published in separate issues of *China and Glass*. One analysis was written during the war and the other was written post-war. Both clearly show his fine grasp of the intricacies involved in surviving this complex and unstable business environment.

Despite this state of affairs, AWCO prepared itself for the anticipated economic post-war boom. By December of 1945 they expanded their work area into a 10,000 square foot decorating department. They were also well represented in the trade as their Charleton line had 4,000 active distributors in the U.S. They were also exporting goods to South America, Central America, Cuba, and the Near East.

Walter renewed his buying trips after the war and his plans were reported in the March 28, 1946 issue of *Retailing*, "... Walter Abels, of Abels, Wasserberg & Co., expects to leave for Europe sometime in May. He will be touring the continent for a few months in search of new merchandise, and will hit 'every new country he can get into'."

The same publication noted his departure on this trip later in June of that year and it contains the one and only quote we have found having been made by his business partner. "... Harry Wasserberg said it was almost like wading to Europe when he saw his partner, Walter Abels, aboard a clipper at LaGuardia field on Sunday. He said the rain was terrible, but the plane got off safely. Walter was heading for France and other countries in search of fine pieces of the type used by Abels-Wasserberg in making lamps before the war. Harry said that if any merchandise is to be found in Europe, Walter will bring it back!"

Later that year, after having returned from Europe, Walter was interviewed about the details of his two-month buying trip through war-torn France, Czechoslovakia, and Italy. The article focused on the industrial conditions presently found in Europe and what might lie ahead. In the August 1946 issue of *China, Glass and Decorative Accessories*, Walter comments about how prices had doubled and sometimes tripled over what they were previously:

'The potteries are practically all working, with production from fifty to one hundred percent of normal, and we did succeed in making some purchases of china and glass. But prices were high, and there is no assurance of delivery.'

Mr. Abels said in Czechoslovakia there is an acute shortage of skilled glass workers because of post-war population shifts. All industries are being nationalized, with government officials in charge of each factory. Prices are set by the central government of the district, and the purchaser has no influence on the price of any merchandise. This is a difficulty for American businessmen used to individual methods. 'The main problem, however, is the skilled labor shortage' Mr. Abels added. 'But the Czechs are ingenious and industrious people, and will undoubtedly solve the difficulties of the present situation.'

In France, Mr. Abels found that, with all the potteries working, they were not producing enough to meet the domestic demand. He did close a contract with one of the finest Limoges china firms, but the china will have to be decorated by hand in the United States, the first time this has been done, Mr. Abels said. This procedure will also save duty on the decorations.

The Italians are making big strides toward recovery, and production is in the level with France. Italy offers pottery and Venetian glass. Mr. Abels made some purchases here and also in Switzerland, where the people have fared better than most of Europe.

One of the biggest difficulties facing buyers abroad is still transportation, Mr. Abels found. The only way to get around is by plane, and reservations should be made months in advance. But in this the American consular services are very helpful, and are interested in helping businessmen foster the interchange of merchandise. In traveling from Paris to Rome, Mr. Abels was given priority to fly in an Armour transport. In general, Mr. Abels found plenty of food to be had at sky-high prices.

Although there were surely some exciting aspects coupled to traveling the continent as the chief executive and buyer for his company, Abels missed his family and was terribly lonely. The letters that voiced his painful separation from his family the strongest were those written as the ship was leaving the American harbor and traveling to Europe. While he had made some friends in Europe, such as Gualtiero Burlamacchi in Italy, Abels did not like being away from his family. He would sometimes bring his wife Elizabeth along and her name appears on some of the ship's manifests for these trips. It could truly be said then that this was a mixture of business and pleasure.

A short analysis of what we presently know about these overseas suppliers mentioned in this article is recapped below.

The Limoges connection is well documented in print from other articles and advertisements of the period. Despite considerable research, information is lacking about the factories involved. Of the two known Limoges suppliers, one had ceased production in 1932 and little is known of the other. It is the authors' belief that most, if not all, of these Limoges firms will be identified in the future. More details on this subject are found under a subsection here titled "The Suppliers."

The Swiss connection was totally unexpected and we have no idea what types of products were purchased from them. We have seen no mention of Switzerland listed as a giftware supplier for the American market.

Although nothing definite was stated here about the items AWCO had bought from Czechoslovakia, there is evidence from Abels' letter that there had been a buying relationship between them and this country.

Prior to reading this article, we already knew that AWCO had bought items from Italy, as we had already purchased several Charleton labeled pieces marked as being made in that country.

During the company's entire period of operation, they imported or produced a large number of decorated objects with styles varying from "Old Paris" to "Art Moderne." They basically knew no decorating boundaries, but, nevertheless, their total catalog of items exhibits a keen sense of good taste and refinement, and that set them apart from the scores of similar competitors.

Many advertisements from this period can be found that display a wide variety of decorated items available from various importers. These items for the most part are gaudy in comparison to the Charleton line and contrast sharply with AWCO's offerings of elegant designs.

In exploring different avenues of research, we were surprised that there was not more direct mention of AWCO in the New York newspapers than the following two articles, which are all that surfaced after an extensive search.

We were able to glean from the December 22, 1948 issue of the *New York Times* that Walter Abels was then serving as the president of the Lamp and Shade Institute of America. Little else of interest to the Charleton collector is in the article and it mainly deals with price increases in the industry due to the rising cost of materials.

A year later, AWCO headlines an article in the business section in the *New York Times* regarding their inability to take further orders due to the crush of holiday business. Walter Abels reports in an article dated December 3, 1949 that in the prior three weeks, the company has been sending on the average of twenty-five telegrams a day to retailers informing them of AWCO's inability to accept their orders. In fact, AWCO employees were working overtime in an effort to complete holiday orders already on the books.

It was stated in the article that this was overall an unusual circumstance and the majority of the lamp industry was not affected in the same way. It was also predicted that 1949 sales volume would be equal to 1948, resulting in another banner year. It was noted that these winter sales were fortunate and were responsible for offsetting "a disastrous spring."

Abels goes on to say that, unlike 1948, there would not be a price increase for their new lines being shown at the upcoming January lamp shows in Chicago and New York.

There were two major lamp shows held for the industry, one in the summer and another held in January. During the late 1940s, the shows in New York averaged an attendance of about 3,300 buyers throughout the five-days of each show. These buyers usually represented large retailers located in metropolitan areas.

There were also many other regional shows held in major metropolitan markets that various firms supported. In all of these shows, buyers would plan and place orders for seasonal deliveries as well as offer and receive input on market trends. Seminars were held in conjunction with these shows for retailers to assist their sales staff so that they were properly trained in order to maximize profits for their stores.

An interesting comment was made in media coverage that manufacturers who had new and attractive merchandise shown on attractive displays received the heavier orders. We think that the fresh designs that AWCO offered on a regular basis was certainly responsible for them being considered "one of the top lamp wholesalers in the New York area."

The price range of lamps that buyers were favoring was table lamps retailing in the $20.00 to $40.00 price range. Popular floor lamps were the ones that could be retailed in the $20.00 to $50.00 price bracket. Lamps that sold for less than $20.00, or were lacking in style, were referred to in the trade as "borax." It seems that during this more affluent period there was a steady decline in the market for merchandise considered to be "borax." Retailers also noted that consumers were "fussy" over the lack of quality for the higher prices being charged.

There were some manufacturers who did not display their nicer imported lamps from France at these shows, but rather kept them in their own special corporate showrooms to be seen by appointment only. We could imagine that AWCO was among these, as they advertised Limoges lamps during this period and they certainly would not want anyone but serious buyers handling these expensive items. We have found mention in several advertisements that a few of AWCO's lamps were to be retailed in the $60.00 range. Some people would consider that high even by today's standards, but imagine the relative expense of these lamps in the late 1940s!

It was during this period of booming business that a young man by the name of Maurizio Burlamacchi was employed by AWCO. He is the son of Gualtiero Burlamacchi, an Italian businessman who was one of Walter Abel's good friends as well as a business associate in purchasing Italian goods. The Burlamacchi name has been associated with the Italian marketplace since the year 1220 (beginning in the silk trade in Lucca, Italy) and is still today a highly respected Italian mercantile firm.

Walter J. Abels (with pipe), Gualtiero Burlamacchi, his son, Pio Burlamacchi, and the dog "Lampo." Near Lucca, Italy, circa 1937-1938. *Photograph courtesy of Maurizio Burlamacchi.*

Young Maurizio came to NYC after his father's death and worked for AWCO for seven months in 1948/49. He was then eighteen years old, having been born on the 14th of May, 1930, and was given a job assembling lamps and shades in the factory located at 63 Greene Street. Maurizio himself says he was treated like a member of the Abels family and he stayed in their home during his first month in America. After residing with the Abels, he rented a room in an apartment on West 87th Street for the remainder of his stay in New York City.

It was through the mention of Maurizio Burlamacchi by Mrs. Eshbaugh that we were able to uncover a crucial link that opened up a fresh avenue of first hand information about AWCO. Another "happenstance."

Not knowing if Burlamacchi was an uncommon name, we did a search on the Internet and found the web site of the buying office of "G. Burlamacchi S.A.S.". We wrote them and told them about the book we were writing and a few days later received the following reply:

> Dear Michael, thank you for your surprising e-mail.
> Regarding Walter Abels and Abels, Wasserberg & Company I think I can be of help to you with a bit of patience.
> Walter was my father's greatest friend and later on gave me a job and put me up in their house in Montclair when I was eighteen and my father had just died. Naturally Mr. Abels and my father worked together in buying Italian goods.
> My father, Gualtiero Burlamacchi, and Walter met probably in 1927 when my father worked for a larger buying office, not his own. They became great friends to which friendship contributed my father's British education. They were together perhaps two or three weeks every year but then corresponded almost daily for business. The last time together must have been 1945, my father was born in 1896 and died in 1947.
> In 1948/1949 I worked six months assembling and shades in their factory in Greene Street. 'Mr. Abels' was like a second father to me.
> Please let me know more in detail what your book is to tell, and if more business or also personal.
> An important man in Abels Wasserberg was Ralph De Felice, designer and production manager.
> If you like, this can be just the start of my information to you. Also I have photographs somewhere put away.
> Looking forward to being in touch, I remain at your full disposal,
> Yours sincerely,
> Maurizio Burlamacchi

Needless to say, we were on "Cloud Nine" after getting this letter. We would finally have an inside track on AWCO as well as the personal reflections of someone who was treated by Abels as "a son." Once again we recognized the importance of the Internet in our research. Once we entered the name "Burlamacchi" in an Internet search engine, it was only a matter of about ten minutes before we had sent our first inquiry to the Burlamacchi firm.

Our second letter to Senor Burlamacchi was basically a broad outline of pertinent information we already had uncovered concerning the company and a detailed list of questions about which he may have intimate knowledge.

With "a bit of patience," we first received from Senor Burlamacchi a manila envelope containing the three pictures shown here. One of them was actually an original color snapshot from 1967. Two of the photographs were taken in Italy and the third was probably taken outside of Walter's last home which was in Bloomfield, New Jersey.

There was no text included with the photographs, and that was puzzling. As it turned out, the fax containing Mr. Burlamacchi's written information had preceded the pictures and had been in a local copy center for almost a month waiting to be picked up. It seems our fax center did not have anything but our first name on the cover letter and the fax was buried in their "dead letter" file. In another week it would have been thrown away!

Rather than rephrase Mr. Burlamacchi's words, we will print here the major portion of the letter we received from him. Except for rearranging a paragraph here and there and the deletion of some personal information that is not germane to the topic, the letter appears here as it was received.

> G. Burlamacchi S.A.S.
> Buying Office
> Corso Italia 32 – Florence, Italy
> September 5th, 2001
> Abels & Wasserberg
> "Information as it came to mind."
>
> As a child before the war I remember driving with my father and Mr. Abels to the hill town of Volterra to buy alabaster lamp bases from "Cooperativa Alabastri Volterra". Mr. Abels wanted fine goods while my father always suggested to him to buy some "tripe" as well.
> In 1945 or 1946 Mr. Abels was in Italy again to buy. The most successful items he bought were a ceramic Guinea Hen and a white cock or rooster used as lamp bases (on a light color American made wood base) made in Florence by Zaccagnini. In Murano Mr. Abels bought glass made mostly by Fratelli Toso and by Barovier & Toso. Evidently sales following that trip were overall not great, because Mr. Abels did not come again for years.
> The Abels Wasserberg factory was in Greene Street (? For sure the subway station, but then the factory I believe was two blocks away east). In the basement I assembled and electrified lamps, on higher floors were the warehouse and Ralph's (De Felice) office and the decorating department with mostly women painting china and glass. Ralph directed everything and solved all technical and artistic problems. Ralph had enormous skill in designing and directing artistic or technical production.

Ralph De Felice and his wife, Grace, in 1965, Bagni Di Lucca, Italy. Ralph De Felice was a partner in the company as well as the factory supervisor and head of the design department. *Photograph courtesy of Maurizio Burlamacchi.*

Mr. Abels rarely came to the factory. Mr. Wasserberg I never saw at all and was seldom even in the office uptown. I understood that Mr. Wasserberg was a "terrific" salesman and selling is all he ever did.

So it was Mr. Abels to be the big boss in the office, Mr. Wasserberg to sell and Ralph De Felice to design and produce and control the factory totally. They were partners, and Mr. Abels used to say that Ralph always obtained the best deals in matters between themselves. Mr. De Felice was a typical southern Italian, from Bari, emigrated as a child 6 or 7 years old with his parents.

He spoke Italian quite fluently, not very tall, quite dark complexion, very strong. He had a beautiful home along Long Island Sound. He lived with his wife Grace, also Italian, and two children, Leonore and Steve.

Like every good American hard working person, Walter was up early in the morning to drive his Studebaker from Montclair into New York with windows wide open in the middle of the winter which was painful to me.

My foreman in the assembling department was a German named "High" and I assure you that everyone worked at "high" speed under him. In the factory I had 30 minutes for lunch, worked 8 hours but often 9 or 10. Working conditions were good but not comparable to today's. I for instance stood up all the time and no break was permitted except the 1/2 hour for lunch in a café outside.

I was paid $0.87 per hour and/or $48.00 a week. Very often I worked overtime or Saturdays. Business was booming in 1949, almost entirely with American made products, while later on many imports were added from the Orient and from Italy. Some of the glass blanks I remember were coming from Pennsylvania.

The factory was a decrepit old building in a sad dark street in the Village, Greene Street I believe, several floors with large elevators, quite functional for the times. There were I believe 120 (?) persons working there in 1949. For the most part very skilled men and women of all extractions, from Germans to Puerto Ricans, but I do not remember any Europeans not already become fully American.

A lady by the name of Frances Martino served in the business office as Walter Abels' personal secretary.

In the lamp department I assembled lamp bases with base, glass, cap, rod, etc. and they better be straight. The logo "Charleton" was considered by us working in "Abels & Wasserberg & Co." nothing more than just a label to be put on (somewhat reluctantly) to give an image or "flavor" which I did not understand. "Abels & Wasserberg & Co." was the name we were proud of.

When I left New York after working 7 months in "Abels & Wasserberg & Co." in May 1949 I started sending all sorts of photographs of goods from which Mr. Abels ordered new items. Very successful were wrought iron wall sconces made by Ferretti in Florence and ceramic lamp bases made by Alessi in Nove Di Bassano.

Soon after Mr. Abels started coming again with Ralph De Felice and their trips continued perhaps for the next ten years; business with Italy being very good.

Walter Abels was a very sincere American gentleman with a sense of humor and a great love for life, very good looking from what I could tell, before he became old. During the war, too old to be in the Army, he drove a fire department truck in New York.

His judgment on life, people, politics or religion was such as to meet my father's way of thinking completely, and as such to earn my admiration always. At home in Italy I have two Oriental lamps with American made shades, a gift to me by Abels, Wasserberg & Co. sent I believe in 1966.

Sorry for the long delay, let us hope that I am just not too late. By mail I will follow up with some photographs I have found. Let us keep in touch.

Yours sincerely,
Maurizio Burlamacchi

In some following correspondences with Senor Burlamacchi, he stated that during his stay with the Abels family that he and Mr. Abels would often engage in conversation about the business in the evening and it was noticeable that this was not something he did with his own children. Maurizio Burlamacchi was the same age as Abels' daughter Jane, and her brother, William Abels, was four years older. This stay with the Abels family commenced after the death of Gualtiero Burlamacchi and was arranged between Maurizio's widowed mother and Walter Abels. In part this was to enhance Maurizio's education and it also resulted in a continued close business relationship between the two families after Maurizio returned home to Italy in 1949.

The firm of G. Burlamacchi is today managed by Maurizio's daughter, Patrizia, and her husband Giulio de Socio. Mr. Burlamacchi is still active in the office that assists foreign companies in purchasing Italian goods. This merchandise is mostly from Florence, Venice, and the surrounding area.

The latest confirmed date for American blank glass being ordered by AWCO is about 1961 and this was for glass lampshades from the Fenton Art Glass Company. According to a note made by his wife Elizabeth, Walter's last buying trip to Europe was taken in June of 1963. On this trip he did visit Italy, and most likely visited the Burlamacchi family.

Between 1956 and 1960, AWCO's marketing direction changed dramatically from their staple giftware line of many years. From Maurizio Burlamacchi we learned that there were a number of reasons for this shift and all were the signs of a business in trouble.

Problems came from several directions. Prices of American goods were rising dramatically at the same time that some of AWCO's older designs were falling out of favor, considered tired and old fashioned. Further, with the tariffs on imported goods falling every year, there was a sharp increase in imports with which AWCO tried to compete. Later the company embraced these imports in order to remain solvent.

Another motivating factor was the dwindling demand for table lamps, which were AWCO's bread and butter. As Ralph De Felice said, *"We don't get those quantities anymore,"* meaning orders for table lamps had dried up. From the appearance of their advertisements, the company was relying heavily upon imports from the Orient. Nowhere to be found are advertisements displaying the finely decorated elegant glassware from American suppliers.

Instead, we find undecorated oriental porcelain statues, landscapes from the Far East painted on rice paper placed in ebony frames, porcelain "Temple" motif table lamps, and hand painted tiles that are matted and framed. Continuing in this vein, they also offered porcelain plates painted with realistic pairs of birds placed upon a background of framed black velvet.

An interesting article from *The Gift and Art Buyer,* dated September 1963, sheds some light on the new direction AWCO took prior to its closure. In a trade journal section concerning news of the giftware industry it was announced that AWCO was moving from number 1540, its space on the fifteenth floor of the Merchandise Mart in Chicago, to a new and larger showroom, number 1214, on the twelfth floor of the same building. The article states that this better positions them on a floor ". . . with a heavy concentration of lamp showrooms." The floor they were formerly on was predominately composed of giftware jobbers.

Although possibly already a staple in their line of lighting fixtures, for the first time, wrought iron Florentine chandeliers with white and gold antique effects are shown in AWCO advertisements. These wrought iron chandeliers were followed by a selection of beautifully wood-carved and ornamented tables, planters, and mirrors. An Italian plate glass table supported upon a bundled sheaf of wheat advertised by AWCO is a real classic. Other similar items advertised include glass topped wrought iron coffee tables with delicately twining leaves in antiqued tones and wrought iron wall plaques in various finishes. AWCO emphasized in their advertisements that these were a mixture of both imported and domestic items. No distinction was made between the imports and domestic items, nor were any manufacturers noted.

Although we think that aesthetically the company was taking a downward turn from their previous high standards, compared with other offerings seen in trade journals of the day, AWCO items were still classier than their competitors. Sadly, in looking at the items pictured in the last full-page advertisement placed in *The Gift and Art Buyer,* we see the result of the difficulties with which they were struggling. The quality of items advertised pales considerably in comparison to those of just a few years earlier.

All AWCO advertisements appear to have ceased abruptly in the spring of 1960. None were found in any trade journal after that date. It seems likely that this was a direct result of less demand for and less profit from the items that then made up the Charleton line.

The last mention of AWCO found thus far in trade journals is in the annual directories of *The Gift & Tableware Reporter* and *The Gift and Art Buyer* from 1963-1964. In both of these publications, AWCO was listed as being both an importer and manufacturer and their location was still at the same address of 23rd East 26th Street, New York City, New York.

A listing in these directories of the types of wares AWCO sold in 1964 includes: bar accessories, gold and silver decorated china, decorated glassware, lamp bases, Chinese art goods, boudoir lamps, desk lamps, figure and novelty lamps, and table lamps. It is interesting that other than a nod to "decorated glassware," there is no detailed mention of the bowls, candy boxes, vases, vanity items, etc. with which they were once heavily involved, and which were cited in previous directories. This shift happened in a fairly short period of time and seems indicative to us as some major changes in the management structure or focus within the company in order to cope with the financial strain.

Just as in their earlier shift to Art Moderne, AWCO did not wholly abandon their traditional floral decorations. Interspersed amidst the advertisements of various Asian influenced items is one from *The Gift and Art Buyer* from August 1957 that shows four table lamps with themes more familiar to us.

We see the return of the "Fruit and Dots" pattern painted on an apothecary jar that was converted into a lamp base. Another apothecary shaped lamp base shows their distinctive "Gold Roses" pattern once again and it also appears on the third lamp in the advertisement as well.

And just when we thought that we had gained some sense of what to expect from the AWCO design staff, we were thrown another curve ball. The fourth lamp is very atypical of AWCO and interesting due to its utilitarian construction. Based on an authentically detailed design of an American military drum complete with an eagle clutching arrows, it carries a strong masculine statement from Colonial times.

These hand painted lamps give evidence that the decorating department at AWCO was still operating, but most likely on a reduced scale, considering the firm's shift toward buying decorated imported goods. Ironically, for a firm that owed a great deal of its reputation to its highly trained staff of designers and decorators, the last advertisement from the company we have found features imported Italian hand painted ceramics. These pieces, although well crafted, blend in more with the wares typical of so many of their competitors and show little of the artistic flair and creativity for which AWCO decorated wares have come to be appreciated today.

A variety of reasons could have caused AWCO to return to their original tastes, and Frank M. Fenton felt one reason the Fenton Art Glass Company (FAGCO) lost volume with this account was due to Fenton's price increases. This was generally the case with all of the American companies, as we would most likely have seen a continuation of decorated glassware from Westmoreland, Consolidated, etc., if it were just Fenton increasing their prices.

American labor prices were also considerably higher than the countries that they were competing against. Although we know that Ralph De Felice, who was the head of the decorating department, stayed on with the company throughout this period, we see no evidence of hand decorated items from the AWCO studio in any of their advertisements after 1957.

It had also been twenty years since the conclusion of World War II and cheaper imports were taking more and more of the market share in America once again. In testament to that fact, in the same September 1963 article from *The Gift and Art Buyer*, we find AWCO capitalizing upon this situation and taking the following course:

> The firm's lamp line features traditional and highly decorative lines utilizing imported bases from many parts of the world. Frequently the designs are originated by American designers, exclusively for Abels-Wasserberg, and executed by foreign artisans in Italy, Spain, Hong Kong, France, Germany and India. Also shown in the showroom are decorative mirrors, Oriental screens, oil paintings and brass and copper imports.

From this little gem of an article we are provided with new items, new materials from which they were being made, and new countries to add to the list of suppliers. We had already seen earlier evidence of AWCO's entrance into Oriental themes from the advertisements of 1956 and they were either trying again or continuing with what proved to be a successful venture.

According to the Abels family, Walter's health began deteriorating during the mid-1960s and he entered into negotiations to sell his interest in the business. Walter did not seemed to be pleased with the way the company was being run during his absences due to ill health and he had little confidence that the people interested in buying him out would be able to stay in business for long.

No mention of Harry Wasserberg is made and it is believed, as mentioned earlier, that he had died several years before. Who succeeded him after his death or controlled his interest in the company is unknown.

Without Walter Abels here to speak for himself, we can only speculate that this direction the company was moving toward was one of the concerns he voiced in letters to his wife. This particular concern was not mentioned, but he did tell her that if things kept going as they were ". . . the whole thing would go bust." It is clear in the letter he wrote that one of the "things," at least, was leadership in the company. This also correlates with the increasing old age of the business partners and the strain of struggling with the business and associated failing health of Abels.

Walter also voiced concerns about AWCO's supply pipeline and stated, "Business with orders is pretty good, and so far that end we think is going alright – but shipments are going out terribly weak." In a letter written ten days later he elaborates by saying, "Just called the office. The men are sending orders all right, but no money coming in and shipments by us only fair."

Walter J. Abels and his wife, Elizabeth, circa 1960-1963, outside of their last home in Montclair, New Jersey.
Photograph courtesy of Maurizio Burlamacchi.

We see here the signals of a company that was experiencing problems not only with cash flow, but with inventory as well. AWCO's management seemed to be losing both paying customers and a sense of direction and Walter clearly saw the danger signs. Hospitalized and not being there to help stave off disaster must have weighed heavily on Abels' mind.

We feel from the anxious tone of these letters written by Walter Abels that he was ready to sell his share of the company and be done with it. Walter voiced his own thoughts and those of another partner in the business who wanted out quickly when he wrote, ". . . because for me and H. Goldberg – we will settle cheap for sure."

These letters were dated at the end of July 1966, and from them we can state definitively that AWCO was still in business at that time. These letters also give us a close approximation to the last days of Abels, Wasserberg & Company.

Without the help of Maurizio Burlamacchi, the fate of AWCO would have remained a mystery. Mr. Burlamacchi has been able to tell us not only about the circumstances surrounding the last days of the AWCO, but also what became of the Charleton name.

AWCO declared bankruptcy and a liquidator was brought forward in an attempt to settle old debts. Mr. Goldberg stayed on for another year to manage the business during this transition. Mr. Burlamacchi writes:

> In the end Beth Weismann bought up the 'Charleton' name and part of the stock. G. Burlamacchi continued to work with Beth Weissman for several years until they in turn closed their own business [Beth Weissman Company]. The high end table lamp business had become very difficult.

At last the facts concerning the disposition of AWCO have been uncovered. Of course, this opened a fresh avenue of research concerning Beth Weissman. As with the "happenstance" we experienced during researching AWCO, our luck proved just as good when it came to researching Beth Weissman.

We were able to locate and interview the last owners of the Beth Weissman Company (BWCO), the Shapiro family. Their whereabouts was made known to us through the fortuitous discovery of an Internet web site for Rose Furniture in High Point, North Carolina, that listed the Beth Weissman Company as one of the lines that they sold (what would we do without the Internet?). We called Rose Furniture and spoke to Phyllis Morgan. She informed us that Rose Furniture had stopped selling BWCO items years ago.

Although we at first thought we had run into another dead end, Mrs. Morgan gave us the phone number of Speer Collectibles in Atlanta, Georgia, and said she thought they could give us further information. There we spoke with Mrs. Bobbi Sasser, who was most helpful. After giving her a quick sketch of our inquiry, we knew we were onto something when she related to us that she also knew Maurizio Burlamacchi. Mrs. Sasser informed us that the Beth Weissman Company was no longer in business, but she could put us in touch with Beth Weissman's grandson, Harold Shapiro.

This was a thrilling revelation and we anxiously called Mr. Shapiro. We tempered our excitement in case there would be little information available about the now defunct company. Fortunately, this was not the case and, between Harold Shapiro and his older brother Michael, we were able to obtain the details that were so critical to understanding the demise of AWCO. Incorporated into this summary are also some details about the Beth Weissman Company that we had previously uncovered in various trade periodicals. While of passing interest at the time, these now naturally took on a deeper importance.

The Beth Weissman Connection

BWCO began about 1932 when Mrs. Beth Weissman desired to sell some of the items she brought back to America that she had purchased in France. She opened a retail concession in a New York City department store located on the corner of 17th and 5th Streets. The department store was named "Paris" and this is where she sold the items she had purchased overseas.

BWCO later moved to a more permanent location at 49th West 23rd Street in New York City. It was situated on the 5th and 6th floors and initially sold only imported giftware. The earliest advertisement for BWCO we have found was in the January 1935 issue of *The Gift and Art Buyer* and the company was already at its new location.

Quite early, and at least by 1935, BWCO had established showrooms in three different locations. Of course they had a showroom in their New York City location, but also had one located on the fifteenth floor, #15105-7, in the huge Merchandise Mart building in Chicago and another at #180 New Montgomery Street in San Francisco.

Somewhere around the beginning of World War II, BWCO was forced to supplement their imported goods with undecorated items that were made in America. During these war years they faced the same problems in obtaining imports that Abels, Wasserberg & Company had experienced.

These blank items did receive decorations, but they were not by BWCO. Instead, these were contracted out to a cousin of Beth Weissman by the name of Sam Lugerner. Eventually, Mr. Lugerner's operation was absorbed into BWCO and he was appointed the chief decorator. In due course, BWCO acquired paint sprayers, kilns for firing the decorations, and an area in which to assemble their lamps. The silk lampshades were made on site and all the sewing of them was done by hand. During this period of expanding sales, the company employed upwards of twenty-five to thirty people (considerably less than the approximately 120 employees of AWCO during this time).

Entering the lamp business was crucial to the BWCO's success. During the war, many items were rationed and any products that relied upon these rationed supplies were in short supply and high demand. The copper needed for the lamps' wiring and the silk needed for the shades were both very difficult to obtain. Sales were very strong and most people buying lamps during the war were less concerned with how pretty the lampshade was than with getting one that was electrified.

After the war, when crucial materials were more readily available, the lamp business blossomed. High tariffs on imported goods were put in place by Congress to protect American manufacturers who geared up their facilities to employ the thousands of soldiers returning home from overseas. Additionally, most of Europe was not in any shape to produce any great quantity of items due to the devastation of the war on its factories and workers.

BWCO utilized its sources cultivated during the war to supply themselves with more innovative items that would have stronger consumer appeal. According to Michael Shapiro, BWCO's best markets were in the larger metropolitan areas such as Los Angeles, Chicago, and New York City. He stated that in general terms the Weissman products were large and flashy and appealed to more urban tastes. He contrasted this by saying that he considered the products of AWCO to be more tasteful and on the quiet side and were very well received in the southern part of the country.

Central elements utilized by both companies were the classic lines and graphics found in genuine antiques. This lent elegance to the items that gave them enduring appeal, a fact that has been borne out over the passage of many years. In fact, Shapiro stated that their motto in the company was "Tomorrow's Antiques Today."

Harold Shapiro stated that the largest supplier of glass lampshades and bases and other items to BWCO was the Beaumont Glass Company. First known as the West Virginia Glass Company, the name was later changed to Beaumont. They operated under that name for their longest period of time in the town of Morgantown, West Virginia.

Although they made a wide array of colored glassware, they are probably best known for their elegant opaque white glass known in the trade as Fer-Lux. We have several vases decorated with gold stars in this treatment and the opalescent fire in the glass is beautiful.

Harold Shapiro also confirmed that BWCO relied upon other American suppliers for glass blanks to decorate, including the Fenton Art Glass Co., Gillinder Glass Co., WV Specialty Glass Co., and the firm of Davis Lynch.

BWCO owned close to 200 different moulds that were kept on hand at Beaumont for their glass production. These moulds were created under the collaborative direction of Sylvia Greenberg and Beth Weissman's son, Philip Shapiro (Philip Shapiro was the father of Michael and Harold Shapiro). Greenberg would design and draw the proposed shape and Shapiro would pass judgment upon the stylistic merit of these designs. These moulds are now stored by the Southwestern Glass Company in Arkansas.

In 1951, BWCO initiated an arrangement to import brass lamps from India. They were the first company to import these items and, to help promote this line, they came up with an innovative marketing idea. Working in tandem with the Indian embassy in New York City, they were allowed to use the embassy as the location for a presentation of these wares. This showing exposed the visitors to a culture that was not understood by many and was surely beneficial to all parties concerned. It was during that time period that BWCO experienced a doubling of its annual gross revenues.

At one point, BWCO owned the exclusive licensing rights to produce lamps that incorporated Wedgwood china in their construction. These were very good sellers, so much so that Wedgwood cut BWCO out of the deal and began making their own lighting fixtures.

BWCO also dealt with very prestigious manufacturers and regional producers in order to import top quality porcelain and glass items. These items were used both for giftware and as lamp parts. The names that have surfaced in the advertisements from trade journal are French Lorraine glass (this may be a region rather than the actual firm), Sevres and French Sarreguemines china. Although not mentioned by name in the advertisements, we have a strong suspicion that a fair amount of the china pictured in these advertisements also came from Limoges, France.

BWCO also established a business relationship with the Italian export firm of G. Burlamacchi. Michael Shapiro spoke very highly of the Burlamacchi family and said that Maurizio was ". . . a prince of a man." In summing up the character of Maurizio, Michael Shapiro said that if he had a bag of diamonds that he needed to give to someone for safe keeping, he would give them to Maurizio Burlamacchi and would never have any reason afterwards to be concerned about their whereabouts.

BWCO also marketed their items through several well-known agencies that spanned the country from coast to coast. It was through these agencies that BWCO products were channeled to various retail outlets throughout America's metropolitan areas. Their names and various locations are mentioned below.

Located inside the Merchandise Mart at 712 Olive Street in Los Angeles, Katherine Zipper & Co. was a well-known agency that has gained a small amount of fame among Charleton collectors. This is due to the fact that their name is linked to advertisements showing decorated Fenton glassware that was hand painted by BWCO. These decorations pictured in advertisements from the March 1946 issue of *The Gift and Art Buyer* mimic the well known Roses and Bows decoration proliferated by Abels, Wasserberg & Company during the same time period.

The importance of this Zipper advertisement cannot be understated. None of these Weissman/Fenton items have ever been found with labels or marks to indicate their decorating origins. They have been confused with Charleton items by collectors for many years. Due to unique characteristics of these decorations pictured in the advertisement, it is now possible by using enlarged and enhanced photocopies to separate the Charleton decorated Fenton items from the ones painted by Weissman. This finding is also buttressed by the fact that none of these Fenton items with this particular decoration have been shown in AWCO advertisements or with Charleton labels or decorators initials.

Other agencies less well-known among collectors that represented BWCO in 1947 were R. & B. Gelbard at the Merchandise Mart in Chicago; Harold J. Abrams of Dallas, Texas; and Arthur Rosengard of Los Angeles. It is at this point in our story that we come to what we feel is one of the most fascinating facts discovered to date.

Sometime during the death throes of the business of Abels, Wasserberg & Company, BWCO purchased the Charleton trademark and a portion of the remaining inventory from the liquidator. These items continued to be sold through the existing network of original AWCO distributors, but the old AWCO showrooms were not utilized.

One of the sweetest parts of the deal was that BWCO convinced the former building supervisor and art director of AWCO, Ralph De Felice, to come and work for them in their design department. This proved to be a great asset for the company. In fact, it was under his tutelage that Harold Shapiro learned the art of design.

De Felice was characterized by the Shapiro family as not only a very gifted individual, but very personable as well. His artistry knew no bounds and he could create beautiful objects whether drawing, painting, or sculpting.

Toward the end of his employment, De Felice cut back on the number of hours he worked, probably in order to enjoy other things of a more personal nature. Ralph De Felice left the employ of BWCO in 1980 and the Shapiro family thinks that he died sometime around 1990.

Fortunately, for BWCO, Abels had a terrific sales force and Michael Shapiro elaborates on one person in particular that covered their southern territory and was hired by BWCO after the purchase of the Charleton trademark.

Michael Shapiro stated that this salesman had been responsible for writing over one half of the total orders that AWCO had received! This gentleman, whose name Mr. Shapiro could not recall at the time of our interview, evidently had a golden tongue and worked hard to develop and nurture a strong loyalty among his accounts.

Unfortunately, this salesman died within about a year after the takeover and BWCO's sales in his territory plummeted. Within a matter of about three years, BWCO had eliminated marketing items under the Charleton label and for all intents and purposes, AWCO ceased to exist.

Despite dropping the Charleton line from their offerings, BWCO did begin to broaden their range of styles in order to appeal to conservative tastes that they had not catered to previously. Although we have been able to document some of the BWCO wares through trade journal advertisements, these show only a very small sampling of the hundreds of different items that they sold over the span of sixty-five years. Hopefully, at some point, we may be able to document some of BWCO's business dealings through company documents, especially the war years and the last years involving the Charleton line; however, the whereabouts of these archives are at this point unknown.

Harold Shapiro stated that there were essentially no efforts to keep old sales records throughout the history of the company. He even related that when the company relocated for a final time in the 1970s that many company records were not transferred to their new location in Farmingdale, Long Island, New York.

BWCO closed in 1993, but the Shapiros have retained the licensing rights to the designs and trademarks of the company[3]. The reason stated for the closure of the company was that they were very proud of the reputation of the company and that to be competitive and follow in the direction that interior design had taken over recent years would compromise their artistic integrity. Additionally, competition in the industry had become very intense as various older competitors were taken over by larger and larger conglomerates and it was becoming impossible to maintain a decent profit margin against firms that had such large volume buying power.

Collecting BWCO items today will be more difficult than collecting those of other, better documented firms such as AWCO. This is mainly due to the lack of research material available to assist in identifying the various patterns and suppliers of blanks that they utilized. That said, it stands to reason that, in time, these items will be better known and prices will escalate as the demand grows along with the collector's knowledge.

Items that were produced by the company may be labeled in various ways. Some of these marks, such as those on glass or metal lamp bases, may be in the form of labels, but most will be ink stamps under the glaze on china and porcelain items.

These labels, in the shape of a shield, will bear the initials "BW" and the words "Gifts of Art". The ink stamps will be worded as "Beth Weiss", "Beth Weissman", or "Bethwood Royal China".

Although the existence of these labels has been verified through the past owner of the company, the authors have not been able to find any of these labels for documentation.

BWCO also decorated items for other companies, one of them being the Trenton China Company of Trenton, New Jersey.

The information that Mr. Burlamacchi and the Shapiro brothers revealed is simply astounding. The Beth Weissman Company was the same firm that, years earlier, had been AWCO's direct competitor. The astonishing fact is not that a competitor bought out AWCO, but that it was a firm whose own decorations are so often confused with Charleton decorations, especially those on Fenton art glass.

Nothing else is known at this point about any further dealings Walter Abels may have had with BWCO, although he did stay in touch with the Burlamacchi family. Walter suffered a great deal from heart problems and a family member feels that condition was perhaps brought about from his rich diet. Walter J. Abels died on Sunday, May 19th, 1974, at the age of eighty years and his wife passed away in August of 1990, at the age of ninety-one.

It is hoped that through the dissemination of the material in this book, new information will surface in several areas. Hopefully there will be leads to the AWCO archives or catalogs, input from former AWCO employees or their friends and relatives, or from collectors who have information and fresh insights.

The Decorators

When they opened their own decorating studio, Abels, Wasserberg & Company purchased undecorated items (blanks) from various glass and ceramic manufacturers and then hand decorated the pieces with designs of flowers, fruit, landscapes, abstract, and geometric patterns. These designs were produced bearing a Charleton label and, at times, one of two different ink stamps[4]. There has never been any evidence found that AWCO produced any trademarked line of wares other than the Charleton line.

The author's have a strong suspicion that AWCO did not develop the Charleton label until they began decorating items in their own studio in February 1942. This supposition is based on the absence of any mention of the Charleton name in their advertisements or industry publications prior to this date. Although the majority of Charleton labeled items are of domestic manufacture, this in itself does not lend strong support to our theory. AWCO did not begin purchasing and decorating these items until the 1940s and the sales grew steadily during and after the war.

The biggest unknown factor that prevents us from going from theory to fact is that we don't have the means to date the imported items that have Charleton labels. Although several different items are shown in advertisements that date after the start-up of their studio, it does nothing to sort out the production dates of the other foreign, unadvertised wares.

The decorating department was under the supervision of Mr. Ralph De Felice. We will hear more about Mr. De Felice later, but let it be said here that he was a highly skilled artist and was directly responsible for the beautiful designs that bear the Charleton label.

It was reported in the December 1945 issue of *The Gift and Art Buyer* that AWCO had fifty-five employees solely engaged in the task of hand decorating. It is now known that the make-up of this group of artisans consisted of a few men, but mostly were women from many other countries who had gained American citizenship. It is also a fact that these artists had acquired their skills in the great establishments of Europe prior to their employment by AWCO. This last statement will become self-evident as you examine the photographs of the artists' superb designs and their professional decorating skills.

The rites of passage required to become a "Charleton" artist involved a year and a half apprenticeship of supervised training in the decorating department. Painting on a curved surface involves considerably more skill than depicting ideas on a flat two-dimensional canvas. Geometric designs that surround the circumference must be in proportion from beginning to end and seamlessly connect with the starting point. Economy of design was important as well, as sometimes the artist painted objects with very small surface areas such as pin trays and cigarette boxes.

It is fairly obvious that, in some cases, two different artists decorated the same item. This suspicion was brought about by the presence of two sets of hand painted initials on the same item. These initials are usually separated in placement, and found painted in different colors, usually one in gold leaf, and the other in one of the colors found in the decoration. Logically this would indicate that one artist would do

Walter J. Abels with his ever-present pipe in a company advertisement. Circa 1967. *Photograph courtesy of Janet Eshbaugh.*

the gold leaf and another the china or enamel paint. The items most commonly found with the artist's initials are decorated Cambridge pieces.

This co-operative effort would make good business sense, as it would streamline the production of the decoration. We can only speculate that certain artists were better suited to different decorations or materials and that these skills were capitalized upon by this arrangement. It was also probable that the chemical properties of the gold paint were such that workers could only tolerate limited exposure to the fumes, or else the use of special ventilation or cumbersome protective equipment was necessary.

The application of mixed media, such as sprayed blushes, hand painting, gold leaf, slip trailing, etc., may have required several firings, performed after each type of decoration was applied. The decorators used china paint for permanence, and the testimony to the durability of this is that many decorated items have suffered no paint loss over a period of fifty years or more.

This china paint was a special formulation that contains finely ground silica, which fused with the base glass when fired. Once a decoration was fired there was no easy way to correct mistakes due to this fused bond between the paint and glass. Each decorating stage increased the labor investment in the item, and a mistake made in the later stages of production was expensive indeed. Occasionally, there can be found some decorated items employing enameled paint, but these are uncommon.

This decorating operation was compounded by the fact that every type of glass or porcelain has a different firing temperature based on thickness, density, and material composition. If this temperature is not properly adjusted for the differing characteristics of each piece, the process could either cause the piece to shatter, or, if the kiln was not hot enough, prevent the paint from fusing with the glass or glaze. Another undesirable effect from this firing process, caused if the kiln temperature is too great, is warping. This is especially true for pieces that are top heavy and have little support near the base, such as fan vases and compotes (see page ###).

When considering the many steps of production (blank acquisition, designing, quality control, etc.) that must take place during the daily operations of a decorating firm, one can then begin to understand the costly and labor intensive undertaking that was involved. Such consideration also helps to foster a greater appreciation for the finished product and all of the artisans involved in creating it.

The Decorations

When we use words such as "distinctive" or "exclusive" in regards to Charleton decorations, it should be recognized that there are always exceptions, and in some cases more than a few. But the collector should realize that the actual decorating span of AWCO's studio was limited to twenty-five years at most, and the types of glass and porcelain blank patterns they utilized will fall within this range. Therefore, using AWCO's limited timeline for decorating, and fairly limited selection of blanks from well-known makers of elegant glass and porcelain made during this period, a tighter focus can be used to discern their handiwork.

The attribution of decoration can sometimes be an onerous task and the work undertaken here is groundbreaking in many areas. Although every effort has been made here to limit errors, sometimes conjecture, even when proven false, can be the nucleus for discussion and learning in the future.

We employed "reverse engineering" during research as an identification method, obtaining information by studying the records of companies that supplied products to AWCO for decorating. The first step of this process was to document items with Charleton labels and then to determine who made the blanks. Once the manufacturer was identified, investigative work was undertaken to see what records might exist as well as interviewing researchers and authors in that particular field. Some items can be dated through the glass and porcelain production records for particular colors or patterns, and with this information, the AWCO advertisements and articles in these journals provide important corroborating evidence.

Items which have no identifying labels are much more problematic. This hazy area of undocumented attribution is of course subjective and always open to interpretation. Many considerations must be used to avoid unwarranted conclusions.

One must now not only identify the item and the years it was produced, but also determine if the original manufacturer was also a decorator. If they were, did they use this or a similar decoration in their line? Did other decorating firms of that time period (there were many) also use their items as decorating blanks?

Over the years there were talented individuals not connected with the commercial industry, or, if so, on a much smaller scale, that produced high quality, fired decorations on whatever pieces caught their fancy. These "cottage industry" items can be the most puzzling due to the lack of available documentation.

In this book we have based our undocumented attributions on our collective experiences and that of other knowledgeable Charleton collectors. We have attempted to make these attributions as accurate as possible through the use of empirical evidence. This includes the existence of the decoration on other pieces with Charleton labels, the motif and strength of the decoration, acid etching, and physical characteristics of the paint. Also considered were the presence, quality, quantity, and style of gold leaf elements. Other considerations were whether the manufacturing source was a known supplier of blanks to AWCO. It was also important to examine items for label remnants, initials, or signatures of the decorators. Comparisons were also made between unidentified decorations with those seen in advertisements from magazines and trade journals.

As tempting as it may be, we have tried to avoid making decisions based on emotion, and if in doubt we have placed the items in the "unknown decorator" category until more information is found. This is harder than it may seem as we sometimes really wanted some items to be Charleton. These items, however, still went in the unknown decorator section, but were captioned in such a way as to indicate our strong suspicions.

In order to standardize some aspects of collecting Charleton and to aid the exchange of information between collectors, we have given names to all of the Charleton designs shown in this book. Prior to assigning a new name, we first determined if AWCO had a trade name for that particular design, as they sometimes did, and then used that. We also queried other collectors for names, especially for names of designs of items they owned and with which we were not familiar.

In selecting names ourselves, we have tried to let the design speak for itself and then to be descriptively succinct so the name is not cumbersome. Often there will be found variations of a particular design. Here we tried to be as objective as possible and only give distinct names to variants if the differences in design might lead to confusion. We have also observed that some variants in decoration can actually affect the value of the item, so this issue has been addressed from time to time.

The vast majority of Charleton decorations to be found are floral decorations, often with pink roses as a central theme. These roses are a major key to locating and identifying Charleton items. Roses in partial and full bloom in a grouping are usually portrayed on items such as plates, trays, bowls, and vases and are usually positioned as if the observer has a direct overhead view. Not only is this stylistically appealing, but this aerial depiction is a good first indicator that the decoration is possibly Charleton. We have chosen in this book to call this decoration "Charleton Roses."

Roses that are painted in partial and full profile are commonly found on tall vases, jugs, and dresser sets. These roses are often linked with garlands bordering the rims, or placed in vertical rows, as well as in a spiral or lattice type arrangement. The roses almost always have some green leaves and stems as a background. Often this background will be interspersed with stems and leaves in gold leaf paint. You may also find some of the roses or leaves are tinted differently, lending an effective "wash" type contrast.

There are a number of larger pieces that have rose blooms that are fully opened. These decorations usually portray the roses as being scaled life-size, and their largeness overshadows the other decorating details. These roses have a styling about them that is quite distinctive and for these items we use the name "Open Rose."

Although garlands, sometimes with gold, blue, or lavender bows located at the top of the rose decoration, are great Charleton indicators, you must use caution as several other companies (most often Westmoreland Glass Company and Beth Weissman) copied this pattern closely. This decoration actually was popular during Victorian times and we have seen this style of painting reflected on many Bavarian and Czechoslovakian items. That is why identifying the blank and its years of production are such key elements in attribution.

Beth Weissman decorated Fenton pieces of the same type that AWCO used with a very similar "Roses and Bows" pattern. Some patterns are so close that proper identification of the decorating firm (AWCO or Weismann) for items with no Charleton label cannot be made. Although some Beth Weissman items were labeled, either these Charleton-like pieces were never labeled or no labels have survived to be reported. There are a few advertisements that picture their decorated pieces and one particular advertisement has led to the positive attribution of their "Roses and Bows" decoration. Actually this was an advertisement placed by the Katherine Zipper Co., who was just a distributor for Beth Weissman and not a decorator. Weissman items on Fenton glassware seem to be limited to Silver Crest and Peach Crest items and direct comparisons of their wares and AWCO's are shown later in the photographs.

The Westmoreland Glass Company (which will also be discussed in detail later in a separate section) manufactured glassware in their own factory and also employed a high quality decorating department. Although using a great many types of decorations, some of which were decals, during the 1950s Westmoreland introduced their best-known hand painted decoration, which they called Decoration #32, "Roses and Bows." This decoration is very similar to the decoration that had been in use since at least 1943 by AWCO.

Although AWCO's use of this decoration predates Westmoreland's #32 "Roses and Bows" by ten years, it can still be a problem for collectors to distinguish between Charleton Roses and Bows decorations and Westmoreland's #32. Even more confusing for collectors is the fact that AWCO's Charleton decoration can be found on the same patterns of glass that Westmoreland used for their Decoration #32. Collectors should study and compare both decorations in attempting to distinguish one from the other.

A technique that AWCO used, and most effectively in this realm of collectibles, was to spray an undercoat of pastel colored china paint in a contrasting shade on the item. Most items with this treatment have either a pink, green, or blue mist. When this mist is employed on Fenton, it will most often be bordered or over-painted with a rose decoration and often accompanied by thickly painted scrollwork.

This mist, when found, will usually be applied on vases, plates, compotes, and in the center of bowls. Often this "mist" will be bordered on either side by the unpainted original color of the glass. A portion of the foot on compotes will sometimes be misted in a star shaped geometric pattern as well. On some vases this mist covers a third of the piece and usually runs to the base or foot.

This mist decoration is not unique to Fenton, although it is found more frequently on that glass than on any other maker's wares. Most likely this is due to the large proportion of Fenton glassware that AWCO decorated.

Of particular note to Cambridge collectors is the decoration which AWCO called "Blue Mist." This decoration is quite scarce and very collectible. This will be discussed in detail in the chapter on Cambridge found later.

There are some glass items, such as certain Consolidated vases, that had the entire exterior spray-painted prior to decoration. This painting is not considered by the authors to be a true mist decoration. Only items that expose the underlying glass or glaze along with the misting will be cataloged as "mist" decorations. There are no examples documented to date that have used this "mist" as the sole decoration.

Unlike some of the other decorating companies of that time period who used a scattering of the same glass blanks that AWCO used, Charleton decorators never utilized stencils, or transfer decoration (partial or otherwise). All Charleton decorations, though varying greatly in technique, were done by hand, and the decorations were also fired. A variety of tools were used to achieve certain effects, such as slip trailing, blocking, or syringe art. In some cases either a latex masking ma terial was used or some type of resin or wax resist was employed in order to create ovals or other designs within an area of blush.

There are a considerable number of Charleton items from various manufacturers that exhibit a soft "doe skin" finish created by treating the piece with acid. The piece is either dipped or brushed with the acid solution and after the correct amount of corrosion has taken place the piece is rinsed with plain water. On crystal pieces there will usually be areas that were masked to prevent etching and these form small oval or circular "windows" of clear glass after the masking material is removed. This satin-like effect is quite striking and was used extensively by AWCO on Fenton Amber and Ruby Snowcrest items. Almost as scarce as the Snowcrest items are the satin finished Fenton items in Crystal that were made exclusively for AWCO.

Another color that sometimes received this satin finish was milk glass. Of the few Fenton milk glass items we have found, they are mostly vanity items with an infrequent vase, bowl, or compote. Almost without exception, all of these items have received excellent decorations.

Fenton's company records indicate that they satin finished the milk glass items for AWCO, but the Snow Crest and Crystal items were probably done at the Abels, Wasserberg studio.

We have documented acid etched pieces from Duncan & Miller and Heisey, but they are few in number and these American made items are considered rare. There are also several examples of acid etched Charleton pieces made in West Germany, but we are not sure if they were decorated in the U.S.

AWCO was very generous with their use of costly gold leaf. Commonly used wide and narrow gold leaf bands can be found in several locations on one piece, mostly on the rim, neck, and the base. Thin gold lines will sometimes be used as the connector from rose to rose, usually in a lattice form, or as stippling.

You will also find gold stems and leaves; these are commonly found scattered uniformly in the background, and most often as a border. These small leaves are usually found grouped two or three on a stem and we refer to them as "sprigs." As far as we can find, only three decorating companies (Amoges, Consolidated Glass Company and AWCO) employed this type of sprig during the Charleton time period.

Found mostly on Fenton, and even then only on a small number of pieces, are the use of squiggly gold leaf "rays" originating from a central decoration in bowls that radiate outwards to the rim. These rays can also be crosshatched in what is very similar to stitching.

The application of this gold leaf appears to have been mostly done by hand painting, but the technique of silk-screening or masking may have been employed to execute gold bands. It is unlikely that silk-screening was used to create the golden rays, stars, roses, or leaves, as each individual decoration is different from all the others. The saw tooth rays that often border some Cambridge and Fenton items are obviously hand painted because of the inconsistent spacing and length of the rays.

In the late 1940s and on into the 1950s, AWCO began issuing some of the most unique decorations they ever developed. The shapes of these pieces also departed from the traditional vanity sets, bowls, compotes, and plates. Instead we find unique platforms for modern decorating. Such things as ovoid vases, pyramids, angular lines on footed bowls, and large tapering decanters were marketed to sophisticated buyers.

Used to decorate these new shapes were modernistic geometric and abstract patterns that had only been hinted at in a couple of earlier patterns. The effect achieved is so different from the standard compotes, vases, etc., with a floral design that, if it were not for the Charleton label, you would never have thought these items were from AWCO. This new look was called "Charleton Modern" in their advertisements, and was certainly reflective of the modern design movement following World War II.

Just as radical as the designs were the techniques employed in applying the decorations. Some pieces were placed upon spinning turntables in order to execute the colored bands. Other items were painted with a base color and then, while the paint was still wet, were daubed with a brush or a sponge form soaked with thinner in order to achieve a mottled effect.

Another method involved "syringe art," commonly used in both the pottery and textile trade. This method required the use of a small handheld paint reservoir (probably a squeeze bulb or syringe) with a narrow spout that allowed the thick paint contained in it to flow onto the piece in raised rib-like lines. Once decorated, the item was then fired for permanence. Sometimes these rib-like lines were overlaid with gold leaf, giving the items a very luxurious appearance.

The sharply contrasting geometric lines that are found on some pieces used a method with the unusual name of "sgraffito." This technique predates Christianity and originated in Japan. It involves coating over of the base color with a thin layer of clay of contrasting color, which is called the "slip." Then, before this wet slip has time to dry, a stylus of some type was used to carve lines in this thin layer revealing the underlying base color. The piece was then fired for permanence.

Their foray into Art Moderne, however, does not mean AWCO abandoned their foundations. During this same period we still can find advertisements and further examples of beautifully decorated items employing their more traditional hand painted roses.

A recent find, a crystal tea jar, is very unique in its decoration. The artists used an undetermined method to achieve a pinkish stucco-like finish over crystal. This material is finely textured and fired for permanence. The color contrasts nicely with the gold theme of the decoration, which is oriental in design.

In broaching the subject of Asian influence on American interior design, AWCO made a startling departure from Charleton Roses in this direction, just as they did with their approach to Art Moderne. We always felt that, aside from their association with foreign imports prior to World War II, AWCO probably purchased items from the Far East to compliment their line. Proof of this association was a long time coming. A piece marked "Charleton" and "Made in Japan" surfaced at auction several years ago, but slipped elusively away before we could document it.

It was only when we uncovered a treasure trove of advertisements covering a time span of ten years from 1946 to 1956 that we truly had our eyes opened to what this company was capable of producing. These full-page advertisements were obtained from a periodical called *The Gift and Art Buyer* that was directed at retailers and wholesalers in the giftware industry.

At the end of this decade of advertisements we found two AWCO advertisements that were just stunning. The first one, dated July 1956, shows an arrangement of oriental items that we never would have associated with AWCO. They are marketed as the "Charleton Kyoto Collection" and, with the exception of a silk paneled screen are very simple in artistic composition.

Not knowing the scale of the paneled screen to the other items pictured leaves the viewer in doubt as to its actual size. It is stylistically accurate for the Orient and it is doubtful that it or any of the other pieces were decorated by AWCO. In fact, some of these advertisements tout the items as having been decorated in the originating country.

The other items appear to be ceramic vases or bowl-like baskets created in very simple, yet tasteful forms. In keeping with their origins, wooden woven-wrapped handles complete the utilitarian shapes and have little adornment by way of decoration. What decoration there is, is organic in nature and appears to be represented in earth tones.

This style of artistry has always had a following, albeit somewhat limited in the U.S. During and after the war, returning servicemen sent or brought home souvenirs from their journeys and soon the market followed suit with "Occupied Japan" porcelain, lacquered vases, lanterns, etc. Displaying this type of art in one's home was not only stylistically pleasing to the occupants – it also communicated a sense of the owners being sophisticated and "world travelers." This was much more intriguing to visitors than Grandma's "Old Paris" vases on the mantel.

Another AWCO offering was made in December 1956. This time the advertisement documents that these items were "Imports from the Orient." Five Blanc de Chine porcelain statues are shown in exquisite detail and the artistry involved in completing them was top notch.

We have not taken the time yet to explore whom these figures might portray or what meaning is associated with their attire or accoutrements. Certainly there may be another story here, but we feel that these items may certainly be enjoyed in their own right as fine examples of Oriental porcelain figurines. To date, none of these Oriental objects have been documented for sale or in collections; but, hopefully, through exposure in this book we will hear more about them from other collectors.

The Suppliers

Published in *The Gift and Art Buyer*, December 1945, is an article entitled "Going on in the Trade" that gives us an idea of the wide scope of suppliers doing business with AWCO. Cited among the complications to be overcome in their decorating trade was the fact that twenty-five factories supplied different types of glass. It is unknown if the term "glass" here may encompass porcelain and china factories as well, so there could possibly have been more suppliers.

This is an area that needs much more exploration in order to determine just who these companies were. Thus far, by identifying items pictured in company advertisements, and examining pieces with Charleton labels, we have compiled this list of known companies that are documented as having supplied AWCO with blank items for decorations:

Glass
Cambridge
Consolidated
Dunbar
Duncan & Miller
Fenton
Fostoria
Heisey
Imperial
Indiana Glass (Dunkirk, Indiana)
Kemple
U.S. Glass/Tiffin
New Martinsville/Viking
Westmoreland
West Virginia Specialty Glass

Ceramics
ARS, Sesto Fiorenrtino
Ceramiche Corte, Bassano Del Grappa, Italy
Limoges
Ronzan, Bassano Del Grappa, Italy
Schumann (china)
Sevres (porcelain)

As may be seen, AWCO used suppliers from all over the world. From the following list of countries we have seen items with Charleton labels that also have separate labels, marks, or ink stamps indicating their country of origin.

France
Italy
West Germany

The following is a list of countries that are documented as being AWCO suppliers and this proof mostly originated in Walter Abels' personal letters, trade journal text or advertisements. To date, no Charleton/AWCO pieces have been found bearing a label of origin from these countries. Poland and Czechoslovakia were added to this list after Abel's personal letters documented purchases being made there. Japan was added after the discovery of the Charleton Kyoto Collection advertisement. At this point we can only logically assume that the Kyoto Collection originated in Japan, although Hong Kong is also possibly the source.

Czechoslovakia
Hong Kong
India
Japan
Poland
Spain
Switzerland

Although AWCO did quite a bit of importing, examples of these items are elusive. Hopefully, due to the durability of Charleton labels, we will be able to greatly increase this list through further collecting as well as input from other collectors.

The Charleton Line

AWCO basically utilized only three types of materials in their blanks. Glass items appear to be the most commonly found, followed by porcelain/ceramics, and then metals. There have been only three pieces of Charleton decorated metal found to date, two of which have the same decoration and are toleware. (Tole means tin or metal and toleware is painted metal. Its history dates to eighteenth century France where it is known as tole peinte.) The third is a very modernistic lamp that was almost entirely constructed of metal. We chose not to include metal in the book's title description due to the paucity of this material.

Early in our collecting career we saw an on-line auction for a Charleton decorated garden statue. It was a gold colored standing figure of an angel and was quite large, about three feet tall or better. The seller did state that the statue had a Charleton label under the base. We cannot recall what material was used, but it is likely that it was either metal or plaster. Obviously, if we could go back in time, this (not so little) gem would now be ours. At the time we had merely a "passing" interest in Charleton, never realizing how quickly that would change! Ah, the one that got away!

Glass

The most common types and colors of glass used by AWCO were white opaque (milk) glass, crested milk glass, cased glass, colored opaque glass, and crystal. If you are just beginning a collection of Charleton, then white milk glass will generally be the least expensive and most plentiful medium to find. Items such as bonbons and compotes in Fenton's Silver Crest and Consolidated vases in milk glass would be a good starting point. You can put together a very nice display in a relative short time without great expense.

If you want to spice this collection with color, then the vanity sets in blue or rose overlay make not only very attractive additions, but can be interesting to collect by themselves. A wide variety of lovely floral decorations exist and new ones surface regularly. Vanity items are available in large numbers, making it easy to piece together complete vanity sets. Bargains are in abundance, so get a feel for the market first before buying expensive pieces.

A bit more expensive, but well worth the extra money, would be the addition of a few pieces of Fenton's Peach Crest. Peach Crest is made by adding a layer of milk glass over a gathering of gold ruby prior to being blown. This is such a striking item that just a few pieces really add impact to your collection display.

Just as there are many collectors, there are many ways to assemble a collection of Charleton, depending upon your personal taste and budget. Group collections are what some people prefer to pursue. By groups we mean, groups of lamps, vanity sets, compotes, vases, candy dishes, plates, etc. Another way to approach this could be in sets. Sets could include not only one company's product, but also a particular mould pattern in various decorations or different mould patterns, even by different companies, with the same decoration. A wide variety of Fenton's crests are still readily available and would make a stunning display.

In our opinion, pursuing a thorough assemblage of Cambridge Crown Tuscan would be the ultimate collection. The Charleton decorations on Cambridge represent the best-designed and executed work AWCO ever produced. The flowing shell pink opalescent glass in finely detailed patterns provides the ultimate canvas for these highly skilled artists.

For whatever reason, Crown Tuscan pieces are easier to find with the Charleton label intact – possibly because most Crown Tuscan items are decorative in nature rather than utilitarian. Lest you be discouraged early on, be aware that there are a number of serious Crown Tuscan collectors with very deep pockets that will bid up scarce pieces at auction way beyond their fair market value. Bringing together a large assortment of this glass will be expensive and can easily span a number of years. Deals may be found if you are patient. Smaller pieces are proportionally less expensive, but larger inexpensive pieces can be found due to ignorance or misidentification on the seller's part. Some of the rarest pieces you may never be able to find. Crown Tuscan collectors are a very tight knit group and generally hold on to the rarities or trade just within their group. We admit that we have looked with envy at some of the Charleton Crown Tuscan items we have seen in private collections.

Ceramics (China, Porcelain, and Pottery)

Collecting Charleton in these materials can be a bit more difficult for a variety of reasons. The manufacturers of these blanks are usually lesser known, thereby making pertinent research material harder to locate. Also, these pieces were apparently not produced by AWCO in any quantity approaching the huge volume of glass they decorated. These items are also very difficult to find with the Charleton label, probably due both to the rougher unglazed bases that provided a less than ideal surface for the bonding of the adhesive on the label and to the more utilitarian and everyday uses of these items. Once again, we find a number of pieces decorated by unknown firms whose floral decorations are easily confused with Charleton.

Other than Limoges, Schumann, some Italian items identified for us by Maurizio Burlamacchi, and possibly Amoges, we have not been able to identify the other ceramic blank manufacturers. Some of the unidentified items found include lamps (both plain and figurine), vanity sets, figurines of people and animals, vases, lavebos, covered urns, plates, and candy boxes.

Most of these items are hand painted over the glaze. AWCO's use of ceramics also has led to the unique finding of two pieces of Charleton that were not decorated with anything other than the uniform and simple color of the glaze, quite unusual for this company. Most likely these pieces were sold just like they were imported. More pieces exist, as evidenced by the pieces shown in bisque and porcelain in their advertisements, but they have not yet been documented in collections.

Through interviews with Maurizio Burlamacchi, more and more of these pieces are thought to have originated in Italy. There was a very strong business relationship between AWCO and G. Burlamacchi and this greatly influenced the European purchases that Walter Abels made.

Metal

Very few Charleton items have turned up in metal objects. We have pictured two pieces of toleware that are both decorated in Gold Roses. There is a tremendous amount floral decorated toleware on the market from other makers. Many of the decorations are similar to Charleton Roses, but the use of gold leaf from these other manufacturers is sparing, if used at all.

Most of these decorated items are from the Nash Company, or Nashco as they were later known. They look so "Charletonesque" that we often cannot resist the temptation of turning them over in hopes of finding a Charleton label.

The only other item that has been found consisting mostly of metal is a unique lamp that the seller described as an "Eames Space Age Lamp." At this point we have no evidence that the lamp was directly associated with Charles Eames. It is quite interesting in design, although we suppose it would require just the right 1960s or early 1970s themed interior to avoid being gauche. This could also have been one of the European lamp imports that are mentioned in a trade journal from 1963.

Another interesting aspect of this lamp is that it has a different AWCO label than any other we have seen. This label is a beige, rectangular paper label. It is in very bad condition, but we could see the word "Wasserberg" and the word "Charleton." It was placed just inside the collar into which a glass globe would have been inserted. An odd place to put a label, to be sure. In fact it took much searching to even find this label. It would have been quite a bit easier to have given up looking for it; but, in the end, our efforts were rewarded. So be sure to check all those old, somewhat odd lamps you may have – they may just turn out to be Charleton.

From a recently discovered biographical sketch of the company found in *The Gift and Art Buyer,* written in September 1963, we know that AWCO was importing metal lamp bases, as well as brass and copper art objects. Although none of these items have been reported to date, various metal fixtures are pictured in the last full page advertisements that AWCO placed in *The Gift and Art Buyer.*

Chapter 2.
Fenton

Of all the glassware on which you may find Charleton decorations, Fenton art glass holds the distinction of being the most plentiful and having the widest variety of delightful decorations. Many collectors see their first Charleton decoration on Fenton and there are many items that can be purchased at reasonable prices. The presence of Charleton artistry on Fenton glass compliments the wide variety of shapes and styles still available today.

The Fenton Art Glass Company is one of the few companies that began operations during the "Golden Age" of glass making (1895-1910) and has operated continuously through today. This is a tribute to the business acumen and hard work of a successive line of Fenton family members and dedicated staff that have been associated with the company from the very beginning.

The founder of the company, Frank Leslie Fenton, was the youngest of seven children, and was born in Indiana, Pennsylvania, in 1880. After graduating in 1897 as the high school valedictorian, he first entertained the idea of being a teacher. But this notion quickly passed and he went to work for the Indiana Glass Company, located in his hometown. Fenton worked hard and within a year he was promoted to plant foreman. By this time, the Indiana plant was under the leadership of the renowned Harry Northwood and was producing some of America's highest quality art glass.

The talent in the glass industry that gathered in the surrounding area during that time was astounding. Names like Heisey, Northwood, William Leighton, Sr., J. H. Hobbs, Percy Beaumont, and Nicholas Kopp are just a few to be mentioned. As a result of the revolutionary ideas and hard labor of these men, many innovative styles and dazzling colors of glass flowed from the factories and into homes throughout America. For the first time, glassware of high caliber was being made cheaply enough that most everyone could afford something to proudly display.

Frank L. Fenton moved shortly thereafter to Steubenville, Ohio, where he was employed at the Jefferson Glass Company. After leaving Jefferson he found work at the Bastow Glass Company. When the Bastow factory was destroyed by fire, he went to work for the Northwood Glass Company, which by then had relocated in Wheeling, West Virginia.

Born with a strong streak of independence, Fenton was too industrious to work for anyone else for long and, having learned the basics of glassmaking, he decided that he could just as easily do this kind of work for himself.

Frank L., and his brother John Fenton, opened the Fenton Art Glass Company (FAGCO) in July of 1905 in Martins Ferry, Ohio. The brothers enlisted the help of two other investors, a druggist named J. C. Dent and a physician, J. O. Howells. J. C. Dent was named the president of the newly formed company and John Fenton was the vice-president. Frank took the role of secretary and general manager, and the other investor, Dr. J. O. Howells, was appointed the company's treasurer. Another Fenton brother, Charles H., was appointed as the head of the decorating department.

For the first two years, the company was a decorating firm only. Purchasing glass blanks from other companies, they decorated these items and resold them. This was a normal course for many fledgling glass companies and, while FAGCO went on to manufacturer their own glassware, many others never went on to that next phase.

FAGCO did not begin manufacturing glass until after the firm had relocated to Williamstown, West Virginia. That area of the country, especially Ohio and West Virginia, is blessed with all of the natural resources needed for the glass industry such as natural gas, coal, clean sand, and water for production and transportation.

By a twist of fate, Frank L. Fenton's former employer, Harry Bastow, came to work for FAGCO in 1906. According to Bastow's account, he was involved in the plant's site selection and oversaw the construction of the glass factory in Williamstown. Other reports downplayed his role with FAGCO and gave John Fenton the lion's share of credit for many of Bastow's claims. At any rate, Bastow was either fired or quit the company in October of 1906.

After FAGCO refused Bastow's claims of exorbitant fees for his supposed services, there ensued a nasty lawsuit. The merits of his case might be weighed by the outcome, as Bastow was asking for $15,000.00 and the judgment rendered to him was for $150.00.

Soon after the departure of Harry Bastow, a gentleman by the name of Jacob Rosenthal came to work for FAGCO. Rosenthal was not only an experienced glassworker and former plant manager, but he was a skilled chemist as well. Indiana "Greentown" glass lovers that hoard chocolate glass know him well for the creation of this rich slag formula. His various skills served him well during his career as the superintendent of FAGCO, and he retired from the company in 1929.

Rosenthal was part of a pool of skilled glassworkers that moved from company to company as work dried up, factories burned down (quite common), or better wages were found in other factories. Despite all the advantages that the area had to offer, many firms never lasted more than a year or two. It took very capable hands to survive the vicissitudes of floods, fires, strikes, economic downturns, and fickle markets rife with heavy competition both at home and from abroad. In this constant flux, workers acquired new skills and useful information that benefited themselves and whoever happened to be their current employer.

The plant construction under Rosenthal's expert guidance moved along efficiently. After a few more exasperating, yet unavoidable delays, the Fenton Art Glass Company produced its first piece of glass on January 2, 1907.

Within two years of the plant's opening, tension mounted between John Fenton and the other members of the family and management. This strain was brought about from a growing concern about his unsound business practices. Without seeking counsel from the other company officers, he spent the company's money rather freely and with little foresight as to the wisdom of his decisions. Never realizing all of the fruits of his labors, John Fenton parted ways with FAGCO and founded his own factory in Millersburg, Ohio, in 1909. In a personal interview, his nephew, Frank M. Fenton, summed up the situation for me this way, "Uncle John got ants in his pants."

Millersburg was built with the funds John Fenton obtained from selling his share of FAGCO back to the family. Unfortunately, under his guidance the company had a short life, opening in 1909 and closing in 1911. He reopened it once again as the Radium Glass Company, but it lasted about a year and went under for the last time in 1912. Now prized by collectors as some of the most beautiful Carnival glass ever produced, Millersburg's Carnival glass is very collectible. Ironically, this glass commands premium prices due to the short supply caused by Millersburg's brief period of operation.

Two more Fenton brothers, James E. and Robert C. Fenton, joined the growing business of FAGCO around the time John Fenton left. Although Robert Fenton was the oldest of the Fenton brothers at the age of 32, he was the last to join the company in 1910.

With innovation and hard work, FAGCO prospered and produced dozens of new and different patterns of glass. They were the first company to produce iridescent (carnival) glass and it was a good seller. In his pithy way of stemming any controversy about which glass company first made carnival glass, with a slight smile, Frank M. Fenton says ". . . anyway, we were the first to claim we made it." They also developed variations of beautiful Victorian patterns such as opalescent Coinspot, Hobnail, and Stretch glass. Along with these pieces, they turned out novelty items, vases and bowls of all descriptions, lemonade sets, and elegant place settings of dinnerware.

FAGCO's entry into the hobnail business in 1939, making bottles for the A. B. Wrisley perfume company, helped to bring the company out of lingering financial trouble from the Depression. Another important account that aided their survival was that of A. F. Dormeyer, for whom FAGCO made mixing bowls. Both of these Chicago firms added greatly to FAGCO's bottom line and ensured the business would continue to operate.

While both of these accounts would eventually turn to other suppliers who were making cheaper machine-made glassware, Fenton wisely never compromised their high standards. When the company decided to introduce various hobnail items in their own line inspired by the bottle made for Wrisley, the line was a tremendous success. Fenton hobnail from this era is still highly prized and collected in today's market.

It was also around this time that Fenton picked up one of the most important outside accounts they would have for many years. The disruption of overseas imports caused by the growing instability of markets in Europe was responsible for many American companies looking homeward for their merchandise. Abels, Wasserberg & Company was one of several others who would turn to FAGCO to supply a major portion of their wares, due to this disruption caused by World War II.

Until this point, AWCO was strictly an import company, buying decorated goods from many different European markets. Beginning with the fall of Poland to Nazi Germany in 1939, and, shortly thereafter, the disruption in shipping over the Atlantic caused by enemy submarines, the pipeline of goods from Europe dwindled rapidly and then virtually stopped altogether.

Walter Abels was quick to make contacts with many American manufacturers in order to keep their inventory stocked. In conjunction, early in 1942, AWCO established a decorating department near their business headquarters in New York City. This allowed them not only to quickly adapt to changes in designs, but also allowed them to offer a higher quality decoration.

AWCO's ability to decorate in-house meant these new decorations could now be coordinated on a combination of wares from different suppliers. The result of this capability is shown in the smartly styled groupings displayed in their advertisements and the gradual assemblage of various sets by collectors.

Most likely there was personal contact between Walter Abels or Harry Wasserberg with Frank L. Fenton. Unfortunately, there are no records reflecting this and Frank M. and Bill Fenton were not directly involved in dealing with AWCO's account during this period. Later on, the independent representatives that serviced these accounts handled all communication between the two companies.

According to information we obtained in a recent interview with Frank M. Fenton, as best he can recall, AWCO and Fenton's business relationship was initiated in 1941. AWCO continued to purchase glass blanks from them until 1958, and then continued purchasing glass lamp parts into the 1960s. Cyrus (Cy) Lowe of the Horace C. Gray Company was Fenton's main representative for AWCO.

It should be no wonder that Abels, Wasserberg & Company relied upon FAGCO to be their biggest supplier of glass blanks, and, in turn, they became one of Fenton's best individual customers during the war years and directly thereafter. There are more different types of Charleton decorations found on Fenton glassware than all other companies combined. The wide choices of shapes and colors available at a fair price made Fenton art glass suitable as the ideal platform for AWCO's elaborate decorations.

After more than fifty years in the glass industry, Frank L. Fenton passed away in May of 1948. The company had lost its guiding light and his death came during a difficult time for the company. The glass boom of the war years was over and competition was strong, especially from factories with automated equipment. None of the Fenton family could easily fill the vacancy left by the death of Frank L. Fenton, but the company was soon reorganized.

Soon after his father's death, Frank M. was appointed as company treasurer, and at the regular board meeting in June 1948 the presidency of the company was formally handed over to him. His uncle Robert served as vice-president and sales manager. However, Robert was over 80 years old and, with his health failing, he passed away in November of the same year. With the death of James Fenton the previous year, and now Frank L. and Robert C. passing in quick succession, the leadership of the company passed completely to the next generation of Fentons.

Frank M. Fenton was born at home on December 1st, 1915. He grew to be quite tall during his early life, and played center for his college basketball team in the Ohio conference. He also studied hard in school where he majored in chemistry and earned a Bachelor of Arts degree.

In school, Frank M.'s unusual height (six feet, seven inches) became a bit of a problem for him. During his basketball days, all of the unwanted attention became so pervasive that he devised a scheme to turn the tables. He had a calling card printed with his height and other personal information and silently handed these out when asked to answer the inevitable questions about his height.

As the years passed Frank could have grown quite weary over the inquires about his height, but rather than brush off those questions, he would often reply with a twinkle in his eye that he is "five feet, nineteen inches." These days he still answers the inevitable question the same way, only adding that because of a slight stoop, he is five feet, seventeen and a half inches. Frank loves to tell stories and they are typically sprinkled throughout with his dry sense of humor. Despite his disarming personality, he is very serious about the glass business. In describing Frank M. Fenton, we have heard of no one who has said it better than William Heacock when he stated that, "Frank Fenton casts a long shadow."

With Frank M. at the helm of the company, his younger brother Wilmer C. (Bill) Fenton was appointed as vice-president and secretary. Bill Fenton was born on November 19th, 1923 and was the "youngster" of the family. He attended Marietta College for three years, but his higher education was interrupted when he was drafted into the service in 1943. After his tour of duty ended, he went back to work for FAGCO and then faced a tough decision regarding his life's endeavor.

For whatever reason, Bill seemed to see little future for him in the family business and felt it was time to chart his course. He was undecided about working for his father at the factory or joining a business venture in Portsmouth that had been proposed to him by an Army buddy while they were still in the service. He was fretting over this decision and called his father for guidance. Frank L. Fenton managed to convince his son that he was needed at the plant. We are sure that Bill Fenton will tell you today that the decision he made was the right choice, as it was the beginning of what is still a long and distinguished career at Fenton.

Until his recent retirement, Bill Fenton headed up Fenton's relationship with the television-shopping giant, QVC. He had previously learned a great deal about the art of salesmanship while working with his uncle, Robert C. Fenton, "Uncle Bob."

Through sound business practices and loyalty from their workforce, FAGCO established itself as a major glass manufacturer. Under the skilful management of the Fenton family they have produced an enormous amount of art glass and other items for the American market. Ranging from dental cuspidors to some of the finest offhand art glass ever made, Fenton's broad range of items can be found all over the world.

Frank M. Fenton provided us with the most treasured gift that any researcher could ask for and that was access to what he calls the "little black books." These are actually just that; black leather bound binders that contain typed records, interspersed with handwritten notes, of FAGCO's orders and shipments to various outside firms. With the orders from AWCO listed in the journals, we were able to compile a very concise record of AWCO's dealings with Fenton.

Although the records are not one hundred percent complete, there are only a few Fenton pieces that have turned up that are not found in these archives. Perhaps the best news is the fact that there are scores of pieces bought from Fenton by AWCO that have not yet turned up, so many surprises are awaiting the patient collector.

Although Fenton never created new moulds or exclusive patterns for AWCO as they sometimes did for other companies, they would, upon request, hand tool the hot glass with special crimping or leave off the outer ring of the crest color. Some items were also done for AWCO in colors that were not offered in the regular Fenton line. Additionally, Fenton would make specific changes at AWCO's request, such as supplying them with Diamond Lace epergnes that had matching horns (lilies) made with smooth exterior surfaces. This allowed the Charleton decorators to portray hand painted roses on the lilies to match the decoration on the interior of the epergne base.

Fenton also supplied them with crested plates – some of which were transformed into decorative clocks. Lamp bases were supplied to AWCO in a variety of patterns and colors. Although AWCO boasted in 1943 that they had over 375 styles of table and boudoir lamps for sale, Charleton lamps made from Fenton glass are very scarce and are an exciting find in today's market.

In an interesting background story written by Helen Klemko, it has been noted that cost never seemed to be the determining factor to AWCO when buying glass blanks. In the early 1950s, Fenton's CEO Frank M. Fenton was meeting with Walter Abels and he asked Walter if he wanted to sit down before he quoted him the cost of a Cranberry Hobnail lampshade he had brought with him. Mr. Abels replied," we don't care how high the price is, as long as it's a good seller!"

The following is an account of some observations we made while visiting the Fenton factory in order to obtain research material. We hope that it may be of interest to the Charleton enthusiasts by somewhat personalizing their collecting experience.

It was important to us to gain some insight into the work that would have been taking place within FAGCO's factory walls during the time that AWCO was operating. Many tasks undertaken in producing art glass at Fenton have not changed a great deal since the 1940s and 1950s. This type of glass making involves a lot of human interaction and the Fenton Art Glass Company is one of those rare family owned and operated businesses that seem to infuse a personal touch into everything they produce.

The entire experience of witnessing the choreography that takes place in creating this beautiful art glass, from the fiery innards of the furnaces to the quiet calm of the large decorating studios, was an education in and of itself. By viewing the various activities, one has the chance to gain a much greater appreciation for the tremendous effort that has to take place in order for collectors to be able to own and enjoy the end results of these labors.

We were understandably nervous as we prepared to meet for the first time with Frank and Bill Fenton for background research for this book. Although Bill is a very busy man, he welcomed us into his office that was brimming over with past, present, and future items for QVC. He enthusiastically discussed a wide range of topics, and his breadth of knowledge of the company's history was amazing.

Later that day, during a question and answer period prior to taking a tour of the Fenton Museum, we asked Frank what his very first job was at the factory. He said that unlike most people, he started at the top and worked his way down. Pausing a few beats, he adds that his father would not give him a job at first, but Uncle Jim put him to work patching the tar roof on the factory. With a slight smile he continued by stating that his next job was working on a yard gang performing maintenance at the factory. After following him around while he was conducting the tour, we soon discovered that this was just a typical "Frankism" that he was apt to include along with his more serious responses to visitor's questions.

In enlightening me as to the relationship that existed between he and his brother Bill during former years, Frank stated it quite succinctly. He considered himself to be the "inside man" making daily decisions at the plant and Bill was the "outside man," on the road calling on customers and managing their sales force.

After many years of sharing the helm of the company, Frank M. Fenton is now the company's resident historian. He still puts in incredibly long hours, even for someone much younger than his eighty-five years. His love of anything glass is evident in all that he does and he does a lot. He was already there at the plant that morning when we first arrived at 9:00 AM and, later that evening, long after the offices had closed, we came across Frank in the Museum deep in a glass discussion with a visitor.

He still makes daily excursions about the plant and when telephoning him at the plant we felt lucky if we could catch him in his office on the first try. Often his phone would be answered by one of the company staff and, after asking if Frank was in, they would reply that he was just seen leaving the sample room, but was heading to the mould shop with a piece of glass.

Although Frank M. doesn't get involved in many of the decisions that were once his responsibility, he is still active in company affairs. The last day we were there he was shuffling through papers in his office, making preparations to conduct an interview with someone for a marketing position. After our return home, we were ending a lengthy afternoon phone call, made in order to follow-up on some questions, and he said that he had to go as he needed to cut the grass at his home.

Both Frank and Bill Fenton are highly thought of by their employees, as are all of the Fentons, and, as we followed Frank around the maze of the plant one afternoon, he was peppered with personal greetings everywhere he went. There was an attitude of great respect that was tendered him by the employees. Respect at times that bordered on reverence. But there is always a relaxed attitude about him that belies his stature. He would occasionally stop and exchange pleasantries with someone, his easy intimacy with them readily apparent and sincere.

Both Frank and Bill collect the glassware they produce, which should be no surprise. However, one aspect of this is rather interesting. Frank told us that none of the Fenton family gets their glass for free, but that everyone, including himself, receives the same discount that is offered to all the employees. Frank also said that after the passing of his father he had to disappoint some family members when they wanted to take home a particular piece for free. Their unheeded lament was often, "But Daddy used to let me have it for nothing!" Although not designed to intentionally hurt anyone's feelings, this was a wise course as the family was growing quickly, and it would have been very cumbersome to keep track of who received what and try to be fair to all.

The type of pleasant business atmosphere we encountered during our visit at Fenton is rare in the workplace these days. It can best be summed up by saying the impression we received from the entire staff was one of casual professionalism. It is not often that one can be warmly welcomed, with little introduction or established reputation, and ask for and receive access to the information we sought.

Visiting this vibrant, bustling factory has been one of the highlights in writing this book. If you have the chance to visit there, be sure to keep an eye out for Frank's head bobbing above the crowd, and, as we are sure he would want us to tell you, "Be sure to stop by the Gift Shop!"

Throughout the years, the Fenton family and dedicated employees have kept the company on an even keel, despite the rough waters they have encountered. The result of their skilled leadership and talented workforce made their glass attractive and available to AWCO, thereby expanding and enriching the catalog of Charleton decorated items accessible to collectors everywhere. Although we personally love virtually every Charleton decorated item we have ever seen, we must confess a strong preference for Charleton decorated Fenton. It was our first love and continues to be, despite the wide range of Charleton available.

Crested Items

As mentioned earlier, AWCO's relationship with FAGCO began in 1941, about the same time that Fenton's crest colors made their debut. The earliest pieces of Fenton glass with Charleton decorations are found on crested items. A crest is an extra ring of contrasting colored glass that is added to the edge of a piece while the glass is still hot. This is a rather tricky addition as the two pieces of glass must be very close in temperature and in their rate of expansion and contraction or the crest will separate during the trip through the annealing lehr.

Ivory Crest and Peach Crest

Although Ivory Crest ranks along with Peach Crest as the first crested colors made by Fenton, no Charleton decorated Ivory Crest items have been reported to date. Aqua Crest, Crystal Crest, and Peach Crest are the best candidates for the honor of being the first Fenton Charleton decorated items. Of these three crests, decorated Peach Crest will be the most abundant of the three colors. Two factors that may have made decorated Peach Crest more plentiful were the wide range of items made and length of production. Peach Crest was produced continuously from 1940 to 1969.

Peach Crest is one of the most striking color combinations in the crest line. Opalescent Milk Glass is layered over a gather (small glob of molten glass) of pure Gold Ruby glass before being blown to obtain these sharply contrasting colors. The addition of real gold to the glass formula makes this an expensive color to produce. Some of the painted decorations on Peach Crest are strongly suspected to be from the firm of Beth Weismann. The numerous items of Peach Crest with gold transfer roses are certainly not Charleton and are most likely from Tyndale.

The most commonly found AWCO decorated items will be on the mould #192, 6" and 8" double crimped Melon vases; #186, 8" double crimped vases; and the #192, 8" Melon jugs. Other items likely to turn up will be hat baskets, hat vases, baskets, and #192 Melon vanity sets. Interestingly, Peach Crest bowls do not appear to have been decorated by AWCO.

Aqua Crest

Like many other colors and treatments that Fenton produced, Aqua Crest items were made intermittently. The first production segment was from 1941 to 1942 and the second lasted from 1948 to 1953. Charleton Aqua Crest pieces were made during both periods and slight differences in the color of the crest will allow you to determine the time span from which a particular piece was made. The darker aqua color crested pieces, whose milk glass has a fiery opalescence, were made during the first issue between 1941 and 1942. The second issue pieces have a lighter aqua colored crest.

Crystal Crest

The other early crest line, Crystal Crest, is one of the most difficult to find crested colors, either with or without a Charleton decoration. Crystal Crest was a very short-lived color – made only for the first six months of 1942. Oddly enough, scarce Crystal Crest was the forerunner to the ubiquitous Silver Crest, which has the distinction of being the most commonly found of all Fenton patterns featuring Charleton decorations.

Surely to be among the rarest of all Charleton decorated Fenton crested items is a piece that just recently came to our attention: a #A-4808-SR 12" four piece Silver Rose epergne. This item was listed on the internet auction house eBay and caused quite a stir among collectors. Many of the older (and newer) large Fenton epergnes frequently sell in the $250.00 price range, but this piece had very special merits that really set it apart, thus allowing it to sell for over $500.00.

Snow Crest

Snow Crest items share aspects of the dual ring Crystal Crest, but they lack the inner crystal ring and instead have a single band of contrasting white opalescent milk glass on the rim. Although the very earliest example of a Snow Crest color by Fenton is Jade Crest[5], produced circa 1942, no items in Jade Crest have ever been documented with Charleton decorations.

Aside from Jade Crest, the earliest known pieces of Fenton Snow Crest were items in Ruby Snow Crest made for the L. G. Wright Company. Fenton's gold ruby formula was used for the glass.

In 1951, Fenton debuted their own Snow Crest line featuring four colors: Amber, Blue, Emerald Green, and Ruby. It was from this production period that AWCO purchased the glass blanks from Fenton to decorate. Charleton pieces to date have only been found on Amber, Emerald Green, and Ruby Snow Crest pieces. To find a Blue Snow Crest item with a Charleton decoration would be a real coup de grace. Decorated Snow Crest items are considered to be some of the most difficult items to find with Charleton decorations due to the limited production time and small numbers and types of pieces made.

Occasionally one can find undecorated Ruby and Emerald Green Snow Crest items without a Spiral Optic treatment. Spiral Optic is a twisting or spiraling pattern in the glass. It is created by first blowing the glass in a spiral optic mould and then blowing it in the mould for the desired shape intended (i.e. vase, bowl, pitcher, etc.). According to Frank M. Fenton, these pieces were possibly part of Fenton's line, but their production was limited to a very brief period, allowing them to be listed in printed price lists, but never pictured in any catalogs. Most Snow Crest pieces lacking this spiral optic treatment will be found with Charleton decorations. The Spiral Optic effect was probably considered too visually "busy" and was thus considered a less desirable platform for painting.

The Charleton decorated Snow Crest items also differ in another way from the regular Fenton issue. AWCO had these pieces satin finished in specific areas to compliment the decorative themes. Satin finishing is the process of using acid, usually hydrochloric, to etch the surface of the glass to achieve a dull or non-shiny finish. Even though FAGCO was quite capable of applying a satin finish on glass, Frank Fenton does not believe that Fenton treated these particular pieces for AWCO. We suspect it was done at AWCO's own facility, as this would have afforded them a higher degree of flexibility and less delay in developing the design.

Charleton decorations found on Snow Crest pieces are among the most elaborate designs that AWCO ever produced on Fenton glass. The white lattices and laurels compliment the milky color of the crest and the satin finished areas effectively isolate the clear, rose decorated panels into separate oval windowpanes.

Charleton Ruby Snow Crest pieces are very rare. The stunning #1925 vase shown later is one of only three or four decorated pieces in this color we have seen to date[6]. Hopefully, more decorated pieces of Ruby Snow Crest will surface and expand the range of known pieces.

While Amber Snow Crest glass is not quite as scarce as Ruby Snow Crest, still only a handful of decorated pieces are documented. A unique item that AWCO chose to include in this group is Fenton's #814 bottle in amber. This item can be correctly identified as either a cologne bottle, when paired in a vanity set, or as a stand-alone (decanter) bottle. Although this particular bottle was never crested, the Charleton decorators placed a wide ring of white paint on the outer rim, creating a faux Snow Crest so that the bottle would match the rest of the line. These bottles use the same stopper as Fenton's #1463 Coin Dot cruet and the #1465 Coin Dot perfume. Some collectors have referred to this as a "King's Crown" stopper, but Frank Fenton states that the correct name is "Coin Dot" stopper.

It is interesting to note that although Fenton used the #814 mould to produce cruets in various optic treatments for their own line, the cologne bottles from this mould were made exclusively for AWCO. In 1999, Fenton once again produced an item from this mould for an outside company. A stopperless cranberry bottle was made for QVC's Heirloom Collection and was decorated to capture the Italian Renaissance period.[7]

Rose Crest

Rose Crest pieces have a crest of pale pink glass that is very close in color to pink "Depression" glass. At first, in 1944, Fenton only used Rose Crest on special mould items made for Weil Freeman. This lasted for about two years. Weil failed to renew their contract with Fenton during 1945 and Fenton later included Rose Crest in their own line.

Charleton decorations and Rose Crest make a delightful, if elusive, combination. Outside of the Weil period, Rose Crest was only available in the Fenton line from 1946 to the early part of 1948. The most common items include fan vases, the #36 small cone shaped vases, 6.5" plates, and the 5" hat baskets.

Emerald Crest

Emerald Crest decorated items are eye catching to say the least. The dark green color of Emerald Crest coupled with Charleton decorations featuring pink roses and gold leaf accents make a grand combination. This color was produced from January 1949 to December 1955, an average time span for several other crest colors. Even with Fenton's production run of almost seven years for Emerald Crest, you will have to search diligently for Charleton items. Those most likely to be found are 6.5" plates, small #36 vases, and nut dishes.

Gold Crest

Gold Crest, like Aqua Crest, was produced in two different periods. This crest color also differs for each time period with the crest from the earlier issue of 1942/43 being a light amber color. In 1963, Fenton reintroduced this treatment, but used their richer Colonial Amber for the crest color. Since the only glass AWCO purchased from Fenton after 1958 was for lamp parts, there should not be any Charleton decorations found on Gold Crest items from the 1963 issue.

Gold Crest was made by Fenton in over fifty different shapes, but finding a decorated piece will not be an easy task. When it does surface, it will most likely be found on the same items on which you find Rose Crest and Emerald Crest.

Silver Crest

At last we come to Silver Crest. This color was introduced in mid-1942 when it replaced the more difficult to produce Crystal Crest line. By eliminating the additional opalescent crest, the new Silver Crest items were less costly and easier to produce. Silver Crest has the distinction of being the most prolific crest color that Fenton ever made. It stayed in Fenton's regular line until 1986 and altogether was manufactured in close to two hundred variations, the widest range of patterns of any crest color, and only second in pattern numbers to Fenton's line of Hobnail Milk Glass. Consequently, due to its broad appeal and the numerous mould shapes available, Silver Crest was AWCO's favorite choice of Fenton blanks. The neutral white background of the opaque Milk Glass also made the best possible color for AWCO to portray their decorations.

The opalescence test is used to determine the production dates of Silver Crest items. Since Fenton discontinued the use of opalescent Milk Glass in 1958, any of the chalky white, non-opalescent items found in Silver Crest can be attributed to 1958 and forward.

Silver Crest is not only the easiest and least expensive decorated Fenton pattern on the secondary market to collect, it also has the distinction of bearing the widest range of different Charleton decorations. The beauty and detail of some of these pieces rivals the best-decorated pieces of Snow Crest. Conversely, some Silver Crest pieces will portray the simplest of designs, yet, despite this economy of decoration, are still very appealing.

Due to the vast number of pieces decorated and the ready availability on the secondary market, assembling a display of decorated Silver Crest can be both affordable and virtually effortless, not to mention enjoyable. There are numerous themes to be collected such as pink roses, blue roses, roses with blue daisies, ivy, fruit, geometric, and blushed floral items with rococo-like accents. Amassing a collection by shape, such as compotes or bonbons, makes a lovely assortment as well since numerous different decorations that can be found on each shape.

Silver Crest vanity items in the #192 Melon moulds are among the most popular Charleton items to collect and lead all other items available in this field. There are a variety of sizes from which to choose, with five sizes of perfume bottles and two sizes of puff boxes available. Elsewhere in the decorated Silver Crest line are various baskets, bowls, candleholders, jugs, and vases.

If you are looking for an elegant touch in vintage bedroom/bathroom accessories, these vanity sets are the ticket. Silver Crest vanity items are also easier to find with Charleton labels and hand painted decorator's initials, which increase their desirability and value. Always be sure to check your reference books to ensure the items you purchase have the correct stoppers. Having the wrong stopper in a cologne bottle can be almost as detracting to its value as having no stopper at all.

Although Silver Crest, due to its popularity and long production period, is considered to be fairly common, there are some very scarce examples to be found. One such example is the scarce #192 large squat Melon cologne bottle. Even more difficult to find is this elusive cologne bottle graced with Charleton decorations, which add to its desirability.

Silver Crest is among the few colors that AWCO used when creating identical decorations on glass blanks obtained from different manufacturers to be paired together. This affords the non-purist the opportunity to assemble a very diverse collection. These pieces from other factories are discussed in later sections, but a collecting tip to keep in mind is that many collectors seem to overlook Charleton decorations on other maker's glass either because these pieces are not factory decorated or they fail to recognize them as Charleton. This seeming indifference or ignorance often makes the prices on many of these items very reasonable.

Silver Crest, like Peach Crest, has been widely used by other outside decorating firms. Some of the decorations are quite similar to Charleton and can be very confusing. By studying known Charleton pieces, one can become quite proficient in distinguishing the majority of these other decorations from Charleton.

There are still some Silver Crest pieces with professionally painted decorations that defy attribution. These will remain anonymous until a piece turns up with an identifying label or other suitable information. Regardless of the decorator, the best advice to follow is to collect what you like. Then, if it turns out not to be Charleton, you can at least still appreciate it for its own beauty and uniqueness.

Tiara or Beaded Melon

Fenton retooled the #192 moulds in 1949 by adding a row of small beads between each vertical melon rib. Fenton named this new pattern the Tiara line (a.k.a. Beaded Melon) and assigned the number 711 to the moulds. Tiara was made in quite a range of overlay colors and Peach Crest. Rose Overlay is a notable exception from the Tiara line, having been discontinued just prior to the production of Beaded Melon.

Turned-out Moulds

Recently uncovered evidence shows a third and final retooling of the original #192 Melon moulds which smoothed out the melon shaped ribs in the moulds. Both cologne bottles and puff jars were produced in these retooled moulds. These items can be found with either satin or shiny finish.

Having no luck in locating either the cologne bottles or the puff jars in any Fenton reference material, we asked Frank Fenton to confirm that these were indeed Fenton. He seemed reluctant to give a definitive attribution which was frustrating since we felt strongly that they were Fenton products.

It was through careful examination of the copies of the AWCO black book records that Frank had sent us earlier that the first clue finally surfaced. There we found mention of Fenton producing some vanity items for AWCO using #192 moulds with the words "turned-out" included in the descriptions. We again contacted Frank, armed with a series of questions from these AWCO/Fenton records. Most importantly, we asked him specifically the definition of the words "turned-out." He seemed to be as puzzled as to the meaning as we were and said he would have to research it and get back to us.

It was during our visit with Frank in June of 2000 that it finally all came together. We brought our copies of the AWCO records with us and were wrapping up some final questions about them that we had not been able to decipher. We had discussed the smooth mould #192 vanity items again a few minutes earlier, but he seemed to have no new information about them. When we were reviewing our notes, we showed him the words "turned-out" found in the black book records. Frank paused and thought for a moment and then he reached over and jabbed his finger at the words highlighted on the copies. "That's where they came from!" he exclaimed. "Those pieces were made from a turning of the #192 moulds, or an additional turning of the #711 moulds." It took a moment to comprehend what he saying, but our excitement rose dramatically as we understood that Frank had solved the puzzle.

Having jogged his memory, Frank went on to say that the first modification to the #192 Melon mould that resulted in the Tiara or "Beaded Melon" line was not well received by customers. As a result, this pattern was only made for a very short period of time before being retired, making them very collectible today.

Fenton, in their constant quest for new items for market, later modified the moulds again by "turning out" or removing the interior raised ribs on the metal moulds using a shop lathe in order for the items to take on the smooth exterior. These smooth sided pieces were never part of the Fenton line, but we are hesitant to say that undecorated ones don't exist since we have learned to "never say never." These "turned-out" moulds have not been found in the Fenton mould storage room yet, but Frank assured me he would keep an eye out for them. Once found, perhaps they will be tagged so we can identify them by a separate mould number. Until then, they will be referred to by us as a "turned-out" cologne or puff box, and so forth.

These new shapes were used quite effectively by AWCO, but never in any great quantity. Evidence so far indicates that the majority of these turned-out items were produced in satin-finished milk glass. The decorations are elaborate and make these unique and beautiful items very exciting to collect.

Overlay Colors

Utilizing blanks made from Fenton's overlay colors further expanded AWCO's representation on Fenton glass. Covering the base color of opalescent milk glass with another, tinted, transparent layer of glass creates overlay colors. These colors, like the crested items, run the gamut from common to very scarce and a few may surprise even the experienced Charleton collector.

Finding Charleton items in Rose and Blue Overlay should be quite easy since, like Silver Crest, AWCO decorated a great many pieces in these two colors. Rose Overlay was produced from 1943-1948 and Blue Overlay from 1943–1953. The Charleton decorations on these pieces cover a wide range of styles, but the rose motif will be the most common design found. Vanity sets are the items most frequently found in Rose and Blue Overlay with Charleton decorations.

Both Amber (Gold) Overlay and Green Overlay, made from 1948 to 1953, are difficult to find even in undecorated items. Made as part of Fenton's Tiara line, few pieces were made utilizing moulds from other lines. Pieces with Charleton decorations are very scarce and appear on only a few shapes. Amber Overlay is more scarce than Green Overlay although both will take quite a bit of time (and luck) to find. Expect to pay premium prices for either color with Charleton decorations, especially if the seller is knowledgeable.

Ranking even higher on the scarcity scale is Ivy Overlay. Made from 1950 to 1953, Fenton's Ivy Overlay is a deeper, richer green than Green Overlay. Also made as part of the Tiara line, Ivy

Overlay appears on a much wider variety of shapes than Amber and Green Overlay. But, again, as with Amber and Green Overlay, Charleton decorations appear on very few shapes. Ivy Overlay provides a very effective background for Charleton decorations. Again, premium prices are to be expected.

Hobnail

Several pieces in decorated hobnail have come to light recently. This pattern was evidently not high on the purchasing list for AWCO and finding hobnail pieces can be considered quite a feat. The Karmans, co-editors of the periodical "Fenton Flyer," pictured several Charleton decorated hobnail pieces in the third installment of their series on Charleton/Fenton in the March/April 2001 issue. Personally, we have found only three Charleton decorated Milk Glass hobnail pieces to date and this pattern remains high on our want list. AWCO bought hobnail pieces from Fenton to decorate in Milk Glass and the pastel colors of Green, Blue, Pink, and Turquoise.

Coin Dot

Lucky is the collector who has managed to secure any Charleton decorated items in Fenton's ever-popular Coin Dot treatment. The painting on these pieces will usually be very small roses or stylized Fleur-de-Lis painted on the dots and the upper border of the pieces. Pieces seen from a distance can be easily overlooked because the decoration can get lost in the glass design. Fenton made Coin Dot in French (white), Blue, Lime, and Cranberry Opalescent glass. No other Fenton opalescent optic glass has been reported with AWCO decorations. Typical items to be found are bowls, jugs, lamps, ginger jars, cologne bottles, puff jars, and vases. As with undecorated Fenton, Cranberry Opalescent Coin Dot items with Charleton decorations will command the highest prices.

Milk Glass

Decorated milk glass in the Fenton line is not nearly as easy to find as one might think. Although milk glass generally is the common poor boy of a glass company's line, Charleton milk glass pieces made by Fenton are very difficult to find. By the term milk glass (properly called opaque white glass), we are referring to opaque white milk glass with no tinted coloration and no applied crest such as Silver Crest, Aqua Crest, and the like. This glass can be opalescent or chalky white, depending on the batch formula and/or the thickness of the item. When discussing milk glass that is tinted, we will preface the term milk glass with the color of the tint.

Pictured in an AWCO advertisement that was found in a *Crockery & Glass Journal* from 1955 is a group of items in Fenton's "Swirl," circa 1954. This pattern was made in several pastel colors as well as milk glass and was produced in approximately twelve different items.

Based on descriptions in the advertisement, AWCO named these pieces in accordance with the base color of the glass, i.e., Rose Blush Pink, Snow Opal, and Jewel Turquoise. No color is listed for Green Pastel and it is possible that they did not decorate this color. With a very short production run, finding these items will require much patience.

Another rare decorated pattern pictured in trade journals was simply called "C" or more commonly "Backward C." This was a very complicated piece of glass for Fenton to produce. The mould alone took the mould maker hundreds of hours to create. It also takes a highly skilled "Presser" to work with this intricate mould as the molten glass must be pressed just right and the amount of pressure applied varies with each pressing. The #9028 comport pictured in the AWCO advertisement is one of only two decorated pieces reported to date. This pattern of glass would seem to be a very fitting background for Charleton decorations so more items in this design are almost certain to be found.

Fenton's New Decorating Department

As might be expected, the ever-popular Silver Crest was the pattern that Fenton chose to usher in the reopening of their decorating studio in the late 1960s. In its beginnings, as previously mentioned, the Fenton Art Glass Company was exclusively a decorating firm somewhat similar to AWCO and, for their first two years, Fenton did not make any of the items they decorated.

Fifty years after closing their decorating department, during a milder period of sluggish sales, Fenton carefully considered returning to hand painting their own glassware in-house in an effort to improve sales. In 1967, Fenton began the search for the right people to staff this new decorating department and, in the summer of 1968, pieces of Fenton glass hand decorated in-house by Fenton appeared for the first time in over half a century. Under the expert direction of the renowned Louise Piper, the studio's first decoration was called "Violets in the Snow." Done exclusively on Silver Crest items, this realistic decoration consisted of sprays of violets offset against the snow-white background of the milk glass. This proved to be a huge success. Two more painted Silver Crest patterns followed in 1969: Yellow Roses and Apple Blossoms.

In the early 1970s, Fenton began the practice of moulding its company logo under the base of its glassware. Since no Fenton items were decorated by AWCO after the late 1950s, there are no Charleton items that have this embossed Fenton logo. At a later time, Fenton artists also began signing their work and there is no documentation of any older Fenton/Charleton items having an artist's signature[8]. Charleton items will sometimes have decorator's initials, but they are quite different in style than Fenton's artists. These distinctions should help the beginning collector avoid confusion between Fenton and AWCO decorated items.

Since these first decorations created by Louise Piper can be found on Fenton glass without the Fenton logo and without the artists' signatures, they could be confusing for the novice collector. However, the limited number of these new in-house decorations and the lack of any significant variance from piece to piece, coupled with the total absence of gold leaf accents, should help eliminate any speculation or confusion about the source of the decoration. With that said, do keep in mind that the Fenton moulded logo is sometimes weakly struck and hard to locate, and the Fenton artist's signatures do not always appear, especially if it is an artist sample or Fenton Gift Shop "Seconds" piece.

Recent Fenton in the Charleton Style

Before closing, we will include something that may be of interest to the ardent collector. Fenton has recently issued a few pieces with decorations that are strongly reminiscent of AWCO's decorated items. We mention this so that the Charleton enthusiast will be aware of these items. These new issues compliment the original Charleton decorations quite well and would blend nicely with vintage Charleton pieces in a collection.

We feel there is one particular item that merits special attention since it was only available through Fenton's hugely popular offerings on QVC. QVC items are never offered as part of Fenton's regular line and are also not available through its regular retail dealer network. This greatly adds to the scarcity and value of Fenton items made for QVC. The item we are referring to is a Cranberry Opalescent Coin Dot rose (ginger) jar with hand painted flowers scattered across the opalescent areas. Although it is pictured on page 151, item #927 of Dr. James Measell's book *Fenton Glass: The 1980s Decade*, this rose jar was actually made in 1992 for QVC. This QVC rose jar could easily be considered the best piece Fenton has ever reproduced in the Charleton style. Although signed by the artist and embossed with the Fenton logo, since this is almost identical in every respect to the original Charleton decorated jar, it could easily be misidentified. The older original Charleton jar is pictured later for comparison.

Fenton later made several more items that capture an essence of the older Charleton. The first two items detailed below are, in our opinion, quite reminiscent of classic Charleton. Of particular note is the "French Rose on Rosalene" melon vase that was a Glass Messenger Subscriber Exclusive for 1997. The glass color of the vase and the painted roses closely resemble the original AWCO Rose Overlay vases, with a few Peach Crest elements as well. The thin gold bands surrounding the neck and base add the final Charleton touch.

From the 1999 Connoisseur Collection comes a beautiful Peach Crest basket with a decoration of roses and gold. The roses and stylized tiny purple flowers are very close to what a Charleton artist would have portrayed. A band of blue blush washes along the staggered border of stippled gold dots. There are even gold latticed accents and sprigs that add even a stronger sense of Charleton artistry.

The following color plates will give the collector a guide to many of the Charleton patterns to be found on Fenton art glass. Each item will be captioned with documentation noting any labels, marks, and other identifying features.

Fenton Ware #7295 Silver Crest three-tier tidbit. Charleton Roses and Gold Spatter decoration, c. 1954. $250-275. Rare. *Courtesy of Rich and Laurie Karman.*

Rich and Laurie Karman, editors of the *Fenton Flyer*, who generously allowed us into their home to photograph their outstanding collection of Charleton decorated Fenton.

Fenton Mould #A-4808SC, 10" high by 12" wide Silver Crest Diamond Lace 4-piece Epergne (notice lilies are not Diamond Lace). Charleton Roses and Gold Spatter decoration, c. 1954-1955. $400-500. Rare. *Authors' Collection.*

Fenton Mould #A-4808SC, 10" high by 12" wide Silver Crest Diamond Lace 4-piece Epergne, bowl interior detail.

Fenton Mould #7213, 9" Silver Crest cake plate, footed. Charleton Roses and Gold Spatter decoration, c. 1953-1954. $150-175. Rare. *Authors' Collection.*

Silver Crest Diamond Lace 4-piece Epergne, bowl crest detail.

Fenton Mould #3513, 9" Rose Pastel Spanish Lace cake plate, footed. Charleton Gold Roses decoration, c. 1956. $100-125. Rare. *Courtesy TWM Antique Mall.*

Silver Crest Diamond Lace 4-piece Epergne, lily detail.

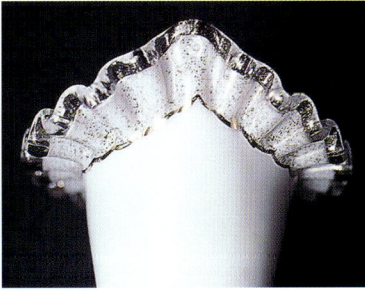

Silver Crest Diamond Lace 4-piece Epergne, lily detail, reverse side.

Fenton Mould #3513, 9" Rose Pastel Spanish Lace cake plate, footed. Top view.

Fenton Ware #5823SC, 11" Silver Crest bowl, fine crimp. Charleton Roses decoration, c. 1958. $100-125. Scarce. *Authors' Collection.*

Fenton Mould #206, 7" Silver Crest square crimp satin finish comport. Charleton Roses decoration, c. 1951. AWCO Charleton label #4425, 1087, or 4922[1]. $100-125. Rare. *Courtesy of Rich and Laurie Karman.*

Fenton Ware #5823SC, 11" Silver Crest bowl, fine crimp. Detail.

Fenton Mould #206 Silver Crest 7" square crimp satin finish comport. Top view.

Fenton Mould #206, 7" Silver Crest footed comport. Charleton Roses decoration, c. 1940s-1950s. $75-85. Note unusual smooth crimp. *Authors' Collection.*

Fenton Ware #7330, 10" Silver Crest footed square bowl. Charleton Roses decoration, c. 1956. AWCO Charleton label #2462. $100-125. Scarce. *Courtesy of Rich and Laurie Karman.*

Fenton Mould #206, 7" Silver Crest footed comport. Top view.

Fenton Mould #206, 7" Silver Crest footed comport, square crimp. Charleton Pink Mist and Roses decoration, c. 1940s-1950s. $85-95. *Authors' Collection.*

Fenton Ware #3920, 8" Milk Glass tall footed hobnail comport, double crimp. Charleton Roses decoration, c. 1954. AWCO Charleton label #828. $85-100. Scarce. *Authors' Collection.*

Fenton Mould #206, 6" Silver Crest comport, square crimp. Charleton Green Mist and Roses decoration, c. 1943-1956. $70-80. Scarce. *Authors' Collection.*

Fenton Ware #3920, 8" Milk Glass tall footed hobnail comport, double crimp. Top view.

Fenton Mould #206, 7" Silver Crest footed comport, square crimp. Charleton Roses decoration, c. 1940s-1950s. AWCO Charleton label #4425. $50-65. *Authors' Collection.*

Fenton Mould #206, 7" Rose Pastel footed comport, double crimp. Charleton Roses decoration, c. 1954-1958. $65-75. *Courtesy of Rich and Laurie Karman.*

Fenton Ware #3920, 7.5" Turquoise Pastel hobnail comport, double crimp. Charleton Roses decoration, c. 1954. AWCO Charleton label #2270. $85-100. Scarce. *Courtesy of Rich and Laurie Karman.*

Fenton Mould #206 Milk Glass satin finished covered candy dish with crystal finial. Charleton Greek Key and Roses decoration, c. 1948-1954. $85-100. Rare. *Authors' Collection.*

Fenton Ware #3920 Turquoise Pastel 7.5" hobnail comport, double crimp. Top view.

Fenton Mould #206, 6" Silver Crest comport, square crimp. Charleton Gold Roses decoration (note unusually heavy gold), c. 1943-1956. $65-75. Scarce. *Authors' Collection.*

Fenton Mould #206 Milk Glass covered candy dish with crystal finial. Charleton Blue Mist and Roses decoration, c. 1948-1954. $85-100. Scarce. *Courtesy of John Walk.*

Fenton Mould #206 Milk Glass covered candy dish with crystal finial. Charleton Pink Mist and Roses decoration, c. 1948-1954. $75-85. Scarce. *Authors' Collection.*

Fenton Mould #206 Milk Glass covered candy dish with crystal finial. Charleton Strawberry decoration, c. 1948-1954. $75-85. Scarce. *Authors' Collection.*

Fenton Mould #206 Milk Glass covered candy. Charleton Raspberry decoration, c. 1948-1954. AWCO Charleton label #4347. $75-85. Scarce. *Authors' collection.*

Top view of lids from Fenton Mould #206 Milk Glass covered candy dishes. Strawberry decoration is on the left; Raspberry decoration is on the right. Note the subtle yet distinct differences between the two decorations. *Authors' Collection.*

Fenton Mould #680, 12" Silver Crest plate. Charleton Roses decoration, c. 1948-1956. $75-85. *Authors' Collection.*

Fenton Mould #680, 12" Silver Crest plate. Charleton Blue Mist with Inlaid Roses decoration, 1948-1956. AWCO Charleton label #4930, 1504, 827, or 2273C[2]. $100-125. Scarce. *Courtesy of Rich and Laurie Karman.*

Fenton Mould #680, 6" Emerald Crest plate. Charleton Green Mist Rococo decoration, c. 1949-1953. AWCO Charleton label #554A. $50-65. *Courtesy of Rich and Laurie Karman.*

Fenton Mould #680, 12" Silver Crest plate. Charleton Green Mist with Inlaid Roses decoration, c. 1948-1956. AWCO Charleton label #4930, 1504, 827, or 2273C. $100-125. Scarce. *Courtesy of Rich and Laurie Karman.*

Fenton Mould #680, 8" Silver Crest plate. Charleton Green Mist Rococo decoration, c. 1948-1956. AWCO Charleton label #4915 or 2273B. $75-85. Scarce. *Courtesy of Rich and Laurie Karman.*

Fenton Mould #680, 6" Silver Crest plate. Charleton Pink Mist and Roses decoration, c. 1943-1958. AWCO Charleton label #4714? (number worn). $45-55. *Courtesy of Rich and Laurie Karman.*

Fenton Mould #680, 8" Silver Crest plate. Charleton Blue Mist Rococo decoration, c. 1948-1956. AWCO Charleton label #4915 or 2273B. $75-85. Scarce. *Courtesy of Rich and Laurie Karman.*

Fenton Mould #680, 8" Silver Crest satin finish plate. Charleton New Orleans decoration, c. 1951. AWCO Charleton label #1101. $95-100. Rare. *Courtesy of Rich and Laurie Karman.*

Fenton Mould #680, 6" Rose Crest clock plate. Charleton Roses decoration, c. 1944-1947. Clockworks by Sessions. $125-150. Rare. *Authors' Collection.*

Fenton Ware #9011, 11" Milk Glass Lacey Edge bowl, shallow. Charleton Roses and Gold Spatter decoration, c. 1954. $100-125. Rare. *Authors' Collection.*

Fenton Mould #203, 7" Silver Crest satin finish bowl, double crimp. Charleton Filigree and Roses decoration, c. 1951. $150-175. Rare. *Authors' Collection.*

Fenton Mould #1522, 10" Rose Crest double crimp bowl. Charleton Arched Roses decoration, c. 1946-1948. $150-175. Rare. *Courtesy of Rich and Laurie Karman.*

Fenton Ware #9026, 11" Rose Pastel Backwards "C" bowl. Charleton Stitched Roses decoration, c. 1954. (Note how the placement of the decoration forms an eight-pointed star pattern.) $100-125. Rare. *Authors' Collection.*

Fenton Ware #3924, 10" Rose Pastel hobnail bowl, double crimp. Charleton Pink Mist and Roses decoration, c. 1954. NWCO Charleton label #2200. $50-100. Scarce. *Courtesy of Rich and Laurie Karman.*

Fenton Ware #3924 Rose Pastel 10" hobnail bowl. Top View.

Fenton Mould #206, 6" Turquoise Pastel comport, double crimp. Charleton Roses decoration, c. 1955. $50-60. Scarce. *Courtesy of Rich and Laurie Karman.*

Fenton Mould #1522, 10" Rose Overlay bowl, double crimp. Charleton Ivory Leaves decoration, c. 1943-1948. $100-125. Scarce. *Authors' Collection.*

Fenton Mould #203, 7" Rose Overlay bowl, double crimp. Charleton Roses decoration, c. 1943-1948. $75-85. *Authors' Collection.*

Fenton Mould #1522, 10" Silver Crest bowl, double crimp. Charleton Open Rose decoration, c. 1956. AWCO Charleton label #2454. $75-85. *Courtesy of Rich and Laurie Karman.*

Fenton Ware #3927, 7" Turquoise Pastel hobnail bowl, double crimp. Charleton Roses decoration, c. 1954. $65-75. Scarce. *Courtesy of Rich and Laurie Karman.*

Fenton Ware #3927, 7" Turquoise Pastel hobnail bowl, double crimp. Top View.

Fenton Mould #203, 7" Rose Overlay bowl, double crimp. Charleton Ghost Rose decoration, c. 1943-1948. AWCO Charleton label #4106. $75-85. *Authors' Collection.*

Fenton Ware #3927, 7" Rose Pastel hobnail bowl, double crimp. Charleton Roses decorations, c. 1954. $65-75. Scarce. *Courtesy of Rich and Laurie Karman.*

Fenton Mould #206, 6" Rose Pastel comport, double crimp. Charleton Gold Roses decoration, c. 1954-1958. AWCO Charleton label #2453. $50-60. Scarce. *Courtesy of Rich and Laurie Karman.*

Fenton Ware #3927, 7" Rose Pastel hobnail bowl, double crimp. Top view.

Fenton Mould #203, 7" Silver Crest bowl, double crimp. Charleton Stitched Roses decoration, c. 1940s-1950s. $50-60. *Authors' Collection.*

Fenton Mould #203, 7" Silver Crest bowl, double crimp. Charleton Stitched Roses decoration, c. 1947. AWCO Charleton label #4423. $50-60. *Courtesy of Rich and Laurie Karman.*

Fenton Mould #205, 8" Silver Crest bowl, double crimp. Charleton Roses decoration, c. 1947-1956. Note the absence of a bow in this decoration. AWCO Charleton label #1124, 1129, 1130, or 1929[2]. $75-85. *Courtesy of Rich and Laurie Karman.*

Fenton Mould #203, 7" Silver Crest bowl, double crimp. Charleton Roses decoration, c. 1954. AWCO Charleton label #4423. $65-75. *Courtesy of Rich and Laurie Karman.*

Fenton Mould #36, 5.5" Silver Crest bonbon, double crimp. Charleton Roses and Bows decoration, c. 1940s-1950s. AWCO Charleton label #4422. $45-55. *Authors' Collection.*

Fenton Mould #205, 8" Silver Crest bowl, double crimp. Charleton Roses & Bows decoration, c. 1947. AWCO Charleton label #4424, 4429, 4430, or 4929[2]. $45-65. *Courtesy of Rich and Laurie Karman.*

Fenton Mould #36, 5.5" Silver Crest bonbon, double crimp. Charleton Pink Mist and Roses decoration (note 6-point star design formed by the decoration), c. 1940s-1950s. $45-55. Scarce decoration. *Authors' Collection.*

Fenton Mould #36, 5.5" Silver Crest bonbon, double crimp. Charleton Green Mist and Roses decoration, c. 1943-1958. $45-55. *Courtesy of Rich and Laurie Karman.*

Fenton Ware #7225, 5.5" Emerald Crest bonbon, double crimp. Charleton Green Sprig decoration, c. 1949-1953. $35-45. *Courtesy of Rich and Laurie Karman.*

Fenton Ware #3926, 5.5" Milk Glass hobnail bonbon, double crimp. Charleton Blue Mist and Roses decoration, c. 1954. AWCO Charleton label #2264. $45-55. *Courtesy of Rich and Laurie Karman.*

Fenton Mould #36, 5.5" Rose Pastel bonbon. Charleton Gold Roses decoration (note unusually heavy gold), c. 1954. $65-75. Scarce. *Authors' Collection.*

Fenton Mould #192, 7" Emerald Crest Jack-In-The-Pulpit or Tulip vase. Charleton Pegged Roses decoration, c. 1949. $150-175. Rare. *Authors' Collection.*

Fenton Mould #206, 6" Emerald Crest square crimp footed comport. Charleton Pegged Roses decoration, c. 1949-1956. $65-75. *Authors' collection.*

Fenton Mould #680 Silver Crest nut dish. Charleton Roses decoration, c. 1943-1956. $45-55. *Courtesy of Rich and Laurie Karman.*

Fenton Mould #206, 6" Emerald Crest double crimp footed comport. Top view. Charleton Pegged Roses decoration, c. 1949-1956. $65-75. *Courtesy of Rich and Laurie Karman.*

Fenton French Opalescent Coin Dot lamp and globe (mould number(s) unknown). Fenton supplied only the glass for the lamps to AWCO. Charleton Roses decoration, c. 1947-1952. $350-400. Rare. *Courtesy of Rich and Laurie Karman.*

Fenton Mould #680 Emerald Crest nut dish. Charleton Pegged Roses decoration, c. 1949-1955. $50-65. Scarce. *Courtesy of Rich and Laurie Karman.*

Fenton French Opalescent Coin Dot 14" tall lamp. Measurement from base to top of lamp fount. Fenton supplied only the glass for the lamps to AWCO. Charleton Roses decoration, c. 1947-1952. $150-175. Scarce. *Authors' Collection.*

Right to left: Fenton Mould #893, 6.5" Cranberry Opalescent Coin Dot ginger jar; Fenton Mould #189, 10" Cranberry Opalescent Coin Dot vase, double crimp. Both with Charleton Roses decoration, c. 1947. Ginger jar: $700-800. Vase: $325-350. Both rare. *Courtesy of Lynn Welker.*

Fenton French Opalescent Coin Dot lamp (mould number(s) unknown). Fenton supplied only the glass for the lamps to AWCO. Charleton Shield decoration, c. 1947-1952. $225-250. Rare. *Courtesy of Rich and Laurie Karman.*

Fenton Mould #1925 Cranberry Opalescent Coin Dot 6" basket. Charleton Roses decoration, c. 1947-1951. $250-275. Rare. *Courtesy of Rich and Laurie Karman.*

Fenton Mould #201 Cranberry Opalescent Coin Dot 5" squat jug. Charleton Roses decoration, c. 1948. AWCO Charleton label #4923. $185-200. Rare. *Courtesy of Rich and Laurie Karman.*

Fenton Mould #201 Blue Opalescent Coin Dot squat jug. Charleton Roses decoration, c. 1947-1950. $135-165. Rare. *Courtesy of Fenton Art Glass Museum.*

Fenton Mould #203 Cranberry Opalescent Coin Dot 4.5" vase. Charleton Roses decoration, c. 1948-early 1950s. AWCO Charleton label #4891. $150-175. Rare. *Courtesy of Fenton Art Glass Museum.*

Fenton Mould #7264, 9" Aqua Crest jug. Charleton Roses decoration, c. 1951-1952. $175-200. Rare. *Courtesy of Rich and Laurie Karman.*

Fenton Mould #92, 4.5" Cranberry Opalescent Coin Dot cologne bottle. Charleton Roses decoration, c. 1947-1950s. AWCO Charleton label #4968. Initial "T" in gold. $175-200. Rare. *Authors' Collection.*

Fenton Mould #192, 8" Peach Crest large Melon jug. Charleton Open Rose decoration, c. 1947. $150-175. Scarce. *Authors' Collection.*

49

Fenton Mould #192, 8" Rose Overlay large Melon jug. Charleton Open Rose decoration, c. 1947. AWCO Charleton label #4703. $110-125. Scarce. *Authors' Collection.*

Fenton Mould #203, 7" Rose Overlay basket. Charleton Roses decoration, c. 1947. $100-125. Scarce. *Authors' Collection.*

Group shot of Fenton Ivy Overlay and Green Overlay pieces. *Authors' Collection.*

Grouping shot of two Fenton Ivy Overlay pieces with Charleton Ivory Leaves and Needles decoration. Left to right: Mould #201 vase and Mould #194 lamp, c. 1951. Vase: $75-85, scarce; lamp: $150-175, rare. *Authors' Collection.*

Fenton Mould #201, 5" Green Overlay squat jug. Charleton Green Rose and Stipples decoration, c. 1949. *Authors' Collection.* $100-125. Rare.

Fenton Mould #201, 5" Ivy Overlay ball vase, double crimp and 5" Green Overlay ball vase, double crimp. Both with Charleton Ivory Leaves and Needles decoration, c. 1949-1951. $75-85 each. Scarce. *Authors' Collection.*

Fenton Mould #201, 5" Ivy Overlay rose bowl. Charleton Roses and Gold Needles decoration, c. 1949. AWCO Charleton label #584. $75-85. Scarce. *Authors' Collection.*

Fenton Mould #1934 Ivy Overlay 7" jug. Charleton Roses decoration, c. 1949. $100-125. Rare. *Courtesy of Rich and Laurie Karman.*

Fenton Mould #1352 Green Overlay 8.5" vase, double crimp. Charleton Green Rose and Stipples decoration, c. 1949. $90-100. *Courtesy of Rich and Laurie Karman.*

Fenton Mould #1934, 7" Green Overlay vase, double crimp. Charleton Magenta Leaves decoration, c. 1949. AWCO Charleton label #578. $100-125. Rare. *Authors' Collection.*

Fenton Mould #186, 8.5" Ivy Overlay vase, double crimp. Charleton Paisley Lattice and Roses decoration, c. 1951. AWCO Charleton label #564. $100-125. Rare. *Authors' Collection.*

Fenton Mould #1925, 10" Gold (also called Amber) Overlay basket, double crimp. Charleton Circled Roses decoration, c. 1948-1953. $200-225. Rare. *Authors' Collection.*

Group shot of three Charleton decorated Fenton Mould #1924, 5" hat baskets and three unknown decorator #1924, 2.5" top hats. *Authors' Collection.*

52

Group shot of two Fenton Mould #1924, 5" hat baskets. Charleton Blue Latticed Roses decoration, c. 1949. Although similar, note the slight differences in the decoration on each basket. $85-95. *Courtesy of Rich and Laurie Karman.*

Fenton Mould #1923, 4" Milk Glass top hat. Charleton Pink Mist and Roses decoration, c. 1951. $50-60. Scarce. *Courtesy of Rich and Laurie Karman.*

Fenton Mould #1924, 5" Gold (also called Amber) Overlay hat basket. Charleton Roses and Rococo, c. 1949. $90-100. Scarce. *Authors' Collection.*

Group shot of Fenton Ruby Snow Crest Charleton decorated pieces. Pieces have been partially acid etched for a satin finish. Note the absence of a Spiral Optic pattern in the glass that most in-line, undecorated Snow Crest pieces have.

Fenton Mould #1925, 8.5" Ruby Snow Crest vase, double crimp. Charleton Circled Roses decoration, c. 1951. $250-275. Rare. *Authors' Collection.*

Fenton Mould #203, 4.5" Ruby Snow Crest vase, double crimp. Charleton Circled Roses decoration, c. 1951. AWCO Charleton label #940. $85-100. Scarce. *Courtesy of Rich and Laurie Karman.*

Fenton Mould #4516, 8.5" Ruby Snow Crest vase, tri-crimp. Charleton Circled Roses decoration, c. 1950-1954. AWCO Charleton label #584. $175-200. Rare. *Authors' Collection.*

Group shot of Fenton Amber Snow Crest pieces, all with Charleton decorations. Pieces have been acid etched for a satin finish. Note the absence of a Spiral Optic pattern in the glass that most in-line, undecorated Snow Crest pieces have. *Authors' Collection.*

Fenton Mould #1925, 8.5" Amber Snow Crest vase, double crimp Charleton Latticed Roses and Diamonds decoration, c. 1951. $175-200. Rare. *Authors' Collection.*

Fenton Mould #1721 Amber Snow Crest 9.5" fine crimped pinch vase. Charleton Latticed Roses and Diamonds decoration, c. 1951. AWCO Charleton label #922. $100-125. *Courtesy of Rich and Laurie Karman.*

Fenton Mould #1925, 5" Amber Snow Crest vase, double crimp. Charleton Latticed Roses and Diamonds decoration, c. 1951. $75-85. Rare. *Authors' Collection.*

Fenton Mould #3005 Amber Snow Crest 11" triangle crimp vase. Charleton Latticed Roses and Circles decoration, c. 1951. AWCO Charleton label #952. $175-200. Scarce. *Courtesy of Rich and Laurie Karman.*

Fenton Mould #814, 8" Amber bottle with "Coin Dot"[3] stopper. Charleton Latticed Roses and Diamonds decoration (note painted on "Snow Crest"). Snow Crest effect at the top of the bottle, c. 1951. $125-150. Rare. *Authors' Collection.*

Fenton Mould #3005 Green Snow Crest 11" triangle crimp vase. Charleton Camellias decoration, c. 1949. $200-250. Rare. *Courtesy of Rich and Laurie Karman.*

Group photograph of the Charleton Fruit and Dots decoration on Milk Glass. All pieces by Fenton with the exception of the square cigarette box whose manufacturer is suspected to be Beaumont. The cigarette box details can be found in the chapter titled Unidentified Manufacturers. *Authors' collection.*

Fenton Mould #814, 8" Milk Glass bottle with "Coin Dot" stopper. Charleton Fruit and Dots decoration, c. 1949-1954. Initialed "K" on the bottom. $125-150. Scarce. *Authors' Collection.*

Fenton Mould #3001 Milk Glass vase. Charleton Fruit and Dots decoration, 1949 and 1951. 7" tall. $75-95. Scarce. *Courtesy of Rich and Laurie Karman.*

Fenton Mould #93 Milk Glass covered candy. Charleton Fruit and Dots decoration, c. 1949-1954. AWCO Charleton label #736 or #615. $125-150. Scarce. *Courtesy of Rich and Laurie Karman.*

Group shot of two Fenton Charleton Laurel and Bow decorated pieces. Left to right: Mould #36, 6.25" Silver Crest fan vase; Fenton Mould #711, 6" Silver Crest Beaded Melon (Tiara) vase, c. 1949. $45-50 each. Scarce decoration. *Authors' Collection.*

Fenton Mould #36, 6" Silver Crest fan vase. Charleton Blue Roses decoration, c. 1943-1958. $45-55. Scarce. *Courtesy of Rich and Laurie Karman.*

Fenton Mould #36 Silver Crest 5.5" bonbon. Charleton Laurel and Bow decoration, c. 1949. $25-35. *Authors' collection.*

Fenton Mould #36, 6" Gold Crest fan vase. Charleton Blue Roses decoration, c. 1943-1944. $65-75. Very scarce. *Courtesy of Rich and Laurie Karman.*

Group shot of two Fenton Charleton Blue Roses decorated pieces. Left to right: Mould #203, 7" Silver Crest bowl, double crimp; Fenton Mould #36, 6" Silver Crest fan vase, c. 1943-1958. Bowl, $50-60. Fan vase, $45-55. *Authors' Collection.*

Fenton Mould #36, 6.5" Silver Crest fan vase. Charleton Red Sunburst & Roses decoration, c. 1948. $50-65. Unusual decoration. *Courtesy of Rich and Laurie Karman.*

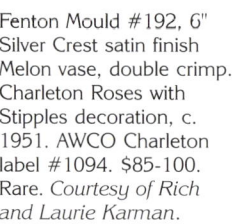

Fenton Mould #192, 6" Silver Crest satin finish Melon vase, double crimp. Charleton Roses with Stipples decoration, c. 1951. AWCO Charleton label #1094. $85-100. Rare. *Courtesy of Rich and Laurie Karman.*

Fenton Mould #36 Rose Crest 4.5" fan vase. Charleton Arched Roses decoration, 1945-1947. $45-55. *Courtesy of Rich and Laurie Karman.*

Fenton Mould #36, 4.5" Rose Crest vase, double crimp. Charleton Arched Roses decoration, c. 1946-1947. $40-50. *Authors' Collection.*

Fenton Mould #192 Silver Crest 8" Melon vase, double crimp. Charleton Blue Mist and Roses decoration, c. 1947-1949. AWCO Charleton label #4189V. $60-75. Scarce. *Courtesy of Rich and Laurie Karman.*

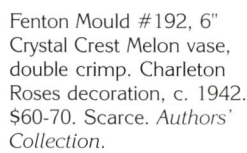

Fenton Mould #192, 6" Crystal Crest Melon vase, double crimp. Charleton Roses decoration, c. 1942. $60-70. Scarce. *Authors' Collection.*

Fenton Mould #36, 6" Emerald Crest cone vase, double crimp. Charleton Green Mist and Roses decoration, c. 1949. $80-90. Rare. *Authors' Collection.*

Fenton Mould #192, 6" Silver Crest Melon vase, double crimp. Charleton Roses and Bows decoration, c. 1947-1952. Note the unusual hash marks just below the neck of this vase. AWCO Charleton label #4170. $40-50. *Authors' Collection.*

Fenton Mould #192, 8" Silver Crest Melon vase, double crimp. Charleton Roses decoration, c. 1947-1949. AWCO Charleton label #4189. $75-85. *Authors' Collection.*

Fenton Mould #192, 5.5" Peach Crest squat Melon vase. Charleton Roses decoration, c. 1940s-1950s. $70-80. *Authors' Collection.*

Fenton Mould #192, 6" Silver Crest Melon vase, double crimp. Charleton Roses decoration, c. 1947-1952. AWCO Charleton label #4188V. $40-50. *Courtesy of Rich and Laurie Karman.*

Fenton Mould #192, 5.5" Peach Crest squat vase. Charleton Roses decoration, c. 1940s-1950s. $65-75. *Authors' Collection.*

Fenton Mould #192 Peach Crest 5.5" Melon vase, double crimp. Charleton Blue Mist and Blue Roses decoration, c. 1943 and 1947. AWCO Charleton label #4428. $75-85. Scarce. *Courtesy of Rich and Laurie Karman.*

Fenton Mould #1925, 6" Peach Crest vase, double crimp. Charleton Pink Mist with Roses and Bows decoration, c. 1952-1954. AWCO Charleton label #1401. $125-150. Rare. *Courtesy of Rich and Laurie Karman.*

Group shot of three Fenton crystal pieces with Charleton Gold Polka Dots on Pink decoration. Note that these crystal pieces were made exclusively for AWCO. *Authors' Collection.*

Fenton Mould #4516, 8.5" crystal vase, triangle crimp. Charleton Gold Polka Dots on Pink decoration, c. 1951-1954. $75-85. Scarce. *Authors' Collection.*

Fenton Mould #192, turned-out, 7" crystal cologne bottle. Charleton Gold Polka Dots on Pink decoration, c. 1951-1954. AWCO Charleton label #1653. $100-110. Scarce. *Authors' Collection.*

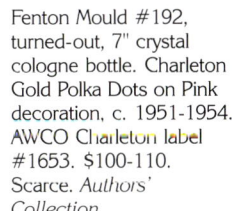

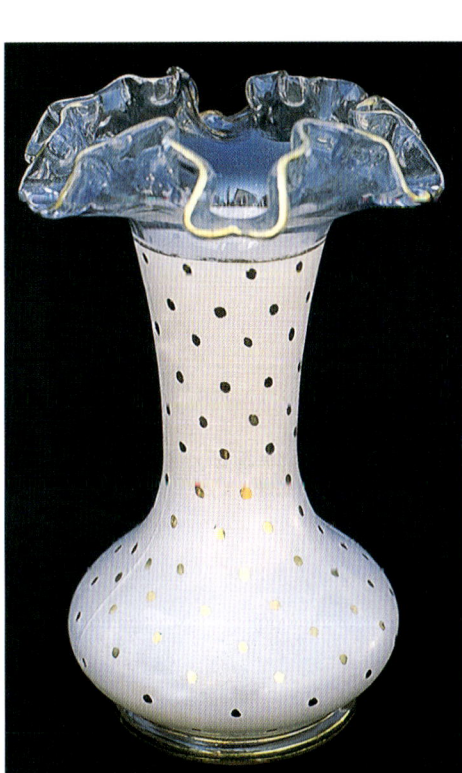

Fenton Mould #186, 8" crystal vase, double crimp. Charleton Gold Polka Dots on Pink decoration, c. 1951-1954. AWCO Charleton label #1651. $75-85. Scarce. *Authors' Collection.*

Detail of Charleton label and retailer's label (Fine Arts Bruner's Santa Rosa, CA) on Fenton Mould #186 crystal vase. *Authors' Collection.*

Fenton Mould #186, 8.5" crystal satin finish vase. Charleton Latticed Roses and Circles decoration, c. 1952-1954. AWCO Charleton label #1410. Insufficient data to price. Very rare. *Authors' Collection.*

Fenton Mould #186 Peach Crest vase. Charleton Roses & Bows decoration, c. 1943-1958. Frank Fenton stated that overheating during the kiln firing of the decoration by AWCO caused the glass to warp and the vase to lean. A worker probably carried this vase out of the factory. Priceless. *Courtesy of John Walk.*

Fenton Mould #186, 8.5" Peach Crest vase, double crimp. Charleton Roses and Bows decoration, c. 1943-1958. AWCO Charleton label #4427. $75-85. *Authors' Collection.*

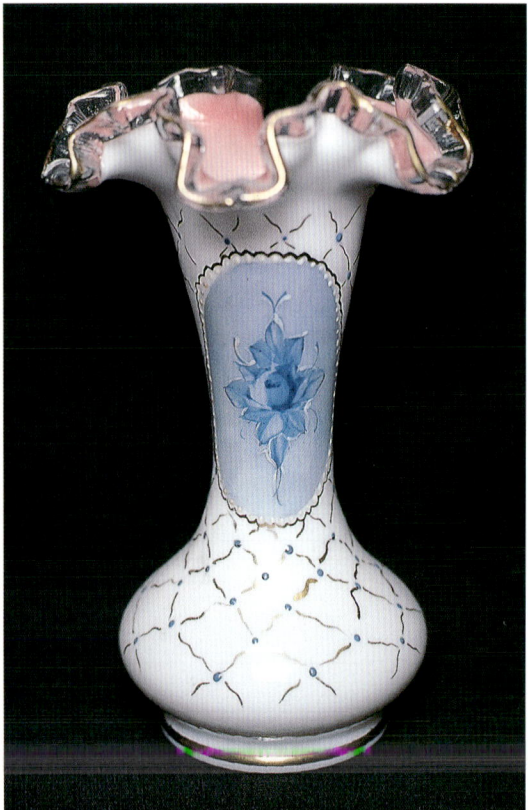

Fenton Ware #4353, 6" Milk Glass fan top vase. Charleton Roses decoration, c. 1954. $100-125. Rare. *Authors' Collection.*

Fenton Mould #186, 8" Peach Crest vase, double crimp. Charleton Blue Rose Medallion decoration, c. 1943-1958. $85-95. Scarce decoration. *Authors' Collection.*

Fenton Ware #7056, 6" Turquoise Pastel swirl vase, fine crimp. Charleton Roses decoration, c. 1955-1958. $75-95. Scarce. *Authors' Collection.*

Fenton Mould #201, 5" Silver Crest satin finish vase, double crimp. Charleton Roses decoration, c. 1951. AWCO Charleton label #1102. $60-70. Rare. *Courtesy of Rich and Laurie Karman.*

Fenton Ware #7056, 6" Pink Pastel swirl vase, fine crimp. Charleton Roses decoration, c. 1955-1958. AWCO Charleton label #2263. $75-95. Scarce. *Courtesy of Rich and Laurie Karman.*

Right to left: Fenton Mould #201 5" Milk Glass vase, square crimp; Consolidated #4112-C, 5.5" Milk Glass vase, double crimp. Both Charleton Roses decoration, c. 1940s-1950s. AWCO Charleton label #4399 on the Fenton vase. Fenton: $50-60 (scarce). Consolidated: $25-35. *Authors' collection.*

Group photograph of the Charleton Red Geometric decoration on Milk Glass with pieces by various glass manufacturers. Each piece will be discussed in detail in the chapter relating to the specific manufacturer. Front row: heart box, Beaumont suspected. Second row, Right to left: leaf tray, Westmoreland; square cigarette box, Beaumont suspected; small covered puff box, Fenton. Third row, Right to left: tall, fine crimped vase, Consolidated; large dresser bottle, Fenton; double crimped, squat vase, Fenton; 7" melon cologne bottle, Fenton. *Authors' Collection.*

Fenton Mould #206 Milk Glass footed covered candy. Charleton Red Geometric design, c. 1948-1954. AWCO Charleton label #738, 4932, or 1503^2. $75-85. *Courtesy of Rich and Laurie Karman.*

Fenton Mould #192, 6" Silver Crest Melon vase, double crimp. Charleton Red Geometric decoration, c. 1947-1952. AWCO Charleton label #4170, 1094, or 4188V^2. $40-50. *Courtesy of Rich and Laurie Karman.*

Fenton Mould #814, 8" Milk Glass bottle with "Coin Dot" stopper. Charleton Red Geometric decoration, c. 1949-1954. AWCO Charleton label #737. $125-150. Scarce. *Authors' Collection.*

Fenton Mould #192A, Silver Crest Melon puff box, Charleton Red Geometric decoration, c. 1949-1958. $45-55. Very scarce in this decoration. *Authors' Collection.*

Fenton Mould #201, 5" Silver Crest ball vase. Charleton Red Geometric decoration, c. 1940s-1950s. AWCO Charleton label #735. $45-55. Very scarce in this decoration. *Authors' Collection.*

Fenton Mould #814, pair of 8" Milk Glass bottles with "Coin Dot" stoppers. Charleton Gold Rose decoration, c. 1949-1954. AWCO Charleton label #2929. $125-150 each. Rare. *Authors' Collection.*

Fenton Mould #192, 7" Silver Crest cologne bottle. Charleton Red Geometric decoration, c. 1940s-1950s. AWCO Charleton label #735. $75-85. Very scarce in this decoration. *Authors' Collection.*

Group shot of Fenton crystal pieces with Charleton Roses with Green Maze decoration. *Courtesy of Fenton Art Glass Museum.*

Group photograph of four Milk Glass Ivy decorated pieces by various glass manufacturers. Each piece will be discussed in detail in the chapter relating to the specific manufacturer. Clockwise from left, Fenton large dresser bottle, Charleton Ivy decoration; Consolidated Bird of Paradise oval covered candy dish, Charleton Ivy decoration; Fenton Silver Crest hat basket, unknown decorator[4]; Fenton covered candy dish, Charleton Ivy decoration. *Authors' Collection.*

Fenton Mould #1522 Crystal covered candy. Charleton Roses with Green Maze decoration, c. 1949. $150-175. Rare. *Courtesy of Fenton Art Glass Museum.*

Fenton Mould #814, 8" Milk Glass bottle with "Coin Dot" stopper. Charleton Ivy decoration, c. 1949-1954. $100-125. Scarce. *Authors' Collection.*

Fenton Mould #814 Crystal 8" bottle with "Coin Dot" stopper. Charleton Roses with Green Maze decoration, c. 1950-1954. AWCO Charleton label #1209 or 1632. $175-225 (with stopper). Rare. *Courtesy of Fenton Art Glass Museum.*

Fenton Mould #93, 6" Milk Glass covered candy. Charleton Ivy decoration, c. 1949-1954. AWCO Charleton label #615A. Handwritten price of $9.50 on label. $150-175. Rare. *Authors' Collection.*

Fenton Mould #93 Milk Glass covered candy. Charleton Blue Drapes & Roses, c. 1949-1954. AWCO Charleton label #736 or #615. $150-175. Very rare. *Courtesy of Rich and Laurie Karman*.

Fenton Milk Glass satin finish vanity set consisting of two Mould #814 bottles and one Mould #93 large puff box. Charleton Roses and Bows decoration, c. 1947-1950. $275-325 set. Rare. *Authors' Collection*.

Fenton Mould #93 Milk Glass covered candy. Top view.

Top view of Mould #93 puff box lid. Note the delicate brown-fringed border treatment. Brown as a prominent color is very unusual to find in a Charleton decoration.

Fenton Mould #192A, 6" Silver Crest satin finish Melon puff box. Charleton Roses with Stipples decoration, c. 1951. $75-95. Rare. *Courtesy of Rich and Laurie Karman.*

Fenton Silver Crest Melon vanity set consisting of two Mould #192 large squat cologne bottles and one Mould #192A small puff box. Charleton Roses and Bows decoration, c. 1949-1958. Note the gold hash marks. $175-200 set. Scarce. *Authors' Collection.*

Fenton Silver Crest vanity set consisting of two Mould #192, turned-out 5.5" cologne bottles and one Mould #192A, turned-out, small puff box. Charleton Pink Mist and Roses decoration, c. 1952-1954. AWCO label #4926 on puff box and #4925 on cologne bottles. $250-275 set. Rare. *Authors' Collection.*

Fenton Mould #192, 7" Silver Crest satin finish Melon cologne bottle. Charleton Roses with Stipples decoration, c. 1951. AWCO Charleton label #1095. $90-100. Rare. *Courtesy of Rich and Laurie Karman.*

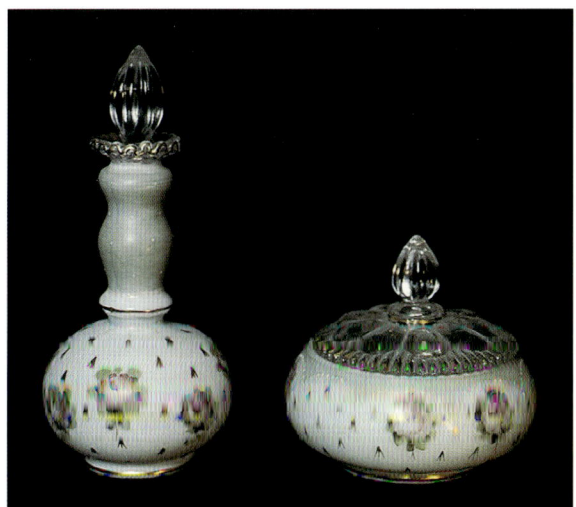

Fenton Mould #192, turned out, Silver Crest Melon vanity set. Set consists of a #192, turned-out 5.5" Melon cologne bottle and a 192A, turned-out, small Melon puff box. Charleton Blue Mist and Roses decoration, c. 1952-1954. Note the darker color of the Blue Mist on this set as compared to the Blue Mist on the previous set. AWCO Charleton label #1406, 4926, or 1661 on puff box; #4188, 4925, or 1404 on bottles. Actual set pictured has AWCO labels with #4925 (bottle) and #4926 (puff box)[2]. $150-175 set. Scarce. *Courtesy of Rich and Laurie Karman.*

Fenton Mould #192A Rose Overlay small Melon puff box. Charleton Pansy decoration. AWCO Charleton label #4608. *Courtesy of Fenton Art Glass Museum.*

Fenton Silver Crest vanity set consisting two Mould #192 5.5" cologne bottles and one Mould #192A small puff box. Charleton Roses decoration, c. 1943-1958. $125-150 set. *Authors' Collection.*

Fenton Mould #192 Rose Overlay 7" Melon cologne bottle. Charleton Pansy decoration. AWCO Charleton label #4607. *Courtesy of Fenton Art Glass Museum.*

Fenton Mould #192 Rose Overlay Melon vanity set. Charleton Pansy decoration, c. 1949-1952. $150-175 set. *Courtesy of Fenton Art Glass Museum.*

Fenton Mould #192 Rose Overlay Melon vanity set consisting of two 7" cologne bottles and one large puff box. Charleton Roses decoration, c. 1943-1947. AWCO Charleton label #G4606 on puff and #4605 on cologne bottles. Initial "D" in green on both bottles. $150-175 set. *Authors' Collection.*

Fenton Blue Overlay Melon vanity set consisting of two Mould #192, 5.5" cologne bottles and one Mould 192A small puff box. Charleton Pansy decoration, c. 1943-1947. AWCO Charleton label #4607 on cologne bottles. $125-150 set. *Authors' Collection.*

Fenton Mould #192 Silver Crest small squat Melon candleholders. Charleton Roses decoration, c. 1943-1949. $50-60 pair. Scarce. *Courtesy of Rich and Laurie Karman.*

Group shot of three Fenton Ruby Overlay Charleton decorated pieces. *Authors' Collection.*

Fenton Mould #192, 7" Blue Overlay Melon cologne bottle. Charleton Roses decoration, c. 1943-1947. AWCO Charleton label #4605. $60-75. *Authors' Collection.*

Fenton Mould #192, 8" Ruby Overlay Diamond Optic vase, double crimp. Charleton Enameled Roses decoration, c. 1951. $100-150. Rare. *Authors' Collection.*

Fenton Mould #192, 11" Ruby Overlay Diamond Optic Melon bowl, double crimp. Charleton Enameled Roses decoration, c. 1951. $150-175. Rare. *Authors' Collection.*

Fenton Mould #192, Ruby Overlay Diamond Optic large Melon covered candy dish. Charleton Enameled Roses decoration, c. 1951. $100-125. Rare. *Authors' Collection.*

Fenton Mould #192A Ruby Overlay 9" Diamond Optic Melon jug. Charleton Enameled Roses decoration, c. 1943-1949. $150-175. Rare. *Courtesy of Rich and Laurie Karman.*

Fenton Mould #192A Ruby Overlay Diamond Optic small Melon puff box. Charleton Enameled Roses decoration, c. 1942-1949. $80-95. Scarce. *Courtesy of Rich and Laurie Karman.*

Fenton Silver Crest console set, group shot. Charleton Turquoise Band and Roses decoration. *Authors' Collection.*

Fenton Mould #203, 7" Silver Crest bowl, fine crimp. Charleton Turquoise Band and Roses decoration, c. 1947. $75-85. Scarce. *Authors' Collection.*

Fenton Mould #1523, 4.5" Silver Crest candlesticks. Charleton Turquoise Band and Roses decoration, c. 1947. AWCO Charleton label #4426. $125-135. Scarce. *Authors' Collection.*

Group shot of six Fenton Silver Crest pieces with Beth Weissman Roses and Bows decoration. Left to right: Mould #36, 4.5" double crimp vase; Mould #203, 4.5" double crimp ball vase; Mould #203 7" double crimp bowl; and Mould #192A Melon vanity set consisting of two small squat cologne bottles and a small puff box. NP (No Price). *Authors' Collection.*

Group shot of four Fenton Silver Crest pieces with Beth Weissman Roses and Bows decoration. Left to right: Mould #192, 8" double crimp vase; Mould #192, 7" Melon cologne bottle; Mould #192, 6" Melon double crimp jug; and Mould #36, 4.5" fan vase. NP. *Authors' Collection.*

Fenton Mould #203 and #205, 7" and 8.5" Silver Crest bowls. Both Beth Weissman decorations, c. 1940s-1950s. Note the similar decorations on each with just a variance in the color of the bows. NP. *Authors' Collection*.

Fenton Mould #711, 6" Silver Crest Beaded Melon vase with suspected Tyndale decoration. Note: this decoration is a transfer. NP. *Authors' Collection*.

Fenton Mould #192, 5.5" Silver Crest Melon cologne bottle. Tyndale blue roses and silk-screened gold fleur-de-lis decoration. NP. *Authors' Collection*.

Group shot of two Fenton Peach Crest pieces with Tyndale decorations. Left to right: Mould #1924 hat basket and Mould #1924 top hat. Both decorations are transfers. NP. *Authors' Collection*.

Fenton Mould #192 Silver Crest cologne bottle. Detail showing Tyndale #427 label.

Fenton Mould #206, 7" Rose Pastel footed comport, double crimp. Unknown gold roses decal, suspected Tyndale, c. 1940s-1950s. NP. *Authors' Collection*.

Fenton Mould #192 Silver Crest cologne bottle. Detail showing silk-screened gold fleur-de-lis.

Fenton Mould #192A Silver Crest small squat Melon cologne bottle. Tyndale decorated. NP. *Authors' Collection.*

Fenton Mould #192, 9" Blue Overlay vase, double crimp. Unknown decorator. NP. *Authors' Collection.*

Fenton Mould #192, 9" Peach Crest Melon vase, double crimp. Unknown decorator. This decoration is different on three sides. NP. *Authors' Collection.*

Fenton Mould #192, 9" Silver Crest Melon vase, double crimp. Unknown decorator. NP. *Authors' Collection.*

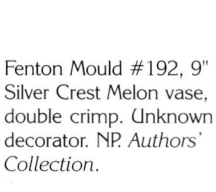

Fenton Mould #192, 9" Peach Crest Melon vase, double crimp. The decoration is different from sides of the vase.

Fenton Mould #192, 8" Silver Crest Melon vase, double crimp, c. 1947-1952. Unknown decorator. NP. *Courtesy of Rich and Laurie Karman.*

Fenton Mould #192, 6" Silver Crest Melon vase, double crimp. Unknown decorator but unlikely to be AWCO, c. 1943-1949. NP. *Courtesy of Rich and Laurie Karman.*

Fenton Mould #192, 5" Silver Crest squat Melon vase, double crimp. Gold leaves decoration, c. 1947-1952. Decorator unconfirmed to date but AWCO likely. NP. *Courtesy of Rich and Laurie Karman.*

Fenton Mould #192, 6.5" Milk Glass Melon vase, double crimp. Decoration has strong similarity to Charleton but unconfirmed to date, c. 1940s-1950s. Note the absence of a crest. NP. *Courtesy of Rich and Laurie Karman.*

Fenton Mould #192, 8" Peach Crest Melon vase, double crimp. Thistle decoration with strong similarity to Charleton but unconfirmed to date, c. 1947-1958. NP. *Courtesy of Rich and Laurie Karman.*

Fenton Mould #201, 5" Rose Overlay vase, fine-crimp. Unknown decorator. Scarce. NP. *Authors' Collection.*

Fenton Mould #186, 8" Silver Crest vase, double crimp. Decoration of African Violets by unknown decorator, c. 1943-1967. NP. *Courtesy of Rich and Laurie Karman.*

Fenton Mould #1523, 5" Silver Crest candleholders. Rose decoration with some similarity to Charleton but unconfirmed to date, c. 1947. NP. *Courtesy of Rich and Laurie Karman.*

Fenton Mould #186, 8" Silver Crest vase, double crimp, interior view.

Fenton Mould #711 Milk Glass Beaded Melon large puff box with very unusual Milk Glass lid. Unknown decorator. Rare. NP. *Authors' Collection.*

Fenton Mould #680, 8.5" Silver Crest plate. Unknown decorator, c. 1948-1958. NP. *Courtesy of Rich and Laurie Karman.*

Fenton Mould #192 Milk Glass large Melon puff box or covered candy with very unusual Milk Glass lid. Decoration with strong similarity to Charleton but unconfirmed to date. Rare. NP. *Courtesy of Rich and Laurie Karman.*

Fenton Mould #192, 5.5" Silver Crest satin finish Melon vase, double crimp. Unknown decorator. Rare. NP. *Authors' Collection*.

Fenton Mould #680 and #192, 5.5" Silver Crest fine crimp nut dish and small squat candlestick. Suspected Charleton Violet decoration, c. 1954. Scarce. NP. *Authors' Collection*.

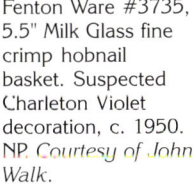

Fenton Ware #3735, 5.5" Milk Glass fine crimp hobnail basket. Suspected Charleton Violet decoration, c. 1950. NP. *Courtesy of John Walk*.

Fenton Mould #680, 5.5" Silver Crest nut dish. Profile view.

Fenton Ware #3735, 5.5" Milk Glass fine crimp hobnail basket. Interior view.

Group shot of two Fenton pieces with suspected Charleton Violets decoration. Left to right: Mould #3937, 7" Milk Glass hobnail bonbon, handled and Mould #36, 5.5" Silver Crest bonbon, double crimp. NP. *Authors' Collection*.

Fenton Ware #3937, 7.5" Milk Glass handled hobnail bonbon. Top view. *Courtesy of Rich and Laurie Karman.*

Fenton Mould #1522, 10" Silver Crest bowl, double crimp. Unknown decorator, c. 1956. NP. *Courtesy of Rich and Laurie Karman.*

Fenton Mould #192 Silver Crest short squat Melon Candlesticks. Suspected Charleton Violet decoration, c. 1948. Scarce. NP. *Courtesy of Rich and Laurie Karman.*

Fenton Mould #36, 5.5" Silver Crest bonbon. Unknown decorator, c. 1943-1958. Note the "blue mist" look to the painting around the edge of the bonbon. NP. *Courtesy of Rich and Laurie Karman.*

Fenton Mould #36, 5.5" Aqua Crest 5.5" bonbon. Unknown decorator, c. 1951-1952. NP. *Courtesy of Rich and Laurie Karman.*

Group shot, all unknown decorator, left to right: Fenton Mould #1924, 4.5" Silver Crest top hat, c. 1942-1948; Fenton Mould #36, 6.25" Silver Crest double crimp vase; Fenton Mould #36, 4.5" Silver Crest double crimp vase, c. 1942-1948, c. 1950. NP. *Courtesy of Rich and Laurie Karman.*

Fenton Mould #680 Silver Crest nut dish, footed. Unknown decorator, c. 1948. NP. *Courtesy TWM Antique Mall.*

Fenton Mould #711, 7" Silver Crest Beaded Melon (Tiara) cologne bottle. Decoration of African Violets by unknown decorator, c. 1949-1952. NP. *Courtesy of Rich and Laurie Karman.*

Fenton Mould #36, 4" Silver Crest fan vase. Decoration of African Violets by unknown decorator. NP. *Courtesy of Rich and Laurie Karman.*

Fenton Mould #36, 4.5" Silver Crest vase, double crimp. Decoration of African Violets by unknown decorator. NP. *Courtesy of Rich and Laurie Karman.*

Fenton Mould #36, 6" Milk Glass fan vase. Unknown decorator. NP. *Authors' Collection.*

Fenton Mould #36, 4" Silver Crest fan vase. Decoration with strong similarity to Charleton but unconfirmed to date, c. 1948. NP. *Courtesy of Rich and Laurie Karman.*

Fenton Mould #36, 4" Silver Crest fan vase, bottom view with (illegible) signature.

Fenton Mould #1923, 7" Silver Crest hat basket. Ivy decoration, unknown decorator[3]. Rare. NP. *Authors' Collection*.

Fenton Mould #36, 5.5" Emerald Crest bonbon. Ivy decoration, unknown decorator. NP. *Courtesy of Rich and Laurie Karman*.

Fenton Mould #203, 4.5" Emerald Crest vase, double crimp. Ivy decoration, unknown decorator. NP. *Authors' Collection*.

Fenton Mould #192 Silver Crest small Melon squat candlestick. Ivy decoration, unknown decorator. NP. *Authors' Collection*.

Fenton Mould #192, 5.5" Silver Crest squat Melon vase, double crimp. Enameled flower and vine decoration, unknown decorator but unlikely to be AWCO, c. 1943-1949. NP. *Courtesy of Rich and Laurie Karman*.

Fenton Mould #192A Blue Overlay Melon vanity set consisting of two short squat cologne bottles and one small puff box. Very unusual enameled grape and leaves decoration. Decorator unconfirmed to date but AWCO likely. NP. *Authors' Collection.*

Fenton Mould #192, 5.5" Rose Overlay Melon vase, double crimp. Unknown decorator, c. 1943-1948. NP. *Authors' Collection.*

Fenton Mould #192, 5.5" Blue Overlay Melon vase, double crimp. Very unusual enameled grape and leaves decoration, c. 1943-1953. Decorator unconfirmed to date but AWCO likely. NP. *Courtesy of Rich and Laurie Karman.*

Fenton Mould #1924, 3" Peach Crest top hat. Unknown decorator. NP. *Authors' Collection.*

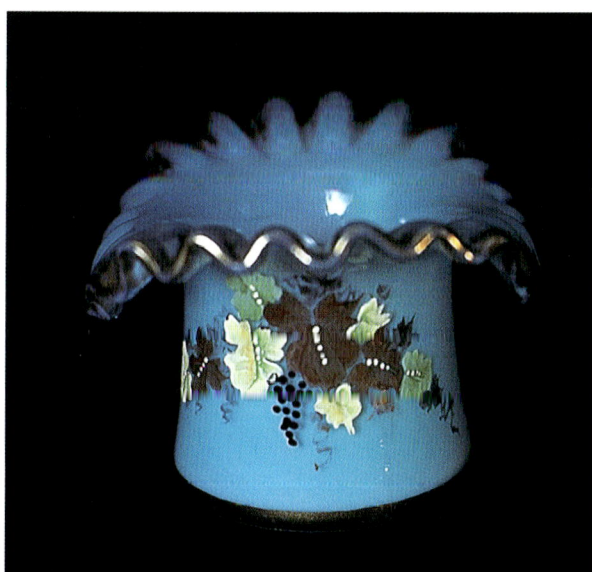

Fenton Mould #1924, 4.5" Blue Overlay top hat. Very unusual enameled grape and leaves decoration, c. 1943-1953. Decorator unconfirmed to date but AWCO likely. NP. *Courtesy of Rich and Laurie Karman.*

Fenton Mould #1924, 3" Rose Overlay top hat. Unknown decorator. NP. *Authors' Collection.*

Fenton Mould #203, 4.5" Silver Crest vase. Unknown decorator. NP. *Authors' Collection.*

Detail showing the Fenton Topaz Overlay basket back stamp.

Fenton Ware #5780 4" Heart Trinket Box. NP. *Author's collection.*

Fenton Blue Topaz Overlay basket. First piece in a series for QVC in the "Charleton Collection." The designs on these items drew their inspiration from Charleton decorations. $96.00. *Courtesy of the Fenton Art Glass Company.*

Fenton Ware #7139 Peach Crest basket with roses decoration from the 1999 Connoisseur Collection. NP.

Chapter 3.
Cambridge Glass Company

Of all the elegant glassware upon which Charleton decorations may be found, Cambridge glass sets the highest standard for excellence in design. We cannot recall seeing any piece of Cambridge glass with an average Charleton decoration. This elegant glassware will not only add the most color and class to any Charleton collection, it will also require of the collector the most expense in order to build a worthy representation of the line.

This first-rate glassware line was established in 1873 by a conglomerate called The National Glass Company, although it would be almost thirty years later before the first piece of glass would emerge from the annealing lehr. During the construction phase, the founders of the company had the good fortune of hiring a superbly talented Englishman, Arthur Bennett, to manage the fledgling company. Mr. Bennett moved from New York, where he was a buyer and an importer of china and glass, to accept employment with Cambridge. Prior to his involvement with Cambridge Glass he knew nothing of the glass manufacturing process.

Named after the small community in Ohio in which it was located, Cambridge Glass enjoyed the abundant natural resources common to many other glass factories in the "Glass Belt." Although owned by National Glass, and initially using moulds obtained from some of their other plants, the Cambridge factory was treated as a separate concern from the other nineteen plants controlled by National. Fortunate enough to own both a coalmine from which, through a special process, gas was extracted and several natural gas wells, Cambridge was better able to manage its operating expenses, thus increasing the likelihood of a successful venture. The first piece of Cambridge glass, a three-pint pressed glass pitcher, rolled off the line in May 1902. From this humble beginning, a glass industry legend was born.

In 1902, National Glass ran into financial difficulties as well as an unexpected depletion of their source of natural gas at the Cambridge site. Several of their other plants burned the following year and the struggling company went bust in the financial panic of 1907. Seizing upon this opportunity, Arthur Bennet took the risk and invested his life savings and, along with a bank loan and a group of investors, purchased the Cambridge Glass Company outright.

Arthur Bennett now stood squarely at the helm of the Cambridge Glass Company and was free to exert more influence over the company's glass colors and designs. Under Bennett's leadership Cambridge crossed a threshold, emerging as a leader in the field of elegant glassware. In addition to using his personal experience as a buyer and importer to guide him in analyzing market trends, Bennett also handpicked his staff and surrounded himself with some extraordinary associates. Actually, the men he chose were not selected for their backgrounds in the glass industry, but, rather, on the merits of their own qualifications.

These men, known as the "Bennett Boys," added greatly to the success of the company and could still be found in managerial positions in the company forty years later. In employing these men, Bennett demonstrated his recognition of the importance of surrounding oneself with smart, talented people. This is a trait shared by all good leaders regardless of the industry or venture in which they are involved.

Initially, Cambridge produced mainly crystal glassware with very limited use of other glass colors. A 1903 catalog lists only four colors in which novelty items were produced – amber, blue, opal (milk glass), and turquoise. There appears to be no rhyme or reason to which colors were made in any particular year. Various colors would appear in one year only to vanish from the line the next year and then reappear once again years later. Within the next twenty to thirty years Cambridge would have a wide spectrum of colors at its disposal, many of these with exotic sounding names like Azurite, Carrera, Dianthus Pink, LaRosa, and the like.

After many robust years of production, Cambridge saw their share of the elegant glass market dwindle and their more costly glass proved noncompetitive. Many factors impacted their market share and among them were growing post war imports, a flood of popular, inexpensive milk glass, and other U.S. competitor's machine-made glass. Although Cambridge experimented with milk glass in the mid-1950s, it perhaps was a case of "too little, too late," and the company closed its doors in July of 1954.

Fortunately, this proved to be only a temporary closing and the Cambridge Glass Company reopened in March of 1955. However, due to the ever-shifting tastes of the American consumer, the company struggled to sell its products. Sold again in 1956, a last ditch effort was made to keep the plant operating, but it never recovered to the point of being profitable and the doors closed for the final time in 1958.

The Cambridge Glass Company produced scores of beautiful glassware in cut patterns, etched patterns, gold encrustation, along with some of the most aesthetically pleasing shapes and designs in the industry. In retrospect, we are personally thankful that Cambridge never lowered their standards of excellence in either material or design in order to survive.

In 1960, the Imperial Glass Company purchased the Cambridge factory and moulds. Imperial went out of business in 1980 and the moulds were redistributed once again. National Cambridge Collectors, Inc., a non-profit organization, purchased all of the etching plates and a major portion of the cast iron moulds. However, due to miscommunication and a lack of funds, other glass companies purchased a few of the remaining Cambridge moulds. Collectors need to be aware of this and do the necessary research to prevent purchasing these new reproductions as vintage Cambridge.

There are several great reference books and websites that the collector can use to appreciate the wide range of design and colors in the Cambridge line. National Cambridge Collectors, Inc. has released a series of books over the years containing reprints of original catalogs and brochures. The mission of NCC is stated as being ". . . dedicated to the preservation and collection of the products of the Cambridge Glass Company." This organization maintains a permanent museum of Cambridge glass in Cambridge, Ohio, and has an outstanding collection of Charleton on Cambridge as well.

In the 1920s and on into the 1950s, Cambridge began embossing some of its glassware with a mould mark which consisted of the letter "C" enclosed in a small triangle. This mark is not always present and even when it is, it can be very difficult to find, as it is often lightly impressed in the glass. It is generally accepted that the presence or absence of this trademark has no effect on the overall value of common Cambridge patterns.

The primary colors of Cambridge that Charleton collectors need to be concerned with are Crown Tuscan, Crystal, Milk (milk glass), Ebony, Ebon, and Emerald Green. We do not include the color Coral, because, for all intents and purposes, it is identical to Crown Tuscan. Although there still remains debate among Cambridge collectors as to the veracity of this statement, Crown Tuscan is the only name used for this color of Cambridge glass in this book. We will leave it to other purists to discuss what can be a controversial subject.

We will not discuss every item from Cambridge that has been found with a Charleton decoration, but rather, we will give a brief summary of some of the scarcer items and notes of particular interest. This summary will discuss these pieces within the color categories they were produced.

Crown Tuscan

Several other major U.S. glass manufacturers, past and present, have used a shell pink color similar to Crown Tuscan. These companies include Boyd, Fenton, Fostoria, Jeanette, Summit, and Westmoreland. The color of Crown Tuscan will vary from a very light pink to a richer shell pink. This is due to variations in the glass batch formula and is not uncommon in the glass industry. Generally, older Crown Tuscan pieces have the deeper pink color and the later pieces have the lighter tint. Charleton decorations on different Cambridge patterns are limited to mostly floral themes, although the number of different shapes found among those patterns offer the collector a wide array of pieces to collect.

We were very fortunate to be able to have access to several private collections of Charleton decorated Crown Tuscan. First and foremost was the fabulous collection owned by avid Cambridge collectors Steve and Helen Klemko. The variety and quality of their collection is simply amazing. We feel certain that their large collection of Charleton "Blue Mist" decorated pieces is one of the nicest in the country.

Steve and Helen Klemko, who generously allowed us into their home to photograph their outstanding collection of Charleton decorated Cambridge.

The Sea Shell line was a favorite pattern utilized by Charleton decorators, evidenced by the plentiful quantity available on the collectibles market. Beautifully designed, this pattern has strong lines, perfect for hand decorating. Probably the biggest bang for the buck in Crown Tuscan is the 7", #SS16 Sea Shell footed comport with the "Harbor" decoration. This is a very substantial moulded piece of glass, much thicker than many of its counterparts and is aesthetically very appealing. There are several design elements that make this item stand out.

First is the central decoration depicting a three sail schooner docked beside what appears to be fair sized building that is most likely a freight warehouse. Charleton landscape scenes similar to this one are very scarce, and have appeared on less than ten different items from other manufacturers to date. Thus far, this is the only Cambridge item found with a landscape scene and this particular landscape is the only type depicted on Cambridge glass.

Positioned along a small bay or river bordered by rolling hills, the overall scene exudes an air of peacefulness. Large pink roses and blue flowers border the lower two thirds of this landscape. The way the picture is composed, effected by the over proportioned roses, gives one a sense of having a supernatural ability to peer past the roses and through the surface of the bowl to a tranquil land faraway. Smaller rose blooms extend to the heavy gilt rays bordering the scalloped edges of the shell. Positioned at the portion of the bowl that flips up at the shell's end are three, gold leaf stylized "ghost" roses. We call them by this name due to the fact that the stylized rose is incompletely painted and it incorporates the color of the underlying glass to complete the rose. This same Ghost rose décor with golden sprigs circles the base and lends it a sense of continuity.

This Harbor decoration appears to have been well received and this is an essential piece for the Cambridge Charleton collector. Due to this fair availability, this item can sometimes be purchased quite reasonably.

There is a variation of the "Charleton Roses" found on this and some other Crown Tuscan items that bears note. These pieces have mauve colored roses rather than the usual bright pink ones. Cambridge collectors have come to call this variation "Chocolate Roses" and that is the name we will use as well. "Chocolate Roses" items are certainly hard to come by and will probably command a higher price if marketed properly.

A strikingly elegant piece to pursue is the 8" #3500/57 Gadroon candy box. This box is not footed and has a low profile. In fact, Cambridge also made this item without the cover and it is known as their #3400/91 relish dish. The interior of the bowl is divided into three sections by a pinwheel shaped divider and three ornately shaped handles grace the exterior of the bowl. The clover shaped lid is offset from the handles further enhancing the overall elegant design. Occasionally the interior of this item will be decorated and these are more desirable.

The 7" #SS11 Shell Nude footed comport never fails to garner attention, especially from lovers of Art Deco. Adapted from the #3011 Statuesque line, instead of the usual candleholder or goblet perched atop her head, this lovely nude supports a 5" or 7" Sea Shell plate. This compote, like a variety of Cambridge pieces, is a composite of several pieces found in other shapes. Utilizing the statuesque nude, the Sea Shell plate, and a blown base, these items were all joined together while the glass was still in a molten state.

This complicated, multi-step process is the main reason the Shell Nude comport has never been reproduced. This type of manufacture is similar to a ballet in that it requires very skilled workers to "carry in" the different pieces at just the right time. The expense and expertise needed to produce this multi-formed item with a blown base makes its future reproduction unlikely.

Several nice pieces in Crown Tuscan pictured in this book were provided by Mike and Cindy Arent. Some of the outstanding pieces they own are the #61 Sea Shell candlesticks, as well as the "Chocolate Roses" Shell center and #16 Sea Shell 6" comport.

There are several other items in the Sea Shell line which are much sought after and command premium prices. The 14" #SS7 torte plate is one the best pieces to include in any collection as a striking backdrop for other Cambridge items. Sixteen interior ribs incorporated in the exterior shell design radiate outward from the center of the plate, adding dimension to an otherwise mostly flat surface. Within this space between the ribs AWCO usually placed either eight or sixteen sprays of flowers to compliment the large floral decoration located in the center of the plate.

Two of the decorations most often found on this plate are the Charleton Roses design and Gardenia. Both decorations are graced with large amounts of gold leaf that blend well with the shell pink glass. This is a very substantial piece of glass and should be handled very carefully, especially when having it shipped. A recent find in this item was a torte plate that had the decorator's initials placed directly below the central decoration. This is an exceptional find and this type of initialing on any Charleton item is very scarce.

The "Holy Grail" of Charleton on Cambridge would have to the 10", #SS40 Flying Lady bowl. It would be considered a good buy if you could purchase one of these decorated ladies for under $500.00. The mould work on this item is just extraordinary, and the sweeping lines create a dramatic sense of motion. This design should be considered to be one of the hallmarks in American art glass representing the Art Deco style.

Cliff McNeil has written a very interesting account involving the Flying Lady bowl, as related to him by Lynn Welker, one of the country's foremost authorities on Cambridge glass. We have recapped the highlights of this account for the benefit of those who are unfamiliar with it.

The Flying Lady bowl was first produced around 1936 or 1937, and it was originally listed in Cambridge catalogs as a flower or fruit center bowl. While quite popular in the town of Cambridge, the risqué depiction of the nude was deemed by some as unsuitable for display when their minister came to call. As a result, the Flying Lady was often hidden in the cellar until after the minister departed.

Another story related by Mr. McNeil concerns how this item actually received its nickname, the "Flying Lady." Just prior to its introduction by Cambridge, the circus came to town and evidently the community was duly impressed by the skills of a German lady who was a trapeze artist. After her departure, the townspeople dubbed this fruit center bowl the "Flying Lady" in her honor and that is how it has been known ever since. Mr. McNeil states that, although the tale ". . . cannot be proven, it is a well known story in the area and certainly lends charm and romance to an already fabulous glass item."

Cambridge Crown Tuscan is among the earliest types of American glassware to be decorated with AWCO's standard floral decorations. It was much later that the "Blue Mist" decoration made its debut in the spring of 1952. An advertisement the April 1952 edition of the *Crockery and Glass Journal* shows several pieces of Cambridge glassware decorated by AWCO. The decoration shown is referred to as "Coral Shell enhanced by a new, hand painted pattern, Blue Mist." The pictures in the advertisement allow easy comparison in order to document the pattern.

For the most part, "Blue Mist" has a unique identifier that aids in its identification: small white stippled dots surrounding the floral decoration. Each of these dots is capped by small interconnected white arches that create a beautiful and interesting accent. (See the detail of "Blue Mist" in the color plate on page ###.)

Although there are other "Mist" type decorations found on Fenton and Consolidated glassware, we will distinguish those decorations from the Cambridge items by noting the subsequent floral decoration, i.e., "Blue Mist and Roses." There are items with a true "Mist" decoration that are not on Cambridge glass, but they are few and far between. Of these, one of the most stunning we have seen is a "Green Mist" crystal lamp pictured in this book in the Lamp section.

Equally enticing as the Flying Lady bowls are the graceful Cambridge Swans that many consider to be the epitome in showcasing a superb Charleton collection. If price is any indicator, it would be hard to disagree with this sentiment given that recently a #1043 8.5" "Blue Mist" Crown Tuscan swan sold for $2,800 on eBay.

Regardless of size, these swans, when found painted, will usually portray the Charleton Rose decoration, although ones with the Gardenia decoration will surface occasionally.

Thus far "Blue Mist" has only been found on Cambridge, and then only on Crown Tuscan, but the possibility of it existing on Cambridge milk glass is not unlikely. Building a sizable collection in this unique and scarce design will require a considerable investment of both time and money; but, after you see the decoration in person you can better appreciate the merits of the pursuit.

In dissecting the April 1952 advertisement mentioned earlier, we find that "Coral" was a term that Cambridge used in marketing Crown Tuscan and, although it actually replaced the name "Crown Tuscan" for a few years, it is believed that the glass formula was basically unchanged. There is, however, a slight difference in the tint of glass made in this later period. The Coral color was noticeably lighter than the earlier production of Crown Tuscan glassware.

For the most part, Cambridge used "Sea Shell" as a designation that denotes any of the Cambridge items that have nautical elements incorporated into the mould itself, such as the various fish and shell designs. One exception to this rule of thumb is the #61 Sea Shell Nude candlesticks, which have no nautical theme in their design. It was marketed by Cambridge in the Sea Shell line in Crown Tuscan and thus received that designation.

Milk

Charleton decorated pieces on Cambridge milk glass (or Milk as it is known in Cambridge circles) were produced for a much shorter time period than Crown Tuscan. Made from January or February 1954 to the first closing of the company in July 1954, Milk prices in relation to the much longer produced Crown Tuscan should reflect this short production period. Of course, to some, the plain white color is not as captivating as the rich shell pink, but it is still a very appealing color as a background for the floral hand painted decorations of Charleton. The thinner items in Milk, such as the shell plates and swans, will exhibit nice opalescence, especially on the edges. This fiery opal color is very attractive and pieces sparkle when placed in brightly lit displays.

Adding Milk pieces to your collection will give nice contrast as well as portray the range of colors that AWCO utilized from the Cambridge Glass Company. Do not expect them to be plentiful, but you can expect them to be more expensive than the same item in Crown Tuscan. We photographed for this book the largest known single collection of Charleton on Milk and that consisted of only eight pieces, all residing in the collection of Charles and Mary Upton. How much you pay will depend on the condition of the decoration, knowledge (or ignorance) of the owner of the piece, and market fluctuation.

Emerald

Cambridge produced items in Emerald green glass in three different time periods: dark Emerald in 1916, a lighter green in the 1920s/1930s, and another dark Emerald from 1949 to 1958. The period of glass produced with Charleton decorations comes from the latter time period of 1949 and it is generally known by Cambridge collectors as "late dark Emerald" to avoid confusion with the glass colors from the other two production periods.

Any item of this color found with a Charleton decoration is very scarce. Only a small quantity has been reported to date. Without a sufficient quantity being traded it is difficult to set accurate market prices, but you can bet that they will be competitive with Crown Tuscan. The gold leaf accents on the rich, dark green glass make an especially attractive combination. Most of the decorations seen by the authors to date all have the same motif, although some recently found pieces have shown some variety. Although there has been little Emerald Charleton to display at this point, others items and decorations will certainly surface and the finds are sure to be exciting.

Amethyst

Although no pieces were available for photographs for this book, prominent Cambridge dealer and glass author Lynn Welker reports that there have been two different pieces of Cambridge Amethyst found with Charleton decorations. Any Cambridge Amethyst items with Charleton decorations should be considered rare.

The first item reported was a pair of #878 Decagon candlesticks decorated with Charleton Roses. The second item was a #3400 Ball Top tumbler with a Clover decoration.

Crystal

Residing in the personal collection of Steve and Helen Klemko is a magnificent 13" #1045 Charleton Crystal Swan centerpiece. You really have to see this piece in person to fully appreciate the impact created when viewing such a large piece of decorated elegant glass. Although Cambridge makes a swan (listed by Cambridge as a punch bowl) one size larger than this one, a Charleton decorated version has yet to be reported.

Another fabulous Cambridge Crystal item is a #575 Cornucopia in the "Eyelet" decoration. "Eyelet" is one of the few patterns that was named by AWCO in their advertisements. The one and only example we have seen is owned by Charles and Mary Upton.

A superb Crystal item also in the Upton's collection is a #P-306 covered candy in AWCO's "Oak Leaf" pattern. Once again, with "Oak Leaf" we have an AWCO created decoration name. This covered candy is one of only two Oak Leaf pieces seen outside of advertisements.

Ebon

Ebon was introduced during the same short time period as Cambridge Milk, from January to July 1954, so the quantity of items available for collectors is in very short supply. Couple this with even fewer Charleton items and you can see why this will be a real challenge to collect even a few pieces. Most items in this color treatment will be found on the pattern known as Cambridge Square.

Cambridge Square was the only new pattern introduced by Cambridge in the 1950s, and, as it turned out, the last new line before the company's demise. Cambridge Square was entirely different from the more traditional styles of elegant glassware the company was known for producing. A strong movement was developing during this time that encouraged the use of "Modern" design in household goods and the look of Cambridge Square, with its clean and angular lines, fit the bill nicely.

It was very well received in the market and generated a fair amount of mention in the trade journals of the day. It was so well acclaimed that the Museum of Modern Art selected the pattern for permanent display in the Gold Design Showroom located in the Merchandise Mart, Chicago.

We first saw a piece of Charleton decorated Ebon last year. It was on eBay and was being marketed as a piece of painted cast iron! It was actually listed as a heavy "Meatle [sic] Bowl," and we found it only because of the mention in the auction description of the presence of the Charleton label on the bottom of the piece.

We were watching the auction closely as it appeared that we might get it rather cheaply and we were hoping to score another Charleton coup. In the last hour of the auction, the price went through the roof and we reluctantly dropped out of a bidding war.

The next year, when making preparations to photograph the Klemko's Charleton/Cambridge collection, Helen suggested that we delay our visit until after the annual Cambridge convention. She had mentioned our prospective book to other collectors and was arranging to borrow several Cambridge items in order that they be photographed and included in this section.

Shortly after our arrival at their home a few weeks later, there, on their table, was the "Meatle" bowl we had bid on! So our paths with this item did cross again, and, even if it was only for a few hours, it was an interesting experience for us just the same. Helen informed us that there had been a real buzz among several of her Cambridge buddies when the word circulated about the ongoing auction, and they were ready when it was coming to a close. Unaware that the word was out, we never really stood a chance against some of those "deep" pockets when, all along, we were hoping to win a real sleeper.

Of course, this bowl was not cast iron, but was a lovely Ebon #3797/165 Cambridge Square pattern covered candy box with a simple yet elegant floral decoration. Along with the candy box, the same owners, Carl and Shirley Beynon, had graciously sent along an Ebon 8" #3797/80 Square pattern footed bud vase with the same decoration as the candy box.

Ebony

During our last trip through Cambridge we had the good fortune to document several exceptional pieces of "Gold Roses" on Cambridge Ebony glass belonging to Mike and Lisa Neilson. This was the first time we had seen any Charleton items in this color and they were just beautiful. This small collection of pieces probably represents one of the largest collections in this color owned by any one collector. No other Charleton decoration has been reported to have been found on this color of glass.

Cambridge Crown Tuscan #SS40, 10.5" Sea Shell Flying Lady flower or fruit center. Charleton Gardenia decoration, c. 1949-1950s. $500-600. Scarce. *Courtesy of Helen & Steve Klemko.*

Cambridge Crown Tuscan #SS40, 10.5" Sea Shell Flying Lady. Interior view.

Cambridge Crown Tuscan Gadroon #3500/42, 12" Urn. Charleton Roses decoration, c. 1949-1950s. $450-500. Rare. *Courtesy of Helen & Steve Klemko.*

Cambridge Crown Tuscan #1043, 8.5" and #1040, 3" type 3 swans. Charleton Gardenia decoration, c. 1949-1950s. #1043, 8.5": $550-600. 3": $150-200. Both rare. *Courtesy of Helen & Steve Klemko.*

Cambridge Crown Tuscan #SS40, 10.5" Sea Shell Flying Lady flower or fruit center. Charleton Roses decoration, c. 1949-1950s. $450-500. Scarce. *Courtesy of Helen & Steve Klemko.*

Left to right: Cambridge Milk #1040, 3" type 3 swan. Charleton Roses decoration. Cambridge Crown Tuscan #1040, 3" type 3 swan. Charleton Gardenia decoration. Milk: $175-225; Crown Tuscan: $150-200. Both rare. *Courtesy of Lynn Welker.*

Cambridge Crown Tuscan #SS40, 10.5" Sea Shell Flying Lady. Front view.

Cambridge Crown Tuscan #SS61, 8.5" Nude Stem Sea Shell candlestick. Charleton Roses decoration. $600-750. Very rare. *Courtesy of Mike & Cindy Arent.*

Cambridge Crown Tuscan #SS10, 5" and #SS11, 7" Nude Stem Sea Shell comports. Charleton Roses & Bows decoration, c. 1949-1950s. AWCO Charleton #4397 (5"). #SS10, 5": $150-175. #SS11, 7": $175-200. Both scarce with the 5" harder to find than the 7". *Courtesy of Helen & Steve Klemko.*

Cambridge Crown Tuscan #SS11, 7" Nude Stem Sea Shell comport. Charleton Roses and Bows decoration, c. 1949-1950s. $175-200. *Authors' collection.*

Cambridge Crown Tuscan #SS11, 7" Nude Stem Sea Shell comport. Top detail.

Cambridge Crown Tuscan #SS11, 7" Nude Stem Sea Shell comport. Charleton Gardenia decoration, c. 1949-1950s. $150-175. Gardenia decoration is harder to find than the Roses & Bows decoration. *Courtesy of Helen & Steve Klemko.*

Cambridge Crown Tuscan #SS7, 14" Sea Shell torte plate. Charleton Gardenia decoration, c. 1940s-1950s. AWCO Charleton label #557. $300-325. Scarce, especially with this decoration. *Authors' collection.*

Cambridge Crown Tuscan #SS7, 14" Sea Shell torte plate. Charleton Roses decoration, c. 1940s-1950s. AWCO Charleton label #4359. $250-300. Scarce. *Authors' collection.*

Cambridge Crown Tuscan #SS9, 9" round three-footed Sea Shell bowl. Charleton Roses decoration, c. 1949-1950s. $125-150. Very Scarce. *Courtesy of Helen & Steve Klemko.*

Cambridge Crown Tuscan #SS42, 8" Sea Shell flower center. Charleton Chocolate Roses[5] decoration. Note the butterfly in the decoration. $175-225. Scarce. *Courtesy of Mike & Cindy Arent.*

Cambridge Crown Tuscan #SS42, 7.5" Sea Shell flower center. Charleton Roses decoration, c. 1949-1950s. $150-175. Very Scarce. *Courtesy of Helen & Steve Klemko.*

Cambridge Crown Tuscan #SS42, 7.5" Sea Shell flower center reverse view.

Cambridge Crown Tuscan #SS44, 6" Sea Shell flower center. Charleton Chocolate Roses decoration, c. 1949-1950s. $125-150. Scarce. *Authors' collection.*

Cambridge Crown Tuscan #1236, 7.5" Keyhole footed ivy balls. Charleton Roses, c. 1949-1950s. Insufficient data to price[6]. Very Rare. *Courtesy of Helen & Steve Klemko.*

Cambridge Crown Tuscan #1236, 7.5" Keyhole footed ivy ball. Close-up.

Cambridge Crown Tuscan #SS49, 10" Sea Shell vase. Charleton Blue Roses decoration, c. 1940s-1950s. $125-150. Scarce. *Courtesy of Shirley & Carl Beynon.*

Cambridge Crown Tuscan #SS66, 4" Sea Shell seafood cocktails or sherbets. Charleton Roses decoration, c. 1949-1950s. $200-250 each. Scarce. *Courtesy of Helen & Steve Klemko.*

Cambridge Crown Tuscan #1238, 12" Keyhole footed flower vase. Charleton Medallion Rose decoration, c. 1949-1950s. $200-250. Rare. *Courtesy of Helen & Steve Klemko.*

Cambridge Crown Tuscan #SS47, 9.5" Sea Shell cornucopia. Charleton Roses decoration. $200-225. Rare. *Courtesy of Mike & Cindy Arent.*

Cambridge Crown Tuscan #274, 10" bud vase. Charleton Roses decoration, c. 1949-1950s. $90-100. *Courtesy of Helen & Steve Klemko.*

Cambridge Crown Tuscan #647, pair of 2-lite candelabrums. Charleton Green Mist[7] and Roses decoration. $700-800 pair. Very rare. *Courtesy of Charles & Mary Upton.*

Cambridge Crown Tuscan #647, a pair of 6" 2-lite candelabrums. Charleton Roses decoration, c. 1949-1950s. AWCO Charleton label 4364. $275-350 pair. Scarce. *Courtesy of Helen & Steve Klemko.*

Cambridge Crown Tuscan #1043, 8.5" and #1040, 3" type 3 swans. Charleton Blue Mist decoration, c. 1949-1950s. Insufficient data to price. Both rare. *Courtesy of Helen & Steve Klemko.*

Cambridge group shot, all Charleton Blue Mist. *Courtesy of Helen & Steve Klemko.*

Cambridge Crown Tuscan #SS11, 7" Nude Stem Sea Shell comport. Charleton Blue Mist decoration, c. 1949-1950s. $150-175. Scarce. *Courtesy of Lynn Welker.*

Cambridge Crown Tuscan #6004, 8.5" vase. Charleton Blue Mist decoration, c. 1949-1950s. $150-175. Scarce. *Authors' collection.*

Cambridge Crown Tuscan #3500/57, 8" Gadroon three-compartment candy box. Charleton Blue Mist decoration, c. 1949-1950s. $275-300. Rare. *Courtesy of Helen & Steve Klemko.*

Cambridge Crown Tuscan #SS16, 7" and #SS14, 9" Sea Shell footed comports. Both Charleton Blue Mist decoration, c. 1949-1950s. #SS16, $150-175; #SS14, $200-250. Scarce. *Courtesy of Mike & Cindy Arent.*

Cambridge Crown Tuscan #3500/57, 8" Gadroon Charleton Blue Mist three-compartment candy box. Interior view.

Cambridge Crown Tuscan #SS21, 6" Sea Shell footed covered candy. Charleton Blue Mist decoration, c. 1949-1950s. $250-275. Rare. *Courtesy of Helen & Steve Klemko.*

Cambridge Crown Tuscan #SS31, 8" Sea Shell four-footed oval bowl. Charleton Blue Mist decoration. $175-200. Rare. *Courtesy of Cambridge Museum.*

Cambridge Crown Tuscan #SS34, 3" and #SS33, 4" Sea Shell ashtrays. Charleton Blue Mist decoration, c. 1949-1950s. #SS34, 3": $50-75, #SS33, 4": 75-100. Both scarce. *4" courtesy of Barbara Wyrick. 3" courtesy of Helen & Steve Klemko.*

Cambridge Crown Tuscan #SS31, 8" Sea Shell four-footed oval bowl. Profile.

Cambridge Crown Tuscan #SS2, 7" Sea Shell salad plate. Charleton Blue Mist decoration, c. 1949-1950s. $90-100. Rare. *Courtesy of Helen & Steve Klemko.*

Cambridge Crown Tuscan #SS34, 3" Sea Shell ashtrays. Tray on left has an overall light blue mist with an unusual edge treatment. Shown for comparison with a standard Blue Mist decorated tray on the right. Insufficient data to price. *Courtesy of Lynn Welker.*

Cambridge Crown Tuscan #3500/57, 8" Gadroon three-part covered candy. Charleton Roses & Bows decoration, c. 1949-1950s. $125-150. Scarce. *Courtesy of Helen & Steve Klemko.*

Cambridge Crown Tuscan 9.5" four-footed three-section Sea Shell relish. Charleton Roses decoration, c. 1949-1950s. AWCO Charleton label #4328. $75-100. *Courtesy of Helen & Steve Klemko.*

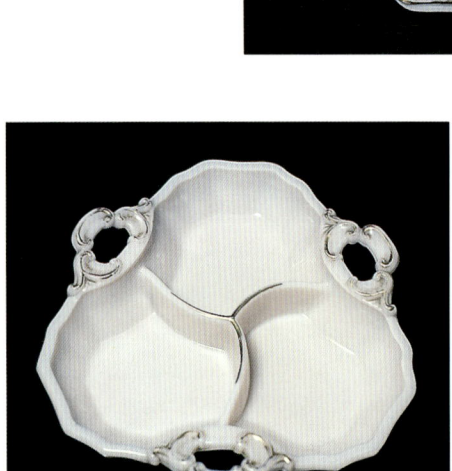

Cambridge Crown Tuscan #3500/57, 8" Gadroon three-part covered candy. Interior view.

Cambridge Crown Tuscan #SS21, 6" Sea Shell covered candy. Charleton Spattered Roses decoration. $100-125. Scarce. *Authors' collection.*

Cambridge Crown Tuscan #3500/57, 8" Gadroon three-part covered candy. Charleton Gardenia decoration, c. 1949-1950s. AWCO Charleton label #714. $125-150. Scarce. *Courtesy of Helen & Steve Klemko.*

Cambridge Crown Tuscan #3400/91, 8" divided relish. Charleton Roses and Bows decoration, c. 1949-1950s. $100-125. Scarce. *Courtesy of Helen & Steve Klemko.*

Cambridge Crown Tuscan #SS21, 6" Sea Shell covered candy. Top detail.

Cambridge Crown Tuscan #SS21, 6" Sea Shell covered candy. Charleton Roses decoration, c. 1940s-1950s. $75-100. *Authors' collection.*

Cambridge Crown Tuscan #SS18, 10" Sea Shell three-footed large bowl. Charleton Roses decoration. $100-150. Rare. *Courtesy of Cambridge Museum.*

Cambridge Crown Tuscan #SS31, 8" oval four-footed Sea Shell bowl. Charleton Roses decoration, c. 1949-1950s. $75-85. *Courtesy of Helen & Steve Klemko.*

Cambridge Crown Tuscan #SS31, 8" oval four-footed Sea Shell bowl. Detail of bottom showing "Hand Painted" AWCO black ink stamp.

Cambridge Crown Tuscan #SS18, 10" Sea Shell three-footed large bowl. Detail.

Cambridge Crown Tuscan #SS18, 10" three-footed Sea Shell bowl. Charleton Roses decoration, c. 1949-1950s. $150-175. Scarce. *Courtesy of Helen & Steve Klemko.*

Cambridge Crown Tuscan #SS18, 10" Sea Shell three-footed large bowl. Detail.

Cambridge Crown Tuscan #SS16, 6" Sea Shell footed comport. Charleton Gardenia decoration, c. 1949-1950s. $75-80. Harder to find than Roses & Bows decoration. *Courtesy of Helen & Steve Klemko.*

Cambridge Crown Tuscan #SS1, two 5" Sea Shell bread and butter plates. Charleton Roses decoration, c. 1940s-1950s. Note the differences in the opalescence and the coloring of the glass. $25-35 each. *Authors' collection.*

Cambridge Crown Tuscan #SS16, two 7" footed Sea Shell comports. Charleton Harbor and Roses, Chocolate Roses variant and Charleton Harbor and Roses decoration, c. 1940s-1950s. AWCO Charleton label #4376 on the Chocolate Roses comport. Chocolate Roses: $75-80; Charleton Roses: $50-65. Scarce in Chocolate Roses. *Authors' collection.*

Cambridge Crown Tuscan #SS2, 7" Sea Shell salad plate. Charleton Gardenia decoration, c. 1940s-1950s. Initialed "H" in green and "A" in gold on the back. $50-60. *Authors' collection.*

Cambridge Crown Tuscan #SS12, 9" and #SS16, 7" Sea Shell comports. Charleton Harbor and Roses, Chocolate Roses variant decoration. 8": $100-125; 6": $75-80. *Courtesy of Mike & Cindy Arent.*

Cambridge Crown Tuscan #SS33, 4" and #SS34, 3", three-footed Sea Shell ashtrays. Charleton Gardenia decoration, c. 1949-1950s. SS34, 3": $35-40. SS33, 4": $40-50. *Courtesy of Helen & Steve Klemko.*

Cambridge Crown Tuscan #SS35, 4.5" Sea Shell cigarette box. Charleton Blue Flowers decoration, c. 1940s-1950s. $95-110. Scarce decoration. *Authors' collection.*

Cambridge Crown Tuscan #SS35, 4.5" Sea Shell cigarette box. Charleton Roses decoration, c. 1940s-1950s. AWCO Charleton label #1656. Gold "70" on bottom. $65-85. *Authors' collection.*

Cambridge Crown Tuscan #SS35, 4.5" Sea Shell cigarette box. Top detail.

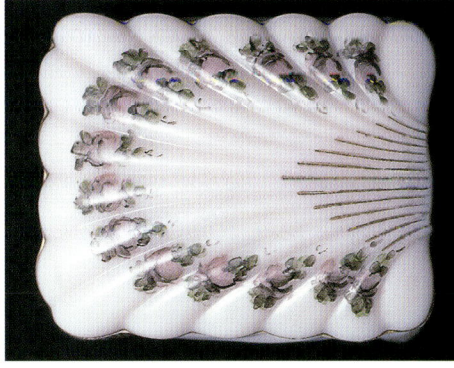

Cambridge Crown Tuscan #SS35, 4.5" Sea Shell cigarette box. Top detail.

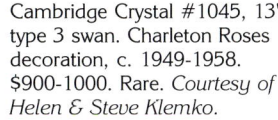

Cambridge Crystal #1045, 13" type 3 swan. Charleton Roses decoration, c. 1949-1958. $900-1000. Rare. *Courtesy of Helen & Steve Klemko.*

Cambridge Crystal #1045, 13" type 3 swan (shown with undecorated small swan for size comparison). Charleton Roses decoration, c. 1949-1950s. #1045, 13": $900-1000. Rare. (Not shown #1043, 8.5": $250-300.) *Courtesy of Helen & Steve Klemko.*

Cambridge Crystal #P.575 cornucopia. Charleton Eyelet decoration. $100-125. Rare. *Courtesy of Charles & Mary Upton.*

Cambridge Crystal #P.306 covered candy. Charleton Oak Leaf decoration. $100-125. Rare. *Courtesy of Charles & Mary Upton.*

Cambridge Crystal #1321, 11" decanter. Charleton Dappled decoration. $200-250. Rare. *Courtesy of Mike & Cindy Arent.*

Cambridge Crystal #1542, 11.5", 20-ounce Lifesaver decanter. Charleton Roses decoration, c. 1949-1950s. $100-125. Rare. *Courtesy of Helen & Steve Klemko.*

Cambridge Crystal #P.306 covered candy. Lid detail.

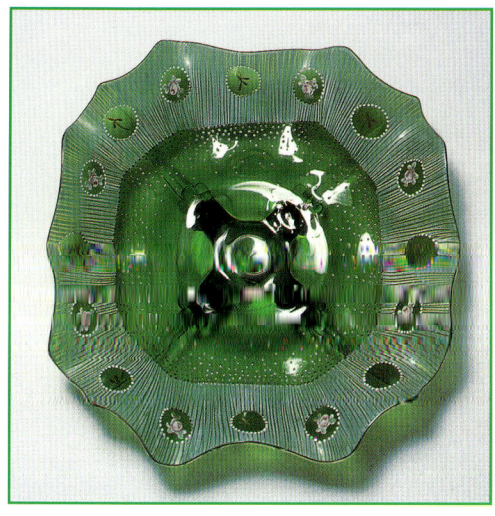

Cambridge Emerald #3400, 13" four-footed crimped shallow bowl. Charleton Pin Stripe and Roses decoration, c. 1949-1950s. AWCO Charleton label #661B. Insufficient data to price. Rare. *Courtesy of Helen & Steve Klemko.*

Cambridge Emerald #SS31, three-footed 8" Sea Shell bowl. Charleton Pin Stripe and Roses decoration, c. 1949-1958. $75-100. *Courtesy of Shirley & Carl Beynon.*

Cambridge Emerald Pristine #499, 6" Calla Lily Candlesticks. Charleton Pin Stripe and Roses decoration, c. 1949-1950s. AWCO Charleton label #667. $225-250 pair. Rare. *Courtesy of Helen & Steve Klemko.*

Cambridge Emerald Cascade #4000/165 covered candy. Charleton Pin Stripe and Roses decoration, c. 1949-1950s. $95-110. Scarce. *Authors' collection.*

Cambridge Emerald #SS35, 4.5" Sea Shell cigarette box. Charleton Pin Stripe and Roses decoration, c. 1949-1958. $75-100. Scarce. *Authors' collection.*

Cambridge Emerald Corinth #3900 Line #136, 5.5" comport. Charleton Pin Stripe and Roses decoration, c. 1949-1958. $75-100. Scarce. *Authors' collection.*

Cambridge Emerald #SS35, 4.5" Sea Shell cigarette box. Top detail.

Cambridge Ebony group. Left to right: #575, 11" cornucopia; #615, 4.5" cigarette box; #1237, 10" Keyhole vase; #3500/55, 6" Gadroon bowl; #575, 11" cornucopia. All Charleton Gold Roses decoration, c. 1949-1950s. Insufficient data to price. All rare. *Courtesy of Michael & Lisa Neilson.*

Cambridge Ebony #1237, 10" Keyhole flower vase. Item detail.

Cambridge Ebony #3500/55, 6" Gadroon bowl. Item detail.

Cambridge Ebony #575, 11" cornucopia. Item detail.

Cambridge Ebony #1237, 9" Keyhole flower vase. Charleton Gold Roses decoration, c. 1949-1950s. AWCO Charleton label #913. Insufficient data to price. Rare. *Courtesy of Barbara Wyrick.*

Cambridge Square #3797/165 Ebon candy box and cover. Charleton Pussy Willow decoration, c. 1954. AWCO Charleton label 2416. Insufficient data to price. Rare. *Courtesy of Barbara Wyrick.*

Cambridge Ebon (satin-finished ebony-colored glass) group shot, both Charleton Pussy Willow decoration. *Courtesy of Barbara Wyrick.*

Cambridge Square #3797/48 Ebon bowl. Cambridge "Birds" decoration. *Courtesy of Cambridge Museum.*

Cambridge Square #3797/78, 9.5" Ebon footed vase. Charleton Pussy Willow decoration, c. 1954. AWCO Charleton label 2415. Insufficient data to price. Rare. *Courtesy of Barbara Wyrick.*

Charles Upton in front of the Cambridge Museum in Cambridge, Ohio. Mr. Upton generously allowed us into his home to photograph his outstanding collection of Charleton decorated Cambridge as well as several pieces in the museum.

Cambridge Milk group. *Courtesy of Charles & Mary Upton.*

Cambridge Milk group. *Courtesy of Charles & Mary Upton.*

Cambridge Milk #W106, 6" Sea Shell comport and #W104, 9" Sea Shell comport. Charleton Roses decoration. 6": $90-100; 9": $150-175. Rare. *Courtesy of Charles & Mary Upton.*

Cambridge Milk #W106, 6" Sea Shell comport. Detail.

Cambridge Milk #W108, 8" Sea Shell three-footed oval bowl. Charleton Roses decoration. $100-125. Rare. *Courtesy of Charles & Mary Upton.*

Cambridge Milk #W101, 4.5" Sea Shell cigarette box. Charleton Roses decoration. $75-85. Rare. *Courtesy of Charles & Mary Upton.*

Cambridge Milk #W107, 6" Sea Shell covered candy. Charleton Roses decoration. $125-150. Rare. *Courtesy of Charles & Mary Upton.*

Cambridge Milk #W114, 7" Sea Shell salad plate. Charleton Roses decoration. $90-100. Rare. *Courtesy of Charles & Mary Upton.*

Cambridge Milk #W111, Sea Shell four-footed round bonbon. Charleton Roses decoration. AWCO Charleton label #2031. $90-100. Rare. *Courtesy of Charles & Mary Upton.*

Cambridge Crown Tuscan #3500/57, Gadroon covered candy. Unknown rooster decoration. NP. *Courtesy of Mike & Cindy Arent.*

Cambridge Crown Tuscan #SS31, 8" Sea Shell oval four-footed bowl and #3500/57 Gadroon covered candy. Unknown decorator. NP. *Courtesy of Mike & Cindy Arent.*

Cambridge Crown Tuscan #3400/102, 5" Globe flower holder. Unknown decorator. NP. *Courtesy of Mike & Cindy Arent.*

Cambridge Crystal 3.75" rose bowl. Unknown decorator. NP. *Courtesy of Cambridge Museum.*

Cambridge Milk #1309, 4.5" Globe flower holder. Unknown decorator. NP. *Courtesy of Mike & Cindy Arent.*

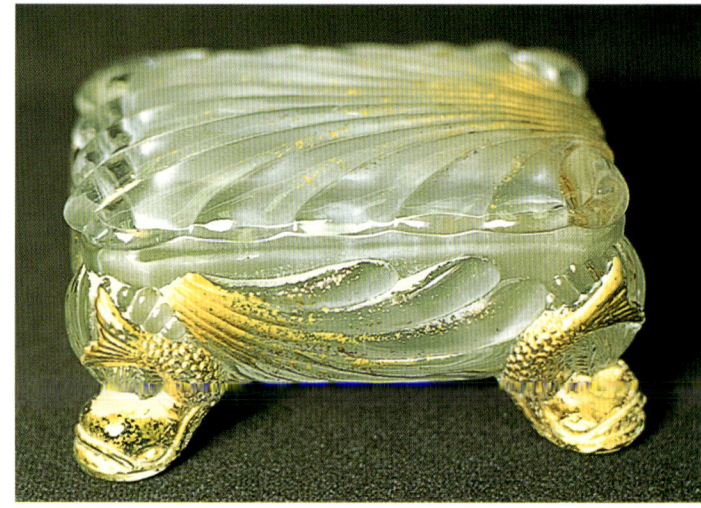

Cambridge Crystal satin finished #SS35, 4.5" Sea Shell cigarette box. Probably decorated by Cambridge. NP. *Courtesy of Cambridge Museum.*

Chapter 4.
Consolidated

Consolidated is the manufacturer that provided the second largest quantity of blanks upon which AWCO placed Charleton decorations. The decorations are mostly of the floral variety, although a few of the modernistic motifs will crop up from time to time. Before we begin exploring the numerous Charleton items from the Consolidated line, we will outline a brief summary of the company and the important people who were associated with it.

The Consolidated Lamp and Glass Company began business in 1893 as the result of a merger between the Wallace and McAfee Company of Pittsburgh, Pennsylvania, and the Fostoria Shade & Lamp Company of Fostoria, Ohio. Headed by F. G. Wallace, President, and Nicholas Kopp, manager, the new company established headquarters at 918 and 920 Penn Avenue in Pittsburgh while still utilizing the manufacturing facility in Fostoria, Ohio. Consolidated was the only U.S. glass manufacturer producing cased glass during the late 1890s. Cased glass is created by layering crystal over colored glass.

The Fostoria, Ohio, plant burned down in 1895, necessitating the search for a new location. The town of Coraopolis, Pennsylvania, came to the rescue by donating a seven-acre tract near the center of the town. In 1896, after completion of the new factory, the Consolidated Lamp and Glass Company moved from Fostoria to Coraopolis.

Prior to 1926, Consolidated primarily made lighting glassware. In its September 1911 edition, *The Coraopolis Record* reported the enormous expansion of Consolidated and that the company was the largest lamp, globe, and shade works in the United States with over 400 employees. In 1926, then company president John Lewis decided to enter the giftware business. It is believed Lewis' decision was in no small part due to the convincing arguments by Reuben Haley. Employed by U.S. Glass from 1911 through 1925, Haley rented space in 1926 in the Consolidated plant for his design firm, Metal Products Company. Not coincidentally, Haley designed all the giftware items for this new venture.

Although Consolidated was well suited to produce Haley's designs of giftware, they did not have the necessary skills to market this line as their forte up to this point had been lighting glassware. An arrangement was made between them and a talented salesman by the name of Howard Selden, who actually managed to obtain exclusive marketing rights for Consolidated's Catalonian and Martelè patterns.

Although Consolidated was forced out of business by hard economic times during the Great Depression, they re-emerged in 1936 to become one of the most highly respected art glass companies in America.

A more detailed history of Consolidated Glass can be found in Jack Wilson's *Phoenix & Consolidated Art Glass 1926 – 1980*. William Heacock was also very interested in this line of research and he collaborated with Mr. Wilson by sharing research in an effort to fully unravel some of the puzzling questions regarding mould transfers and duplication of early patterns by both companies. William Heacock also wrote several articles on Phoenix/Consolidated and they were published in several editions of his "Collecting Glass."

In the realm of Phoenix/Consolidated collectors, milk glass items are given very little attention. Other than a token display of a few items and a reprint or two of company catalogs, there are few color photographs and little printed material to educate collectors in the various patterns and shapes Consolidated produced. Milk glass in the Consolidated line just doesn't have the cachet to compete with sculpted Dancing Nymph vases or ultra-modern Ruba Rhombic.

Although information on Consolidated's milk glass lines may be hard to come by, this perceived oversight seems intentional for the most part. We would not expect most Consolidated collectors of the fancier sculpted patterns to get too excited over any collection of decorated milk glass, even if it is Charleton. Even fewer Consolidated collectors are versed on AWCO's relationship with Consolidated and proper recognition of the beautifully decorated pieces out there is long overdue.

Regardless of that, Jack Wilson and Bill Heacock have provided us with more useful reference information on Consolidated's milk glass line than will be found anywhere else. Without these catalog reprints, most of the Consolidated mould numbers and decorations would be unknown to the collector.

Any indifference to Consolidated's milk glass line is a boon to the Charleton collector as many pieces are available for little cost and the scarcer treatments are very undervalued. We have collected many large pieces for less than twenty dollars, even with the Charleton labels intact. In the color plates that follow you will see for yourself that Consolidated glass was not overlooked by AWCO and they spent considerable time and expense in lavishly decorating it. These good prices and ready availability are gradually dwindling as a growing number of knowledgeable collectors enter the market.

A real problem in collecting some of the more elaborate vases is that unknowing owners will often misidentify the pieces as "Bristol" or "Victorian" glass and overvalue the pieces. Trying to obtain these pieces for their true market value can be difficult if not impossible, most likely due to the owners having invested too much in the pieces themselves. Sometimes you just have to "bite the bullet" and pay a ransom in order to take that really elusive item home with you.

Evidently, AWCO relied heavily upon Consolidated to supply them with blanks during the milk glass boom of the late 1940s and on through the 1950s. The lines they purchased were limited and consisted mainly of the Regent and Con Cora patterns. But they did use a nice variety of shapes from these lines so a wide selection is available.

Consolidated's first large foray into milk glass was marketed as the Con-Cora line. This line also reintroduced some items using older Catalonian and Florette moulds and they marketed them under the Con-Cora umbrella. These items were sold either decorated or as plain milk glass.

Consolidated Con-Cora in-house decorations were very well done and the items were fired for permanence. Three decorations are depicted in Consolidated catalogs on Con-Cora: Roses, Ivy, and Violets with Forget-Me-Nots. The artist often, but not always, initialed the decorated pieces in this line.

Consolidated's Violets decoration is very easy to identify, as there is usually a solitary white Violet amidst the other blue and lavender ones. AWCO has never produced a violets floral decoration similar enough to Consolidated's to be of concern to the Charleton collector.

Consolidated's Rose decoration can be a little tricky as Charleton and Consolidated have very similar characteristics. Gold sprigs scattered about are identical to ones found on many Charleton items. Other similarities include the same consistency and color of china paint used for the roses and leaves, even some of the leaves are shaded differently as on Charleton. The construction of the Consolidated rose buds are also very similar, although the development of detail on the buds is usually not as complete as AWCO's.

There are a couple of differences between the Charleton Roses decoration and Consolidated's to aid in the identification. The drape of the garlands connecting the single rose buds in the Consolidated decoration is quite a bit different than the garlands usually associated with Charleton. There is also no other use of gold leaf other than the sprigs on Consolidated Roses and the overall decoration appears as being rather sparse on the large vases. We strongly suggest that the Charleton collector purchase a piece or two of Consolidated Roses to get better acquainted with their design.

Consolidated's Ivy decoration has been a real problem for us to keep sorted out. Ivy appears to be the most common of the three decorations on Con-Cora. Perhaps this is merely our perception, as we tend to concentrate more on this pattern when out buying Charleton for a couple of reasons. Mainly, we really like this pattern and we have started our own little Consolidated Ivy collection. And, of course, we need the Consolidated Ivy pieces for research and, hopefully, having more items will make finding differences in the these two similar decorations easier to recognize.

We have examined many pieces of Ivy and little variance can be found between the two decorators. Both use three and five lobed leaves, both often use a thick brown vine that weaves throughout the leaves, and the paint color, size, and leaf placement are each well matched.

Now we shall go out on the proverbial limb and state our case for separating Ivy decorations by AWCO from Consolidated. Determinations made without the company labels are greatly subjective, but there has to be a starting point for making these classifications.

On pieces we know to be AWCO, those that have Charleton labels, there is a usage of gold leaf foliage or berries which is not present on the Consolidated pieces. This makes for a strong identifier. When you see a Consolidated piece of glass with gold berries, leaves, or heavy gold leaf bands, then you are almost certainly looking at a Charleton item. No Ivy pieces with this use of gold leaves or berries can be seen pictured in the Consolidated catalogs thereby virtually eliminating any chance that such pieces have been decorated by Consolidated.

However, Consolidated does use gold leaf accents on the crimps, pattern rings, and the bases of many of their Ivy items much the same as Charleton. But one thing that Consolidated does use, and which has not been found on Charleton items, are dark green bands on the crimps or smooth edges on some of the pieces. This green edge is easily identified in the company catalogs and is most often found on pieces with flat ground rims.

The green spiral spring-like tendrils on the Consolidated pieces pictured in the catalogs as well as the pieces in our collection seem to be larger and longer than the ones found on the Charleton items, even on smaller items. This difference is slight and is also tenuous due to the fact that, to date, no large vases of labeled Charleton Ivy have turned up for further comparison.

Not all Ivy decorated pieces of either company have the berry clusters and, when they do, these clusters do vary. On one of our Charleton items that have these clusters, the berries are portrayed as stippled dots of green. On another piece, which is believed to a Consolidated decoration, the berries are stippled white. In the Consolidated catalogs, pictures of the Consolidated Ivy decorated pieces are too small and grainy to see if the white berries are actually there.

When looking at some Consolidated items with Ivy decorations and no labels, we are reluctant to state with any certainty which company decorated it. With no Consolidated company records to use in order to determine which pieces AWCO bought from Consolidated, we are on shaky ground in a lot of instances.

Grouped within the Con-Cora line is a pattern inspired by Imperial's Candlewick line that Consolidated called "Beaded Edge." The Beaded Edge items from Consolidated with their "Roses" decoration also have the gold leaf sprigs found in Charleton decorations. This, as one would imagine, causes confusion between Charleton decorations and Consolidated. There are no documented Charleton items on Consolidated Beaded Edge to date, but AWCO did decorate crystal items in the Imperial Candlewick line so it would not be surprising to see some items turn up.

Just as a general note on Imperial Candlewick and Consolidated Beaded Edge items, the outside edge of the beads on Candlewick are flame polished smooth whereas the edges of the Consolidated items have rough mould lines. Westmoreland's Beaded Edge has much smaller beads so there is no chance of confusion with either of the others.

Another pattern of note in the Con-Cora line is the Florette cookie jar. Florette actually dates back to 1894 in the Consolidated line and its reintroduction appears to have been quite successful. Collectors sometimes call Florette "Quilted Pillow" and, while that is an excellent descriptive name, we shall refer to it by its original name.

The Florette cookie jars came in two different sizes, the #3758 which is 6.5" high, and the #5100 which is the 9" high. To date we have only found the 6" jar with a Charleton decoration. If AWCO decorated the larger jar, it has not yet been reported.

Here again, Consolidated's Rose decoration on this piece could be confused for Charleton. Consolidated's use of gold on the buttons on this item is close to what AWCO did with it. But the Charleton jar has much smaller roses and the gold leaf on the buttons has a sunburst shape. This is one of the nicer pieces of Charleton Con-Cora and can still be found for a reasonable price.

It is not known if AWCO produced an Ivy decorated Florette cookie jar since none have been reported to date. Certainly its existence remains a good possibility and we would love to hear from collectors if they have one in their collection.

Consolidated's success with Con-Cora induced them to develop and release another catalog of decorated milk glass known as the Regent line. This line is confusing for collectors due to the fact that the Regent line also included some of the earlier Con-Cora patterns with the same decorations. Consolidated also added some older patterns into the Regent lineup such as Catalonian, Florette, and Florentine.

The decorations on Regent pieces include the same three as on Con-Cora pieces with the addition of seventeen new decorations. Since none of these new Consolidated decorations are likely to be confused with Charleton, they are not detailed in this account[9].

There are, however, some new shapes in the Regent line that AWCO chose to decorate. These Regent patterns seem to have received more elaborate detailing than the items found in Con-Cora.

The ginger jar known to collectors as the temple or rose jar (shape numbers #4020, #4021, and #4022 depending on size) is a good example. This ginger jar can be found in some very striking decorations. Its classic Grecian lines are perfect for these elaborate motifs and are highly sought by collectors.

Another simple yet very effective piece that AWCO bought from Consolidated is the #2321 milk glass vase. We can find no particular name for this vase, but it is not an ordinary shape. The best and simplest description is that it is a large ball vase flattened on either side. We have taken to calling it an "ovoid" vase for lack of a better name. This vase is shown in Jack Wilson's book, but has no name associated with it in the catalog and Wilson does not list it at all in his price guide. It is a very difficult Charleton item to find, but well worth the search.

One extraordinary piece to be on the lookout for is Consolidated's large #2591 milk glass 10" oval candy box in the Martelè pattern and decorated in Charleton Ivy.

The word Martelè was first used in association with hand wrought silver and it is an apt appellation for this Consolidated design. This pattern was designed by the renowned Rueben Haley in 1925, and was first introduced by Consolidated at the 1926 annual Pittsburgh buyers' exhibition. Critics touted the Martelè line as the best example of work in the U.S. reflecting the influence of René Lalique.

The Martelè line consisted of a variety of different sculpted themes such as dancing girls, flowers, fish, and dragonflies. The Charleton piece we have has the Iris pattern on the outside of the box with another Martelè design, Bird of Paradise, embossed on the inner lid. All of the Martelè patterns have a deep carved appearance and the mould work is some of the best that was commercially produced in America.

Charleton decorators used gold leaf to cover the entire exterior of the Iris design on this box. This effect is very luxurious and the piece easily stands out in a crowd. The lid has an "S" shaped finial with a gold line tracing its top and an embossed area of gold leaf scrollwork circles the outer portion of the lid. Enclosed within this border are large green ivy leaves on a weaving green vine. Sprinkled throughout the ivy are clusters of tiny hollow gold berries.

This is a very heavy, thick milk glass piece and must be handled with care. We recently purchased another of these decorated boxes just like the first, but without the Charleton label, so they are out there on the market, but are fairly scarce. This association of Martelè items with Charleton decorations has never been reported before so the market prices may be more reasonable now than at a later date. We would not be surprised to see more Charleton items in the Martelè line come to light, as the various patterns should have been quite appealing to AWCO as blanks.

As mentioned previously, Consolidated artists did initial their work from time to time and this can be useful. These initials can be hard to find and were sometimes skillfully blended into the artwork. It is not, however, the ultimate tool to determine if a piece is Consolidated decorated or Charleton. We have a Consolidated Regent vase, spray painted a powder blue over the exterior of the milk glass. It is a #4038 10" bulbous vase with a large Open Rose decoration. This decoration has decorator's initials on the face of the vase within the decoration, as well as a Charleton label #4039. We have only seen two other Charleton pieces signed near the decoration and they were labeled as well.

For his book, Jack Wilson was provided with a brief list of initials of known Consolidated artists who signed their work, and, as would be expected, the initials from our vase do not appear in his list[10]. Useful as it may be in some instances, it is doubtful that the list Mr. Wilson provides in his book is comprehensive, as Consolidated surely would have employed more than nine decorators, so, without the Charleton label, a vase such as this could easily be misidentified as having a Consolidated decoration.

It is quite exceptional to find Charleton items that have the artist's initials within the decoration. The general rule is artists' initials on Charleton decorated pieces are found on the bottom of the item or under the inner lid of covered items. If more than one artist's initial appears, one will often be in a different handwriting and color. We suspect that the initials done in gold leaf indicate the artist who did the gold leaf and the initials in painted colors indicated who actually painted the china paint decorations.

There is the possibility that AWCO bought items already decorated from Consolidated and distributed them under the Charleton name. They established a pattern of doing this type of thing with imports in their early days and we don't know when, if ever, this practice was discontinued.

From trade journals of the period, we know that there were at least two other wholesale companies who were offering decorated Consolidated Glass under their own name during the late 1940s to 1950s. We will briefly discuss these companies to make the collector aware of the possibility of encountering professionally decorated glassware that does not seem to fit in the established categories we have been discussing.

The most prolific of these two companies decorating Consolidated glass was the "The Rainbow Art Company" of Huntington, West Virginia. Originally their specialty was decorated glassware and later, in 1954, they became a subsidiary of Viking Glass. Three vases pictured in a Rainbow trade advertisements are also from the same Consolidated moulds that AWCO utilized. The advertisements are in black and white so we must rely upon the verbal descriptions in order to visualize the colors on these pieces.

These vases were probably of high quality as they used enamels and gold paint in their decorations. They were fired twice for added durability of the decoration, which must have added considerably to the overall production costs.

These Rainbow vases with hand painted floral decorations are problematic due to the overall similarity to Charleton. Upon enlarging one of these advertisements for these vases, we could see what appeared to be a gold-banded rim and it also shows large rose sprays on both the body and upper neck with copious foliage. This pattern was called "Tudor Rose" and was one of two patterns Rainbow advertised heavily nationwide.

We have what we believe to be a Rainbow "Tudor Rose" vase in our collection. It is decorated on a Consolidated #5C, 11" milk glass, fine crimp vase. By careful comparison of several details visible in the enlargement, our vase matches strongly on four points of the decoration. Coupled with the fact that this is one of the moulds depicted in the Rainbow advertisement, we are satisfied with this attribution.

A head to head comparison with Consolidated's own rose decoration rules this out as being Consolidated decorated. Although we had initially purchased this vase thinking it was Charleton, after comparing research material we feel we have been able to sort out the true decorating firm.

The other pattern Rainbow promoted widely was called "Dogwood" and the decoration is very reminiscent of Consolidated's sculpted glass "Dogwood" pattern. This Rainbow piece is very striking in person. It was advertised as "white milk glass with hand painted Dogwood design in lustrous ruby and gold." For us, as collectors and lovers of decorated glassware, this decoration is particularly enticing. The Rainbow "Dogwood" pattern is quite typical of what one might expect to find executed by AWCO on a temple jar and is a prime example of a decoration that could easily have been misidentified without proper research.

Producing items for a line of over three hundred items in a seven day, around the clock schedule indicates that Rainbow was a big producer and had quite a presence in the market in the late 1940s. Rainbow was not shy at all about getting their wares out in the public eye. Television host Tommy Bartlett is shown in an advertisement presenting two #4021 "Dogwood" temple jars to guests on ABC's "Welcome Travelers" nationwide broadcast in 1948.

There are also Consolidated hand decorated items that have been found with the words "DeLuxe" stamped on the bottom. From period trade advertisements, it appears that "DeLuxe" was a name employed by Rainbow and the decorations are indeed similar.

Another lesser-known company, Beaver Valley Glass Company, advertised gift items in glass, crystal and colors. A decorated Consolidated vase is pictured in their advertisement, but it has not been determined if this company was a decorator or just a distributor. Since their painted items were different in style from any other decorated piece of Consolidated, Beaver Valley Glass may very well have been a decorator. Further investigation will be needed for a true determination, however.

Consolidated Con Cora #4012, pair of 6" Milk Glass vases. Charleton Roses decoration, large variant, c. 1940s-1950s. $25-30 each. *Authors' Collection.*

Consolidated Con Cora #4014, 9.5" Milk Glass vase. Charleton Pastoral decoration, c. 1949-1952. $125-150. Rare. *Authors' Collection.*

Consolidated Con Cora #4012, 6" Milk Glass vase. Detail.

Consolidated Con Cora #432, 9" Milk Glass vase. Charleton Medallion Roses decoration, c. 1940s-1950s. AWCO Charleton label #4473. $150-175. Rare. *Author's Collection.*

Consolidated Con Cora #4012, 6" Milk Glass vase. Charleton Green Mist and Gold Needles decoration, c. 1940s-1950s. AWCO Charleton label #4983. $65-75. Rare. *Authors' Collection.*

Consolidated Con Cora #432, 9" Milk Glass vase. Reverse view.

Group shot of three sizes of Consolidated Con Cora Milk Glass ginger jars. Right to left: #4022-22A, 11"; #4021-21A, 9"; #4020-20A, 7". *Authors' Collection*.

Consolidated Con Cora #4022-22A, 11" Milk Glass ginger jar. Detail of Charleton Bamboo and Roses decoration.

Consolidated Con Cora #4022-22A, 11" Milk Glass ginger jar. Charleton Bamboo and Roses decoration, c. 1940s. AWCO Charleton label #631. Gold initial "K" on bottom. $175-200. Rare. *Authors' Collection*.

Consolidated Con Cora #4021-21A, 9" Milk Glass ginger jar. Charleton Lavender Flowers decoration. AWCO Charleton label #4471. $100-125. Scarce. *Authors' Collection*.

Consolidated Con Cora #4020-20A, 7" ginger jar. Charleton Blue Mist and Roses decoration, c. 1940s-1950s. AWCO Charleton label #4894. "Hand Painted" black ink stamp on bottom. $125-150. Rare. *Authors' Collection.*

Consolidated Con Cora #4021-21A, 9" ginger jar. Charleton Chinese New Year decoration, c. 1940s-1950s. AWCO Charleton label #629. "Hand Painted" black ink stamp on bottom. $125-150. Rare. *Authors' Collection.*

Consolidated Con Cora #4020-20A, 7" Milk Glass ginger jar. Charleton Roses and Rings decoration, c. 1940s. AWCO Charleton label #4779. Green initial "H" and gold "53" on bottom. $75-100. Scarce. *Authors' Collection.*

Consolidated Martele #2553, 10" Bird of Paradise Milk Glass oval candy box. Charleton Ivy decoration, c. 1956. Note the s-shaped finial. AWCO Charleton label #1004. $125-150. Rare. *Authors' Collection.*

Consolidated Regent #2321, 6.5" Milk Glass vase. Charleton Floral Bouquet decoration, c. 1950s. AWCO Charleton label #4787. $60-75. Scarce. Note the unusual flattened sphere shape of this vase. *Authors' Collection.*

Consolidated Martele #2553, 10" Milk Glass Bird of Paradise candy box. Top view.

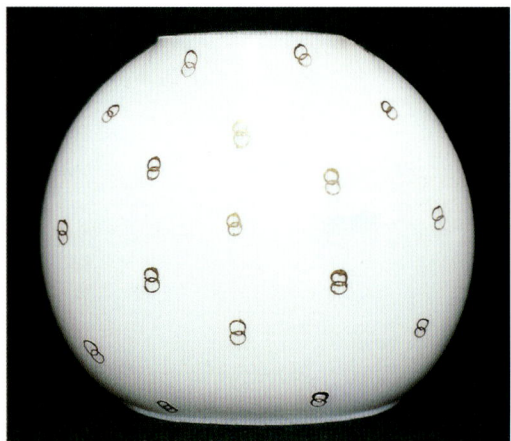

Consolidated Regent #2321, 6.5" Milk Glass vase. Reverse view.

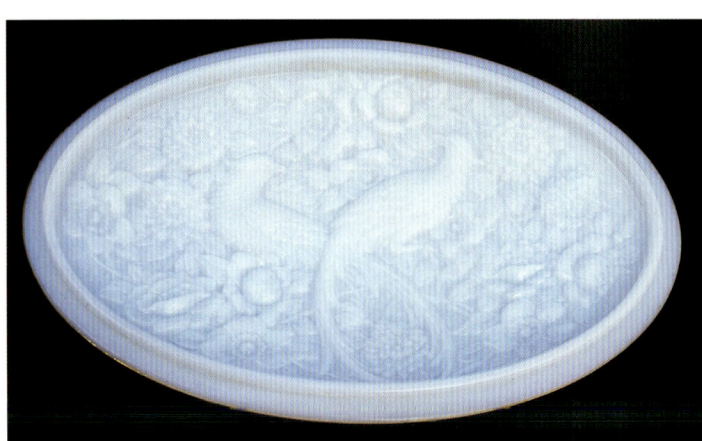

Consolidated Martele #2553, 10" Bird of Paradise Milk Glass oval candy box. Lid interior.

Consolidated Con Cora #3758/59, 6.5" Milk Glass Tufted Pillow cookie jar. Charleton Sunburst and Roses decoration, c. 1950s. AWCO Charleton label #4360. $125-135. *Authors' Collection.*

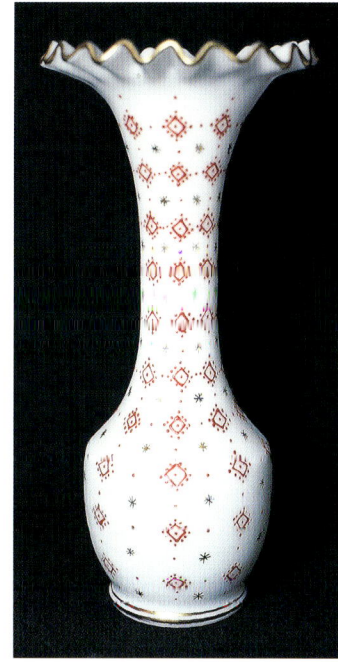

Consolidated Regent #5-C, 11" Milk Glass vase, fine crimp. Charleton Red Geometric decoration, c. 1950s. AWCO Charleton label #740. Initialed "J" in gold on the bottom. $75-85. Scarce. *Authors' Collection*.

Consolidated Con Cora #4038, 10" Milk Glass vase. Charleton Roses and Rings decoration, c. 1940s. AWCO Charleton label #4475A. $75-90. Scarce decoration. *Courtesy of Barbara Wyrick*.

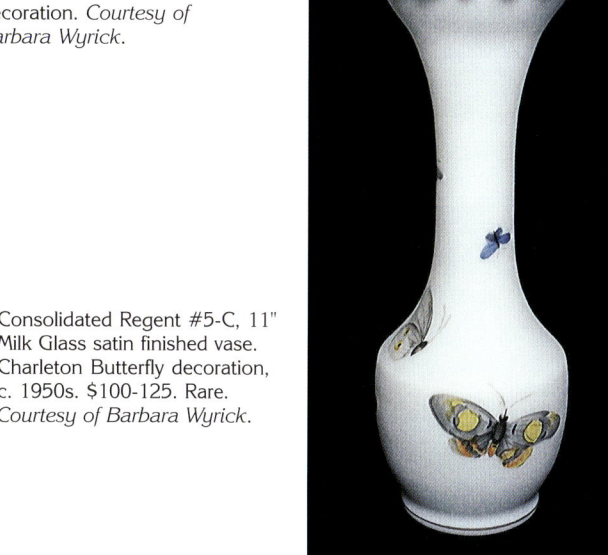

Consolidated Regent #5-C, 11" Milk Glass vase. Charleton Pink Mist and Roses decoration, c. 1950s. AWCO Charleton label #4467. $65-75. Scarce. *Authors' Collection*.

Consolidated Regent #5-C, 11" Milk Glass satin finished vase. Charleton Butterfly decoration, c. 1950s. $100-125. Rare. *Courtesy of Barbara Wyrick*.

Consolidated Regent #5-C, 11" Milk Glass vase. Charleton Grey Mist and Roses decoration, c. 1950s. $65-75. Scarce. *Authors' Collection*.

Consolidated Regent #5-C, 11" Milk Glass satin finished vase. Detail of decoration.

115

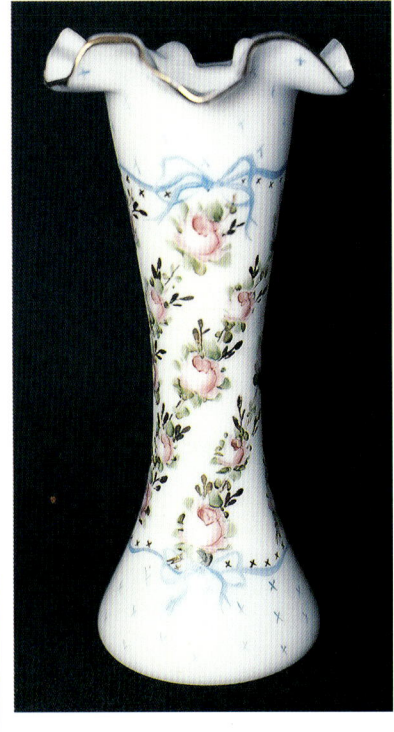

Consolidated Regent #8-C, 11" Milk Glass vase. Charleton Roses and Bows decoration, c. 1950s. $65-75. Scarce. *Authors' Collection.*

Consolidated Regent #8-C, 11" Milk Glass vase. Charleton Yellow Mist and Roses decoration, c. 1950s. $65-75. Scarce. Note the very unusual Yellow Mist decoration has only been found on one other Charleton decorated item. *Authors' Collection.*

Consolidated Regent #8-C, 11" Milk Glass vase. Side view.

Consolidated Regent #6X13, 10" Milk Glass cylinder vase. Charleton Roses decoration, c. 1950s. $75-85. Rare. *Authors' Collection.*

Consolidated Regent #6X13, 10" Milk Glass cylinder vase. Charleton Leaf and Bands decoration, c. 1950s. Initial "R" in green. $85-100. Rare. *Authors' Collection.*

Consolidated Regent #4112-C, pair of 6" Milk Glass vases, front and rear views. Charleton Roses decoration, c. 1950s. $25-35 each. *Authors' Collection.*

Detail of Consolidated lamp. Note that the circles are actually *cut* into the glass, that is a very unusual practice for AWCO. We do believe AWCO cut the glass after purchasing it from Consolidated. It is also quite likely that AWCO put the satin finish on the vase.

Consolidated satin finished crystal 16" lamp. Made from Consolidated's Con Cora #4039 vase (not known to be a regular in-line item in crystal). Charleton Roses decoration, c. 1940s-1950s. Consolidated supplied only the glass for the lamps to AWCO. The metal parts would have been purchased from a lamp supplier and assembled by AWCO. $125-150. Rare. *Authors' collection.*

Consolidated Regent #4038, 10" Milk Glass vase. Marked "DeLuxe USA Inc." on bottom. Probably Rainbow Art Glass[8]. NP. *Authors' Collection.*

Consolidated Regent #4038, 10" Milk Glass vase. Detail of "DeLuxe" mark.

117

Consolidated Regent #5-C, 11" Milk Glass Fine Crimp Vase. Rainbow Art Glass decoration, c. 1950s. NP. *Authors' Collection*.

Consolidated Regent #5-C, 11" Milk Glass Fine Crimp Vase. Detail of decoration.

Consolidated Regent #4020-20A, 7" Milk Glass ginger jar. Unknown decorator, c. 1950s. NP. *Authors' Collection*.

Consolidated Regent #5-C, 11" Milk Glass vases, fine crimp. Rainbow Art Company "Dogwood" decoration in ruby and gold. NP. *Authors' Collection*.

Consolidated Regent #5-C, 11" Milk Glass vase, fine crimp. Detail of decoration.

Group shot of Consolidated (not Charleton) Ivy decoration. These items are not Charleton decorated, therefore, we have not listed any prices. *Authors' Collection.*

Consolidated Regent #6001, 11" Milk Glass three-ringed vase. Consolidated (not Charleton) Ivy decoration, c. 1950 s. NP. *Authors' Collection.*

Consolidated Con Cora #5631/32, 13" Milk Glass "Spin-A-Cake" 2-piece footed cake plate. Consolidated (not Charleton) Ivy decoration, c. 1940s-1950s. Initialed by Consolidated artist "HM" (Helen Mixter). NP. *Authors' Collection.*

Consolidated Regent #7-C, 10" Milk Glass vase. Consolidated #1326 Violet decoration, c. 1950s. (Note the Consolidated "signature" of a lone white-colored violet amidst the purple violets.) NP. *Authors' Collection.*

Consolidated Regent #4112-C, 6" Milk Glass vase and #4063C, 8.5" Milk Glass vase. Consolidated Roses decoration, c. 1950s. The #4063C vase has the initials "HM" for Consolidated artist Helen Mixter. NP. *Authors' Collection.*

119

Consolidated Regent #4112-C, 6" Milk Glass vase. Consolidated #1434 Assorted Flowers decoration, c. 1950s. NP. *Authors' Collection.*

Consolidated Con Cora #5637/38, 8.75" Milk Glass candy box and lid. Consolidated #1510G Roses decoration, c. 1940s-1950s. Initials by Consolidated Artist "WH", Wally Hindle. NP. *Authors' Collection.*

Consolidated Regent #4112-C, 6" Milk Glass vase. Consolidated #1505G Magnolia decoration, c. 1950s. NP. *Authors' Collection.*

Consolidated Con Cora 6" Milk Glass ivy ball. Consolidated #1326 Violet decoration, c. 1940s-1950s. NP. *Authors' Collection.*

Consolidated Regent #4021-21A, 11" Milk Glass ginger jar and #4039, 12" Milk Glass vase. Consolidated #1510G Roses decoration, c. 1950s. NP. *Authors' Collection.*

Consolidated Regent #1171, 4" Milk Glass vase. Consolidated #1500G French Daisy decoration, c. 1950s. NP. *Authors' Collection.*

Chapter 5.
Westmoreland Glass

Another major company from which AWCO bought glass blanks is The Westmoreland Glass Company (WMGCO). Research indicates the glass Abels bought from Westmoreland was almost exclusively white milk glass. Although Westmoreland is widely remembered for their dominance of the milk glass boom that began in the 1950s, many collectors also seek out their beautifully cut, etched, and decorated colored glass. This glassware was certainly equal to the best of many of the other large twentieth century American glass companies.

Westmoreland's earliest beginnings can be traced to 1883 when a group of men incorporated a company called the East Liverpool Specialty Company in East Liverpool, Ohio. This first organization was strictly involved in packing jelly into glass containers and then selling it, and, at this point, was not involved in glass manufacture. Unfortunately, the company folded rather quickly after the company's treasurer was discovered to be an embezzler who cleaned out the company funds and fled to Bermuda.

At this point, Major George Irwin, who was involved in the earlier company, persuaded the other founders to persevere and relocate the company to Pennsylvania in 1888. The fact that there was a natural gas well for the manufacturing facility (a rare utility in those days) helped convinced the others to move, but Major Irvin also offered another inducement. The businessmen were offered the chance to buy surrounding land at fixed prices in hopes that the land value would appreciate at a subsequent auction. A later auction was also held for the remaining lots to entice glassworkers to relocate to the area with an added benefit of free gas for their homes.

Perhaps to remove the curse of its first beginning, the company was renamed "Specialty Glass," but remained a glass company in name only until buildings could be constructed to house the factory. These building projects drained all of the available cash of the newly reformed company, necessitating additional capital. Fortunately, two new investors realized the potential of the business and bought into the failing company.

Charles H. West and his older brother George invested $40,000 earned from their previous dry goods business and George's sale of a large tract of land. This amount of money would be close to one million dollars by today's standards. This large investment gave them a controlling majority (53%) of Specialty Glass stock and, shortly thereafter, George became president of the company and Charles was named the secretary/treasurer.

This reorganization and West's investment prompted yet another name change and the company became the Westmoreland Specialty Company. The new name was a combination of the new owners' last name and the Pennsylvania county in which the firm was located. This company was involved in more than just the production of fine tableware. They also produced commercial products such as headlight lenses for Pierce Arrow automobiles, and red glass disks with the word "Stop" embossed on them that were marketed directly to automobile owners. They even made pressed and cut glass doorknobs that were found in the finer homes of that period.

The name would later change once more to the Westmoreland Glass Company in 1924, as the word "Specialty" in the previous name seemed to mislead some customers into thinking that the company would take orders for any type of product. This new name remained unchanged for sixty years until the company permanently went out of business in January 1984.

Around 1909, a gentleman by the name of Ira Brainard invested in Specialty Glass. He and his family, most notably his grandson, J. H. Brainard, would become a major force in the operations and survival of the company during the coming years. Actually, Ira was a close friend of his nearby neighbor Charles West, and together they moved in the higher social circles and met together for weekly bridge games. They were such close friends that Charles would later use "Brainard" as the middle name of his son Samuel.

As WMGCO established itself as a major elegant glass producer, another family company was built on adjacent property and was soon shipping out of the factory site. This company, "West Brothers," was developed by George West and continued in the early tradition of producing filled glass candy and condiment containers. It was quite successful and led to the construction of a grinding mill for corn and a vinegar factory for the preparation of mustard. The vinegar factory was so large that it not only made enough for their internal use, but was also able to shipping 300 barrels of vinegar a week to other customers. At one point it was said that the West Brothers plant was the largest producer of prepared mustard in the United States. These mustard and vinegar productions also kept the sixteen pot furnaces busy supplying all of the needed glass containers.

The history of the Westmoreland Glass Company is a fascinating one and further details of their legacy can be found in two other reference books. *Westmoreland Glass 1950 1984*, contains an account of Westmoreland's company history that was penned by glass author Lorraine Kovar. Ms. Kovar, who authored three comprehensive volumes detailing Westmoreland glass (WMG), is a very dedicated collector of elegant glass and her well-researched books are meticulous in detail. Her books contain many catalog reprints, which she has managed to preserve. From her books, the Charleton collector can find a wealth of pattern information, as well as numerous color photographs essential for the identification of decorated items from the Westmoreland line.

Charles West Wilson's *Westmoreland Glass* is another excellent reference, but deals mostly with the early company's glass and history. The historical text and large photographs of the elegant glassware shown in his book are simply outstanding. Mr. Wilson was well suited to this task as he is the grandson of Charles H. West. His intimate insights and preserved handwritten accounts from various Westmoreland family and factory workers make for interesting reading.

We queried Lorraine Kovar about obtaining information of Westmoreland's relationship with AWCO and were disheartened to hear that one of the company's past owners, David Grossman, had ordered the company records burned by their janitor. Apparently some of the catalogs and such were saved by a couple of people that recognized their value, but most of the information was destroyed.

This loss makes the task of building a comprehensive list of the mould patterns and glass colors sold to AWCO by Westmoreland nearly impossible. Assuming that all of the WMGCO business records were destroyed in the incinerator, the only way now to reconstruct this record will be to locate the AWCO business files.

There is scant information that exists about Westmoreland glassware that was decorated outside of the factory, so we can get only a glimpse of the type of wares and decorations that were produced by AWCO. Fortunately, we have a beginning, as the Westmoreland books that have been authored are very useful for determining pattern names, colors, in-house decorations, and dates produced.

Westmoreland glass with Charleton decorations on the secondary market is in very short supply. There are also many glass collectors who are not familiar with AWCO's association with WMGCO, causing Charleton decorated pieces to be often overlooked and misidentified as being from Westmoreland's own decorating department.

This is quite understandable for several reasons. Of course, there is the aforementioned difficulty arising from the lack of factory records, but adding to this problem is the fact that very little of Charleton decorated Westmoreland glass retains its original Charleton label. This is quite odd considering the number of Charleton labels found on glassware from other companies.

Another contributing factor is that AWCO's and WMGCO's "Roses and Bows" and "Rose" decorations were very similar to one another and placed on identical shapes of Westmoreland glass. This duplication often meant that there was no reason to suspect the involvement of an outside decorating firm. Subsequently, these pieces were most often identified in collections as being entirely Westmoreland.

Westmoreland utilized rose sprays as decorations on their glass as early as 1906. Later, in the teen years, these flowers were created using raised enamel paints, also known during that era as "Cameo" painting. The raised enameled rose often included a scattering of forget-me-nots, which is quite typical of later Charleton designs. Also incorporated into these flowers were thin gold bands of cross-hatching or lattice. This theme can also be found on Charleton decorated glass as well. These floral and gold leaf decorations were influenced by decorated Bohemian glass from the same era and both types of this early-decorated glassware are still commonly found today.

In the late 1930s, this more laborious and costly Cameo painting ceased and the paint employed by the WMGCO decorators was switched to the thinner china paint more commonly used on china ware. The later decorations remained thematically quite similar to the older ones excluding the addition of new accents and themes. Familiarizing yourself with Westmoreland's glassware from this earlier period should remove any concern of confusion with Charleton decorations since the Westmoreland glass decorated by AWCO comes from the decades of the 1940s and 1950s.

Westmoreland continued their earlier tradition of these floral decorations into the milk glass craze of the late 1940s and 1950s. The popularity of milk glass swept the country and soon almost every glass company was pumping it out in huge volume. For all intents and purposes, WMGCO ceased the production of colored glassware in order to meet this spiraling demand for milk glass.

Although there were many Westmoreland milk glass patterns that were ideally suited for Charleton decorations, either they were ignored by AWCO or have yet to be reported. The possibility of Charleton decorations on patterns such as "Doric" only fuels the passion to search for new examples.

One of the more curious facts about AWCO's use of Westmoreland glass is that we find very little of the variation in artistic expression evidenced on Fenton, Cambridge, and various European glassware. The decorations most commonly found are roses, fruit, and a few landscapes. We are hoping that, with time and awareness, more pieces will surface to expand the limited catalog present today.

There are some exceptions to this limited decoration range and they are found when AWCO added Westmoreland glass into a grouping of other companies' glass, all of which have received the same decoration. Obviously, AWCO had no qualms about mixing pieces from various companies to suit their needs, thus making collecting Charleton decorated items that much more fun and diversified.

With the exception of two pieces of crystal, we have not found Charleton decorations on any Westmoreland glass other than white milk glass. There is a good possibility that other colors will surface, as there is such a wide range of colored glass that AWCO could have utilized for their decorations. Even though Westmoreland made a prodigious amount of beautiful milk glass patterns, AWCO appears to have only utilized a few of them, and even they were not decorated in great numbers. Reasons for this limited usage remain speculative, as there are no facts present at this point to determine the cause.

Charleton decorated Westmoreland milk glass can be found on pieces with or without the WMGCO moulded logo. Finding unlabeled decorated glassware with the Westmoreland logo does not give any degree of certainty that it was decorated in-house by Westmoreland glass decorators. Lorraine Kovar confirmed that there is a substantial quantity of Westmoreland glass on the market that has no mould mark, as Westmoreland was not fastidious about engraving their mark in new moulds made to replace the older ones after they were worn out.

Westmoreland/Charleton pieces seem to have few of the identifiers, such as the gold leaf decorator initials, that are found on some Cambridge and Fenton glass items. There is, however, another marking that is a most helpful clue when seen on Westmoreland glass (and some others) lacking a Charleton label.

Beaded Edge plates appear to have been a favorite pattern of milk glass for AWCO and these are often found with the words "Hand Painted" stamped in very small type on the backs of the plates. Black ink was used and was not fired on for permanence, therefore, it is easily damaged or removed if rubbed or washed. This stamp has been found in conjunction with the Charleton label and should serve as a positive identifier once you are familiarized with this particular stamp. There is no indication that the WMGCO ever used this stamp for their own decorated wares.

This ink stamp should not be confused with a similar ink stamp used by the Kemple Glass Company on their decorated milk glass plates. The Kemple stamp has a much larger typeface which is easy to distinguish from that of the Abels stamp once compared.

A very rare example of an AWCO marking has only been found on Westmoreland glass. This is a blue triangular ink stamp that may sometimes be found on the back of Westmoreland's rectangular pin tray. Only two examples of this stamp have been reported to date.

Although WMGCO painted numerous patterns of fruit, flowers, animals, and figures on their Beaded Edge plates, there are several ways to discern the Charleton pieces. Other than the label or ink stamps, the most useful identifier is the placement of wide bands of gold leaf close to the border of the plate. Westmoreland did not use this motif and it will serve as the best guide when scouring the marketplace.

The presence of gold leaf painted on the beads is another clue that you are probably not dealing with a Westmoreland decorated item. Be sure to compare any decoration unknown to you with the known examples painted by Westmoreland.

One unique decoration utilized by AWCO, on the Beaded Edge plates (BE-16), is that of large pink roses and stems portrayed over a black wash background. We have two plates with this theme: one uses a large double rose while the other features a single rose. These Beaded Edge Charleton plates have the entire surface decorated, again, very unlike WMGCO. Both plates have the black ink stamp on the back and have gold leaf decorating the outer surfaces of the beads on the edge. This decoration has been confirmed as AWCO by label and depictions in advertisements.

Another remarkable decoration that has only recently been discovered on several Beaded Edge plates is a landscape scene that depicts either a person or persons seated on a hillside by the water seemingly lost in thought. This is one of those finds that shocks the senses into a new awareness as drawn depictions of people on Charleton glass were undocumented up to this point and should be considered quite scarce.

Using Kovar's reference books is a must when comparing decorations on Westmoreland glass. Her reference material is very accurate, having been gleaned from the actual company catalogs. Having this material is quite helpful as WMGCO produced a number of hand painted decorations on these plates.

However, there is a note that the collector needs to be made aware of when using Kovar's *Westmoreland Glass 1950 – 1984, Volume II* as a decoration guide. On page 49, there is picture of a plate labeled "BE-16" in the top center of the lower right photograph. This gold-banded Beaded Edge plate with a depiction of fruit, with the pears being the predominant theme, is actually a Charleton plate. We have two similar plates, and both are ink stamped so as to remove any doubt as to their origin. Although her photograph of the plate is rather small, once you compare the decoration with the other "fruit" motifs surrounding it, you can see the distinctive contrast of the two different styles.

As previously stated, when Lorraine was writing her book she was not very familiar with AWCO decorated Westmoreland glass and the style is similar to that of other fruit motifs done in-house by Westmoreland. This is the only example of Charleton misidentification that we have found in any of her books on Westmoreland.

Rather than discuss a specific pattern next, we would like to delve into the particulars of a decoration that is probably the most confusing found on any Charleton item. This pattern is Westmoreland's Decoration #32, "Roses and Bows." The pattern first appears on Westmoreland glass in the 1950s and was initially called "Roses with Lavender Bows," but the word Lavender was dropped within a short period of time after its introduction.

Both Beth Weismann and AWCO used this same decoration in the early 1940s, AWCO's use being ten years earlier than Westmoreland's. There is a good possibility that the Charleton version was still being produced simultaneously with WMGCO's Decoration #32 into the 1950s, hence the confusion. But by studying the two decorations, there are certainly differences in the styles used, and WMGCO's Decoration #32 appears to be more organized and cleaner in detail and execution.

The similarities between Weissman and Fenton are discussed elsewhere and, since there has been no speculation or documentation that Weissman was decorating Westmoreland glass, we will leave the Weissman pieces out of the equation in this section.

One of the nicest examples of Charleton on Westmoreland glass we have is found on an "Old Quilt" milk glass covered honey box. Old Quilt, also known earlier as "Checkerboard," has been found as early as 1910 in a Butler Brothers catalog. Our piece is not only Charleton labeled, but also has the common WMGCO mould mark used after the 1940s. This lovely pattern has such intricate mould work that it readily lends itself to the skilled hand decorator for exquisite detailing.

Westmoreland also decorated Old Quilt in-house with several different decorations, including the #32 Roses and Bows. As you will see in the photograph of the Charleton decorated Old Quilt item, while it certainly has roses, there are no lavender bows and the decoration is distinctive from WMGCO's Decoration #32 in several ways. This piece has the Charleton trademark "Pink Mist" treatment on the finial, lid, and foot as well as gold leaf sprigs scattered throughout the roses. The Pink Blush treatment is quite striking when placed on the sculptured crisscross diagonal lines found on the sides of the box.

Actually, Westmoreland decorated some of these Old Quilt diagonal lines in a similar way and there is an interesting story associated with this decoration. This story, as related by Lorraine Kovar, involves the wife of Philip Brainard, a descendent of Ira Brainard, an early major investor in the WMGCO. Apparently Mrs. Brainard would visit the factory from time to time and paint Old Quilt pieces with alternating squares of black and gold and then these items were given as personal gifts to friends.

WMGCO also dabbled in this type of decorating on Old Quilt in-house as well, but it proved to be too time consuming and the gold leaf used was quite expensive so production was very limited. There are no records of which items of Old Quilt were done, so it could appear on most any item of Old Quilt.

Two new patterns of Westmoreland glass have turned up in Charleton recently. One is a 7" English Hobnail milk glass basket decorated with Roses and Bows. Although it is not labeled, there is no doubt of the decorator due to the overall layout and the placement of numerous small gold X's.

The second item is a Charleton/Westmoreland split handle basket. This basket was only made in two patterns, the ever-plentiful Paneled Grape and the Pansies pattern. It is upon the Pansies (PB-1, line #757) pattern that the Charleton decoration has been seen. Again, the Charleton decoration is so stylistically different from the WMGCO's in-house decoration that there is little doubt as to the attribution.

Another curious example of this Charleton decorated Pansy basket we have seen had the split handles drooping down into the center of the bowl. This is just an example of the folks at AWCO using too high of a temperature in the decorating kiln. More than likely, this item was taken home by one of the workers.

While finding Westmoreland glass with Charleton decorations may be a somewhat difficult task, it is well worth the effort. Perhaps as collectors and dealers become more knowledgeable about Charleton decorated Westmoreland glass, it will become easier to find.

Westmoreland 7" Milk Glass English Hobnail basket. Charleton Roses and Bows decoration, 1950s. $85-100. Rare. *Authors' Collection.*

Westmoreland #OQ-35, 5" Milk Glass covered honey box. Charleton Pink Mist and Roses decoration, c. 1950s. AWCO Charleton label #4907. $75-85. Scarce. *Authors' Collection.*

Westmoreland 7" Milk Glass English Hobnail basket. Bottom detail.

Westmoreland #OQ-35, 5" Milk Glass covered honey box. Detail of lid.

Westmoreland Milk Glass vanity set consisting of two 5" cologne bottles and one 4.5" powder jar. Charleton Blue Mist and Raspberries decoration. $175-225 set. Rare. *Authors' Collection.*

Westmoreland Milk Glass Puff Box lid detail. Charleton Blue Mist and Raspberries decoration. AWCO Charleton label #4150A (beige paper label).

Westmoreland #1, 8" Milk Glass Club Shell and Loop plate. Charleton Pink Mist and Roses decoration, 1950s. AWCO Charleton label #568. Handwritten "A" in green on the bottom. $60-75. Scarce. *Authors' Collection.*

Westmoreland #BE 16, 8.5" Milk Glass Beaded Edge plate. Charleton Black Mist and Roses decoration, 1950s. $60-75. *Authors' Collection.*

Westmoreland #BE-16, 8.5" Milk Glass Beaded Edge plate. Charleton Black Mist and Roses decoration, c. 1950s. AWCO Charleton label #4935B. Black ink stamped "Hand Painted" on back. $60-75. *Authors' Collection.*

Westmoreland #BE-16, 8.5" Milk Glass Beaded Edge plate. Charleton Fruit and Flowers decoration, 1950s. "Hand Painted" black ink stamp on back. $60-75. Scarce. *Authors' Collection.*

Westmoreland #BE-16, 8.5" Milk Glass Beaded Edge plate. Charleton Porter Apple decoration. AWCO Charleton label #1012A. $60-75. Scarce. *Authors' Collection.*

Westmoreland #BE-16, 8.5" Milk Glass Beaded Edge plate. Charleton Castle on the Hill decoration, c. 1950s. Note the painted human figures on this plate which is one of a very few decorations depicting people that have been documented to date. "Hand Painted" black ink stamp on back. $75-80. Scarce. *Authors' Collection.*

Westmoreland #BE-16, 8.5" Milk Glass Beaded Edge plate. Charleton Butterfly and Fruit decoration, c. 1950s. "Hand Painted" black ink stamp on back. $65-75. Scarce decoration. *Authors' Collection.*

Westmoreland #BE-16, 8.5" Milk Glass Beaded Edge plate. Charleton Harbor and Tower decoration, c. 1950s. Note the painted human figures on this plate which is one of a very few decorations depicting people that have been documented to date. $75-80. Scarce. *Authors' Collection.*

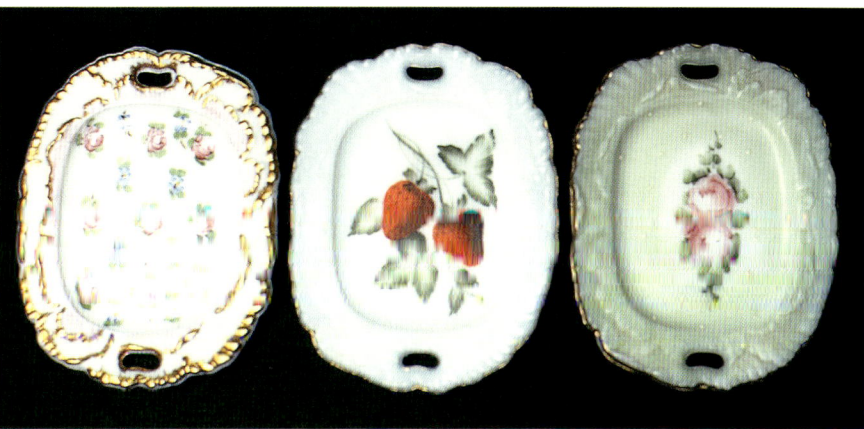

Three Westmoreland #14, 4" Milk Glass trays. Charleton Pink Mist and Roses, Strawberries, and Green Mist and Roses decorations, c. 1950s. Triangular blue ink stamp on Pink Mist and Roses tray. AWCO Charleton label #1509 on Strawberries tray and #639 on Green Mist tray. $30-40 each. *Authors' Collection.*

Westmoreland #BE-16, 8.5" Milk Glass Beaded Edge plate. Charleton Harbor and Castle decoration, c. 1950s. Note the painted human figures on this plate which is one of a very few decorations depicting people that have been documented to date. $75-80. Scarce. *Authors' Collection.*

Westmoreland #14, 4" Milk Glass tray. Charleton Strawberry decoration. $30-40. *Authors' Collection.*

Group shot of items with AWCO's Charleton Strawberries decoration. Clockwise from top, Fenton Mould #206 Milk Glass covered candy, $75-85, scarce; Westmoreland #14 pin tray with AWCO Charleton label #1509, $30-40; Westmoreland #324-2 leaf-shaped tray, $45-55, scarce. *Authors' Collection.*

Westmoreland #324-2, 6" Milk Glass leaf tray. Charleton Red Geometric decoration. AWCO Charleton label #743. $45-55. Scarce. *Authors' Collection.*

Westmoreland #324-2, 6" Milk Glass leaf tray. Bottom of tray.

Group shot of Westmoreland #1923 Milk Glass leaf dessert plates or bonbons with Charleton Roses decoration. *Authors' Collection.*

Westmoreland LF-2, Line #1923, 6" Milk Glass leaf dessert plate or bonbon. Charleton Roses decoration, c. 1950s. $35-40. *Authors' Collection.*

Westmoreland #BE-1, 6" Milk Glass Beaded Edge bowl, oval, crimped. Charleton Roses and Bows decoration, c. 1950s. $50-60. Scarce. *Courtesy of Helen & Steve Klemko.*

Westmoreland #EH-46, 5.5" Milk Glass English Hobnail bowl. Charleton Roses decoration, 1950s. $45-50. Scarce. *Authors' Collection.*

Westmoreland #EH-46, 5.5" Milk Glass English Hobnail bowl. Interior view.

Westmoreland #RO-3, 5.5" Milk Glass Rooster on Nest with basket weave base; #SR-1, 8.5" Milk Glass Standing Rooster; #HN-2, 5.5" Milk Glass Hen on Nest with basket weave base. All Charleton Roses decoration, 1950s. Rooster on Nest: $65-75; Hen on Nest: $60-70; Standing Rooster: $75-125. Beware of reproductions! *Courtesy Bob & Darlene Corriher.*

Westmoreland #SR-1, 8.5" Milk Glass standing rooster. Charleton Roses decoration, 1950s. Note painted base. $75-125. *Courtesy Bob & Darlene Corriher.*

Westmoreland #SR-1, 9" Milk Glass standing rooster. Charleton Roses decoration, c. 1950s. OWCO Charleton #4162. $75-125. Scarce. Beware of reproductions! *Courtesy of Helen & Steve Klemko.*

Westmoreland #HN-2, 4" high by 5.5" long Milk Glass Hen on basket weave base. Charleton Roses decoration, c. 1950s. $75-125. Scarce. Beware of reproductions! Reproductions will have the circular Westmoreland mark. *Courtesy of Helen & Steve Klemko.*

Westmoreland #1872-2, 9" Milk Glass sleigh. Charleton Roses decoration, 1950s. $100-125. Rare. Beware of reproductions by Summit Art Glass. *Authors' Collection.*

Westmoreland #1211-1 Milk Glass octagon-shaped one pound covered candy. Westmoreland #32 Roses and Bows decoration, 1950s. Note: although the decoration has no bows, Westmoreland still called this Roses and Bows. NP. *Authors' Collection.*

Westmoreland #1872-2, 9" Milk Glass sleigh. Reverse view.

Westmoreland #1211-1 Milk Glass octagon-shaped one pound covered candy. Decoration detail.

Westmoreland #WB-2, 10" Milk Glass Wedding Bowl. Westmoreland Roses & Gold Filigree decoration, c. 1950s. NP. *Courtesy of Helen & Steve Klemko.*

Westmoreland 6.75" Milk Glass Bristol-style vase. Unknown decorator. NP. *Authors' Collection.*

Chapter 6.
AWCO Decorations on Items by Unknown Manufacturers

This section contains an eclectic collection of Charleton decorations on blanks that are by unknown manufacturers. Some are imports from Italy and West Germany. Others are of unknown origin. These blanks were made of either glass, ceramics (including porcelain), or in unusual instances, metal. In mentioning metal, we are not referring to stands or lamp bases, but rather the object itself is primarily made of metal (toleware). Regardless of their origin, all of the items shown in this chapter have Charleton decorations.

We will be using the word "new" in this section quite a bit. There were certainly a lot of surprises in store for us in the stunning new shapes, materials, colors, and styles that came together in quantities large enough to merit their own section.

Some of these foreign blanks were purchased by AWCO abroad. After World War II, Walter Abels traveled Europe in order to keep his company supplied with the best in glass and ceramics. Of such importance were his travels, mention is made of these excursions in the trade journals of the day.

In a short write-up in *Retailing* in March of 1946 we find the following, "Walter Abels, of Abels-Wasserberg & Co., expects to leave for Europe sometime in May. He will tour the Continent for a few months in search of new merchandise, and will 'hit every country he can get into'."

A short time later the June 6, 1946 issue of *Retailing* recorded his plane's departure from La-Guardia airport for that trip. Harry Wasserberg reported. ". . . the rain was terrible, but the plane took off safely."

A short account sums up the nature of the trip by saying, "Walter was heading for France and other countries in search of fine pieces of the type used by Abels-Wasserberg in making lamps before the war. Harry (Wasserberg) said that if any merchandise is to be found in Europe, 'Walter will bring it back!'."

Despite these items having a mystery concerning their manufacturer, there is compensation in the fact that they all have their Charleton labels. Without these labels, it is doubtful that many of these items could have been identified due to the departure of the AWCO artists from traditional Charleton decorations.

The mention of this departure is not intended to denigrate the items, as the decorations found on these pieces rivals the best decorations found on any other Charleton objects from known makers. Hopefully, after experts and other collectors have examined the photographs in this section, we will be able to solve some questions regarding the makers.

Despite the differences just mentioned, AWCO still utilized many high quality blanks from these unknown makers on which to display their artists' handiwork. It should be emphasized here that rarely did AWCO ever attempted to capitalize on the reputations of the manufacturers who supplied them blanks.

Although to AWCO the important and inherent beauty of the form and color of the glass or porcelain blank was always given due consideration, that factor seemed to be mostly secondary to the decoration. They could have certainly enhanced the prestige of their wares had they so chosen by mentioning their suppliers, such as Fenton, Cambridge, Heisey, and others, in their advertisements, but their pride resided in their artwork. For the most part, AWCO stakes its own claim on these items by simply referring to them in advertisements as "Charleton China" and "Charleton Porcelain."

In this section will be seen a combination of styles as AWCO began to produce more items with abstract and modernistic designs that flourished during the 1950s. There are still other traditional motifs on these unknown items, although the period from which they were produced is unknown. Although AWCO was not timid about pushing the artistic experimental boundaries, there is no indication that AWCO ever abandoned their trademark roses and floral sprays.

A new surprise was in store for us as we began to find items that were Charleton labeled, but were unadorned beyond a simple one color glaze. It is not known if these plain wares were special orders by the customer or if AWCO diversified their style in order to have something for everyone. These findings radically altered the visual cues we used when scanning the aisles of the antique stores and malls.

In our early days of collecting items for this book, it was fairly easy to set our "auto-pilots" and only pause to examine the floral designs on Fenton, Cambridge, and Consolidated glass. Now, although still quite worthwhile and enjoyable, this broadened spectrum has slowed our pace considerably when shopping, as it requires considerably more concentration.

Trade journals advertisements document some of these "Charleton Modern" pieces as they were called by AWCO. These pieces have never been reported and there are a lot of exciting finds that await the diligent collector.

Crystal 9.75" vase. Possibly Indiana Glass. Charleton Dappled decoration, c. 1950s. See the Cambridge chapter for the decanter in this decoration as well as the other pieces shown in the Advertisement chapter. $75-85. Rare. *Authors' collection.*

Crystal 7" vase. Charleton Spun Gold decoration, c. 1940s-1950s. AWCO Charleton label #2936P. $75-85. Rare. *Authors' collection.*

Crystal 9.75" vase. Interior view. *Authors' collection.*

German Cased Glass 21" tall decanter and two 9.75" tall cologne bottles. Glass is crystal cased over Milk Glass. Charleton Arabian Nights decoration, c. 1950s. AWCO Charleton #3130 on decanter; no Charleton labels on cologne bottles. Each cologne bottle has a sticker which reads "Made in Western Germany"; the decanter does not have this sticker. $150-160, large decanter; $60-75 each, cologne bottles. Rare. *Authors' collection.*

Group shot of various pieces with Charleton Zigzag decoration, c. 1940s-1950s. This decoration technique is known as "Sgraffito". *Authors' collection.*

Ceramic 10.5" vase. Charleton Zigzag decoration, c. 1940s-1950s. AWCO Charleton label #2053. "1853" impressed on bottom. $50-60. Rare. *Authors' collection.*

Ceramic 9.5" decanter. Charleton Zigzag decoration, c. 1940s-1950s. AWCO Charleton label #2061. "1853" impressed on bottom. $60-75. Rare. *Authors' collection.*

Ceramic 7" ovoid vase. Charleton Zigzag decoration, c. 1940s-1950s. AWCO Charleton label #2062. "1860" impressed on bottom. $50-60. Rare. *Authors' collection.*

Ceramic 5" covered candy box. Charleton Zigzag decoration, c. 1940s-1950s. AWCO Charleton label #2063. "1866" impressed on bottom. $60-75. Rare. *Authors' collection.*

Ceramic 7" ovoid vase. Charleton Harlequin decoration, c. 1940s-1950s. AWCO Charleton label #2106. "1860" impressed on bottom. $75-85. Rare. *Authors' collection.*

Crystal 8.5" tea jar. Charleton Tea Drinkers with Pink Stucco finish decoration, c. 1940s-1950s. AWCO Charleton label #1608. Probably U.S. Glass. Insufficient data to price. Rare. *Courtesy of Barbara Wyrick.*

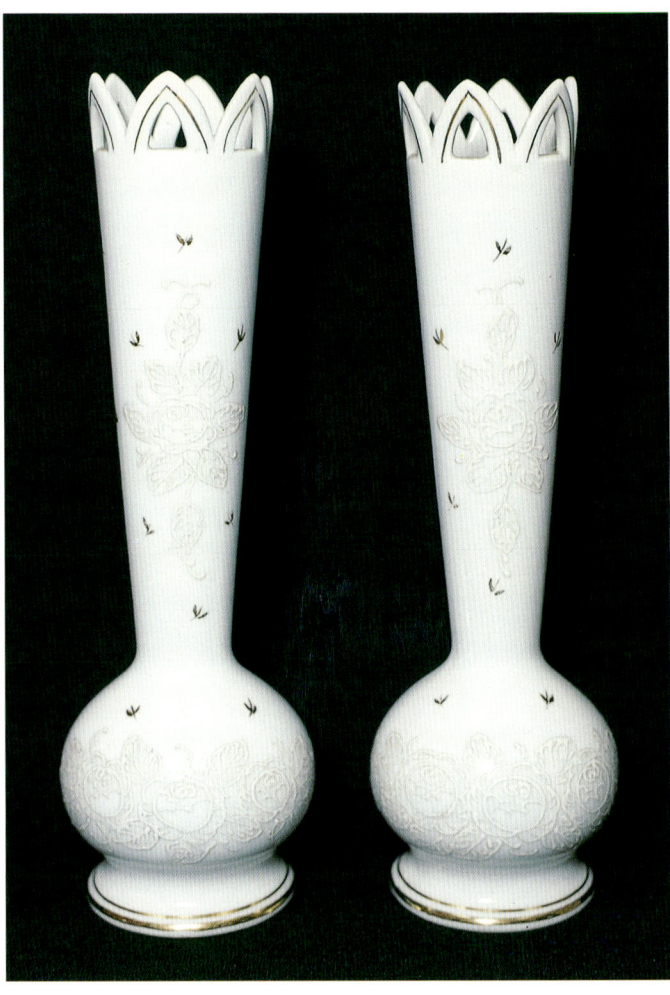

Pair of porcelain 12" reticulated vases. Charleton Ivory Roses decoration, c. 1940s-1950s. AWCO Charleton label #2548. $40-45 each. Rare. *Authors' collection.*

Pair of porcelain 12" reticulated vases. Detail. *Authors' collection.*

Porcelain 9" candlesticks. Charleton Roses decoration, c. 1940s-1950s. $85-100 pair. Beige paper AWCO Charleton labels (numbers illegible). Rare. *Authors' collection.*

Group shot of porcelain pieces with Charleton Roses decoration. *Authors' collection.*

Porcelain 9" Apothecary jar. Charleton Roses decoration. AWCO label #4507. Rare. $85-100. *Authors' collection.*

Porcelain 12" urn. Charleton Roses decoration. "9141" embossed on bottom. The base is bolted onto the body of the urn. AWCO Charleton label #4206A. $150-175. Scarce. *Authors' collection.*

Italian porcelain 6" cornucopia made in Bassano del Grappa, Italy. Charleton Roses decoration. AWCO label #4289B. "47" written in gold on the bottom. Rare. $75-85. *Authors' collection.*

Porcelain shell dish, 5". Probably made by Amoges. Charleton Roses and Bows decoration. $40-50. Scarce. *Authors' collection.*

Cased opaque white glass cut to emerald green 8" vase. Charleton Pastoral decoration. Possibly Bohemian and, if so, this is the first example of Bohemian Charleton decorated glass found to date. $125-150. Rare. *Authors' collection.*

Milk Glass 10" Oak Leaf dresser bottle. Probably Kemple. Charleton Roses decoration. AWCO Charleton label #4228. $40-50. Scarce. *Authors' collection.*

Milk Glass 10" Oak Leaf dresser bottle. Detail. *Authors' collection.*

Milk Glass 9.5" Leaf & Scroll dresser bottle. Probably Kemple. Charleton Brown Roses decoration. $40-50. Scarce. *Authors' collection.*

Milk Glass 9.5" dresser bottle, not original stopper. Probably Kemple. Charleton Roses decoration. $40-50. Scarce. *Authors' collection.*

Milk Glass 9" vase. Possibly Consolidated. Charleton Blue Mist and Roses decoration. $50-60. Scarce. *Authors' collection.*

Milk Glass 9.5" vase. Probably Kemple. Charleton Roses decoration. AWCO Charleton label #4055A. $40-50. Scarce. *Authors' collection.*

Group shot of two Milk Glass 6" vases. Left to right: Charleton "Ship Ahoy" decoration, AWCO Charleton label #4226B, and Charleton "Trifle in Glass" decoration, AWCO Charleton label #4226A. All probably Kemple. Both have a "Z" or "N" in gold handwritten on the bottom. $50-60 each. Scarce. *Authors' collection.*

Two Porcelain 6" cologne bottles. Suspected to be Amoges. Charleton Roses decoration. AWCO Charleton label #4609. Embossed "8827" on bottom. $125-150 pair. Rare. *Authors' collection.*

Group shot, two Porcelain 6" cologne bottles. Left to right: Charleton Roses decoration, Amoges applied rose decoration (marked "Amoges Hand Painted"). Note the similarity in the shape of the Charleton decorated bottle with the Amoges bottle. This leads us to believe the Charleton bottle was made by Amoges. *Authors' collection.*

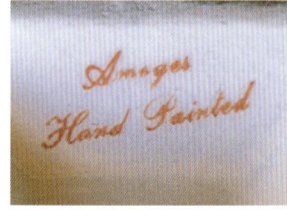

Amoges Porcelain 6" cologne bottle. Detail of Amoges mark on bottom.

Porcelain 6" cologne bottle. Rear view.

Pink Cased Glass 6" cologne bottle. Charleton Double Pin Stripe and Roses decoration. AWCO Charleton label #2211. Also has label that reads "Made in West Germany". Rare. $75-85. *Authors' collection.*

Pink Cased Glass 6.5" vase. Charleton Double Pin Stripe and Roses decoration. AWCO Charleton label #2214. Also has label that reads "Made in West Germany". Rare. $50-60. *Authors' collection.*

Group shot of Porcelain items with Charleton Progressive Rose decoration. *Authors' collection.*

Porcelain 5.5" dresser box, rectangular. Suspected to be Limoges. Charleton Progressive Rose decoration. AWCO Charleton label #4851. "Hand Painted" stamped in black ink on interior of the lid. $35-45. Scarce. *Authors' collection.*

Pair of Porcelain 4" pin trays. Suspected to be Limoges. Charleton Progressive Rose decoration. $20-25 each. Scarce. *Authors' collection.*

Two porcelain 5" dresser bottles. Suspected to be Amoges. Charleton Progressive Rose decoration. AWCO Charleton label #4513 (beige paper label). $40-45 each. Scarce. *Authors' collection.*

Pink satin finish 5" covered candy box. Charleton Roses decoration. Label on bottom reads "Hand Painted Made in Germany US Zone". AWCO Charleton label #2244. $75-80. Rare. *Authors' collection.*

Porcelain 5" dresser bottle. Detail of beige paper Charleton label.

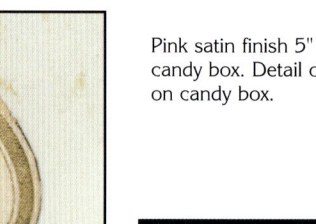

Pink satin finish 5" covered candy box. Detail of labels on candy box.

Porcelain 3" powder jar. Suspected to be Amoges. Charleton Progressive Rose decoration. AWCO Charleton label #4514 (beige paper label). $40-45 each. Scarce. *Authors' collection.*

Crystal satin 7" cylinder jar (missing top). Possibly WV Specialty Glass or Tiffin. Charleton Gold Roses decoration. AWCO Charleton label #2913. $60-75 (with top). Scarce. *Authors' collection.*

Crystal 6" heart-shaped dresser box. Suspected to be Dunbar. Charleton Roses decoration. $50-60. Rare. *Authors' collection.*

Milk Glass 4" heart-shaped dresser box. Suspected to be Beaumont. Charleton Roses decoration. AWCO Charleton label #1788. $50-65. Rare. *Authors' collection.*

Crystal 6" heart-shaped dresser box. Side view.

Milk Glass 4" covered heart-shaped box. Suspected to be Beaumont. Charleton Red Geometric decoration. AWCO Charleton label #732. $55-65. Scarce. *Authors' collection.*

Milk Glass 6.5" three sectioned candy box. Charleton Roses decoration. Initials "KB" are within the decoration. $60-75. Rare. *Authors' collection.*

Milk Glass 4.5" covered cigarette box. Suspected to be Beaumont. Charleton Rose decoration. AWCO Charleton label #4230C. $50-60. Scarce. *Authors' collection.*

Milk Glass 6.5" three sectioned candy box. Interior view.

Milk Glass 4.5" covered cigarette box. Suspected to be Beaumont. Charleton Fruit and Dots decoration. $50-60. Scarce. *Authors' collection.*

Milk Glass 4.5" covered cigarette box. Suspected to be Beaumont. Charleton Red Geometric decoration. Initial "I" in gold on the bottom. $50-60. Scarce. *Authors' collection.*

Milk Glass 3.25" pin tray. Charleton Blue Mist and Roses. $25-35. *Authors' collection.*

Porcelain figural of two ladies measuring 8" long by 6.5" high. AWCO Charleton label #3984. "Italy" is handwritten under the glaze. Although this does have a Charleton label, this has not been decorated. Insufficient data to price. Rare. *Authors' collection.*

Porcelain Louisiana Cavalier and Lady figurines, each 9" tall. AWCO Charleton #4291. Original price tag for $7.50 remains, c. 1940s. $60-75 pair. Scarce. *Authors' collection.*

Porcelain figural of two ladies. Detail.

Dresden-style 9" lady porcelain figurine. AWCO Charleton label #4397. $75-85. Rare. *Authors' collection. (Note: There should be a matching gentleman but he remains elusive to date.)*

White Ceramic Lavabo. Reservoir 13" high by 8.75" wide; basin 5.5" high by 12" wide. Charleton Granite decoration. AWCO Charleton label #1975. $50-60. Scarce. *Authors' collection.*

White Ceramic Lavabo. Reservoir 13" high by 8.75" wide; basin 5.5" high by 12" wide. Charleton Gold Roses decoration. AWCO Charleton label #1898B. $90-100. Scarce. *Authors' collection.*

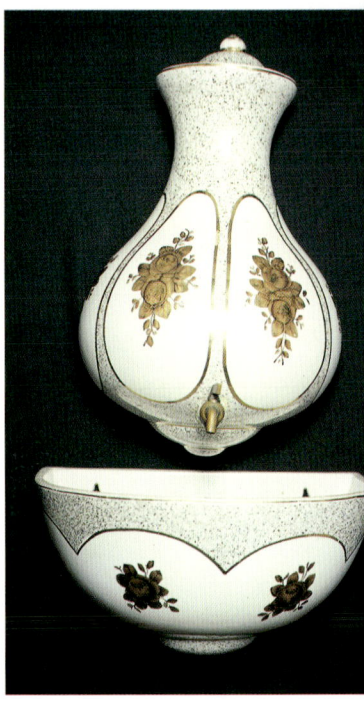

White Ceramic Lavabo. Reservoir 13" high by 8.75" wide; basin 5.5" high by 12" wide. Charleton Gray Marble decoration. AWCO Charleton label #1898. $75-85. Scarce. *Authors' collection.*

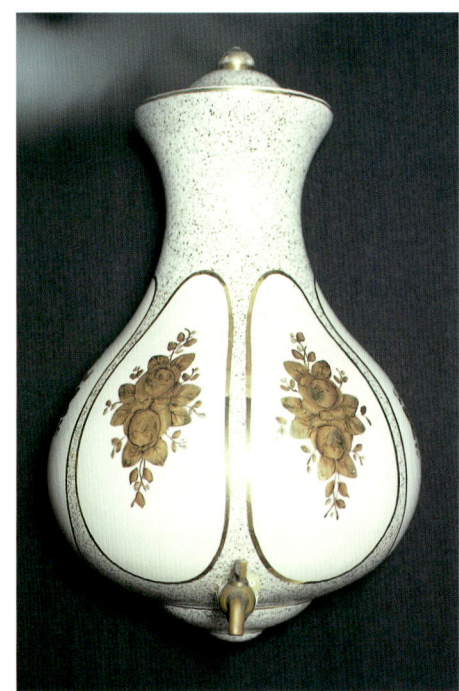

White Ceramic Lavabo. Charleton Gold Roses decoration. Detail of reservoir and lid.

Pink Ceramic Lavabo (shown without basin). Reservoir 13" high by 8.75" wide. Charleton Pink Marble decoration. AWCO Charleton label #1898A. $75-85. Scarce. *Authors' collection.*

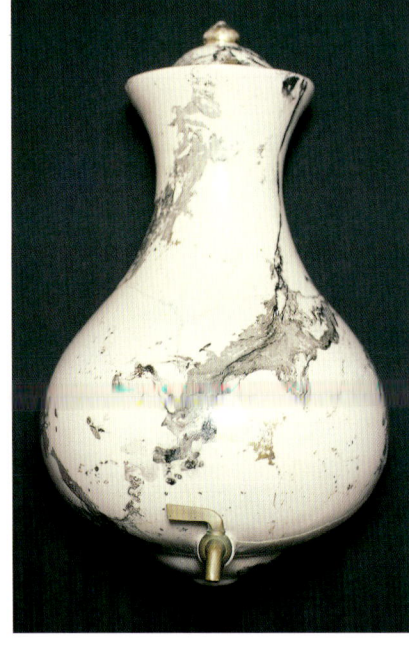

White Ceramic Lavabo. Charleton Gold Roses decoration. Detail of basin.

Toleware Metal 9.5" vase. Charleton Gold Roses decoration. AWCO Charleton label #2789. $50-60. Scarce. *Authors' collection.*

Toleware Metal 8" covered candy. Detail of interior showing gold sponge effect.

Toleware Metal 8" covered candy. Charleton Gold Roses decoration. AWCO Charleton label #2784. $65-75. Scarce. *Authors' collection.*

Toleware Metal 8" covered candy. Detail of bottom showing handwritten "AW+Co" and Charleton label. *Authors' collection.*

Ceramic 5.5" double switch plate. Charleton Roses decoration. AWCO Charleton label #2281D. $40-50. Rare. *Authors' collection.*

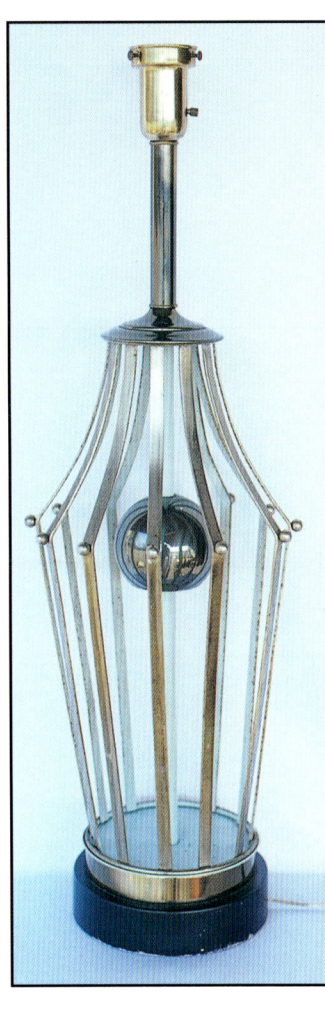

Eames-type metal lamp. Charleton decorated, c. 1950s. $75-85. Rare. *Authors' collection.*

Crystal 11" lamp. Measurement from base to top of lamp fount only. Charleton Roses and Green Maze decoration, c. 1950s. $75-100. Rare. *Authors' collection.*

Crystal 11" lamp. Measurement from base to top of lamp fount only. Charleton Green Mist and Roses decoration. $150-200. Rare. *Authors' collection.*

Crystal cased glass 15" lamp. Charleton Roses decoration, c. 1950s. $125-150. Rare. *Authors' collection.*

Pink Ceramic 19" tall monument lamp. Measurement from base to top of the ceramic body. Charleton Roses decoration, c. 1940s to 1950s. $65-75. *Authors' collection.*

Porcelain 8 Day mantel clock, 8" tall. Charleton Gold Roses and Butterfly decoration, c. 1950s. AWCO Charleton label #2306B. "V4038 5,59" hand engraved into metal back plate of clock. Clockworks by Florin. $100-125. Rare. *Authors' collection.*

Porcelain 8 Day mantel clock, 8" tall. Side view.

Pink Ceramic 19" tall monument lamp. Detail of decoration.

Chapter 7.
All Other Known Manufacturers

Rather than constructing brief chapters for each of the following items, we have grouped them all together in this one area. Although produced by well-known manufacturers, these items at this point are very few in numbers. Each maker in this section will be subtitled and there will be brief summaries of most of the companies. We are certain that as the Charleton collecting field grows, many of these makers will merit their own sections in future editions.

Duncan & Miller

The George Duncan Glass Company was one of the longest operating glass companies in America. Your interpretation of the company's timeline determines the number of years they operated, but in a broad sense you could say it was over one hundred years.

Although George Duncan had been involved in the glass business as early as 1856, he did not get involved in a substantial way until 1867, when he bought into Ripley & Company, which had been founded two years earlier. By 1874, he and his family owned enough interest in the company to change its name to George Duncan & Sons.

Just a few years after this, George passed away and his son, James E. Duncan, and son-in-law, Augustus M. Heisey, oversaw the business. This was the same Augustus Heisey whose own name would also become synonymous with elegant glassware years later.

The company of George Duncan & Sons would be absorbed into the large glass collective known as United States Glass in 1891 and known in the concern as Factory D. James Duncan seems to have been squeezed out of a leadership position of the company after this consolidation. According to Neila Bredchoft's *Early Duncan Glassware,* he "retires from active business for the present, although still a young man." Interestingly, Duncan's factory membership with U.S. Glass was short-lived, and was dissolved a year later after a fire destroyed Factory D.

This also ended the business association of Augustus Heisey with the Duncan factory. He continued to work for U.S. Glass in a position as their Commercial Manager. He later opened his own firm known as A. H. Heisey & Company, and they began producing glass in 1896. We will examine AWCO's relationship with Augustus Heisey in a later section.

The Duncan organization, however, survived this disaster and pressed forward. Despite local rumors, there seemed to have been no effort or desire on their part to rebuild the plant on its former site, or continue their association with U.S. Glass. But as fate would have it, many years later, U.S. Glass would appear once again on the Duncan scene.

The George H. Duncan Sons' Company, as it was called for a brief time, went into operation after they relocated to Washington, Pennsylvania. Here they built an entirely new factory and the first glass was made on February 9th, 1893. Many collectors feel that Duncan glass was not "really" made until after this transition and do not have a great interest in collecting their earlier glassware.

Within a short period of time the firm would become known as the Duncan and Miller Glass Company. This has been shortened over the years to Duncan Miller and this is the name commonly used by collectors.

The "Miller" in Duncan and Miller came from the name of John Ernest Miller (often printed as J. Ernest Miller). Ernest had become a partner, along with brothers James and Harry B. Duncan, in this new company.

Actually, Ernest's association with the George Duncan Company was not a new one. His name was found mentioned as early as 1880 in the *Crockery and Glass Journal* where he was noted to be employed by Duncan as the skilled foreman of the mould shop.

As a designer, he is best known for the creation of Duncan's highly acclaimed "Three Face" pattern. His beautiful wife, Elizabeth Blair Miller, was to have her likeness frozen in time, as she was the model used to depict the three identical faces encircling the stems on this pattern.

The 1920s, and especially the Great Depression of the 1930s, were the glory years of Duncan & Miller. This is when their most widely acclaimed patterns were introduced; patterns that are still very popular with glass collectors today.

These designs can mostly be credited to Duncan Miller designer, Robert A. May. His work shows obvious influences of René Lalique, and the opalescent glass produced in soft pink and blue pastels have become Duncan's trademark. The smooth flowing lines are classic by nature and are almost impossible to walk by without a second glance when browsing in antique stores.

These patterns were made for a number of years and eventually found their way into the decorating studios of AWCO. The known Duncan Miller patterns that Charleton collectors should be concerned with are Teardrop, Canterbury, Sylvan, Murano, Grecian Urn, along with various figural glass animals and cornucopias. The decorations can be found on opalescent glass, crystal, and milk glass.

Although it may be your desire, AWCO decorated Duncan Miller is not readily going to be a large part of your Charleton collection. The pieces found on the market are few and far between. Altogether, we have seen in person and in pictures about a dozen or so decorated Duncan items.

These decorations have all been on par with the nicest AWCO has done. Look for the usual Charleton Roses to appear as well as naturalistic painting on glass animals. As more pieces are reported, there is a good possibility that the AWCO decorations on Duncan Miller will go beyond the standard floral designs.

Leslie Piña, noted glass author and history professor, has written and recently published an excellent reference book on Duncan & Miller titled *Depression Era Glass By Duncan*. This is the best overall book for Duncan & Miller collectors as it shows the company's early patterns as well as pieces made right up to the closing of the factory.

The large, superb photographs are a delight to examine and she includes (but does not identify the decorator) two pieces of handpainted decorated glass as well. These two pieces have the same decoration, and this design was unknown to us until we first examined her book. We decided to call this decoration "Leaf and Dots" due to the depiction of delicately serrated leaves placed among numerous tiny gold circles. Pictures of these items are not included in this volume, so we will briefly describe them for the interested collector.

The first piece with this previously unknown decoration is found on a 3.5" #538 Grecian Urn produced in milk glass. Leslie lists this sized item as being a cigarette holder, and although these one-piece urns were quite simple, they stand out by having clean lines and are graced with a generous square foot. There is a good possibility that the larger handled urns by Duncan were utilized by AWCO, as there are several decorated urns from other manufacturers found in the Charleton line.

The second piece in this Leaf and Dots pattern is an absolutely captivating 10" milk glass swan, identified as Duncan's #30 Pall Mall pattern. This ample piece allows for an expansion of the decoration and really does justice to the finely detailed leaves and profusion of scattered gold dots. The swan and the urn were both designed to appeal to the growing market for accessories in the "Modern" style.

The poised, flowing lines are soothing to the eye, and these elegant swans came in a variety of sizes and styles. They "nest" inside one another as well, creating a visually interesting display.

No details were available as to why the company was closed and sold off in 1955. But once again, U.S. Glass came into the picture when they bought most, if not all, of the Duncan Miller moulds as well as the use of their trademarked name. U.S. Glass continued to produce many different glass items from these Duncan moulds and discerning the difference between some of these pieces can be challenging. There are some differences in the tint of the colored glass, but the crystal items are said to be very confusing.

Duncan & Miller Sylvan #122, 7.5" crystal swan. Charleton Roses decoration, c. 1940s. $100-125. Rare. *Authors' collection.*

Duncan & Miller Canterbury #115, 9" pink opalescent crimped bowl. Charleton Gold Leaves and Bows decoration. AWCO Charleton label #4889. $50-60. Scarce. *Authors' collection.*

Duncan & Miller Sylvan #122, 7.5" crystal swan. Detail.

Duncan & Miller Canterbury #115, 8" pink opalescent two-handle, two-compartment oval relish. Charleton Stitched Roses decoration. $60-75. Scarce. *Authors' collection.*

Duncan & Miller Murano #127, 10" Milk Glass bowl. Charleton Roses decoration. $75-85. Scarce. *Authors' collection.*

Duncan & Miller Swirl #121, Shape #2, 14" crystal cornucopia. Charleton Roses decoration. $150-165. Scarce. *Authors' collection.*

A. H. Heisey & Company

The A. H. Heisey glass company produced some of the best designs in elegant glassware that were offered by American glass manufacturers. Unfortunately, their relationship with AWCO was very limited and it will require a lot of searching to find examples of their glass with Charleton decorations.

A. H. Heisey was a very capable businessman who had quite a resume. He is best known for the glass company he founded in 1895, but he also had a variety of other interests as well. Augustus H. Heisey was actually born in Germany in 1842, but was raised in Merritown, Pennsylvania. At the tender age of nineteen he held his first job in the glass industry with his employment at King & Co. in Pittsburgh in 1861.

This time period also marked the beginning of the American Civil War and Heisey served a distinguished enlistment fighting for Company C of the 155th Regiment of the Pennsylvania Zouaves. He was engaged in several battles and suffered a slight wound during the North's successful defense of Little Round Top in the Battle of Gettysburg.

After his release from the Army he continued his vocation in the glass industry and, after trying a couple other small firms, he went to work for Ripley & Company. This move was to be the beginning of many changes in his personal and business life.

The Ripley company is where Heisey was to meet his future wife, Susan Duncan. She was the daughter of George H. Duncan and soon after their marriage in 1871 the Ripley firm soon took on George Duncan's family name. Augustus was appointed to be in charge of sales for this new firm and he stayed with the firm for twenty-three years. George H. Duncan & Sons was to later become the now familiar concern of "Duncan & Miller."

Towards the end of his tenure with the company, George H. Duncan & Sons merged with the conglomerate U.S. Glass where Heisey held the title of commercial manager. In 1893 Heisey left U.S. Glass and pursued the mining business in Arizona for a few years. However, his desire to be in the glass business never left him and he traveled back east. In 1895, he began construction of his own factory in Newark, Ohio.

This was the beginning of the Heisey glass company that is highly respected among glass collectors today for their production of top quality elegant glassware. The innovative designs found on the beautifully pressed and cut pattern glass they manufactured are highly sought by collectors today. They had some of the best artisans employed to produce these items and their reputation is second to none.

Although successful for some sixty years, the company struggled to keep up their sales volume after the changing of consumer's tastes after World War II. With rising labor costs and outdated styles, they closed their doors in December 1957. Their moulds were purchased by the Imperial Glass Company and later by other parties, and there have been some reproductions from these Heisey moulds by other companies.

One of their most popular patterns during the early years of the 1940s was called "Lariat." It is generally believed that Lariat was created by Heisey to compete with the huge success of Imperial's "Candlewick" line of elegant glass. If this is true, then it worked to a large degree as Heisey had a difficult time making enough new Lariat moulds to fill the demand. This was partly due to the shortage of steel created by the restrictions on certain materials during the war.

They also had a great deal of success with various crystal animal figurines portrayed in whimsical poses. These stylistic animal figures are still very popular and command high prices across the line.

It is mainly these two patterns, Lariat and the animal figurines, that will occasionally surface with Charleton decorations.

Group Shot of Heisey Crystal Lariat pieces with Charleton decorations. All items are described in detail below. Note that the decoration on all pieces with the exception of the fan vase is enameled. *Authors' collection.*

Heisey #1540 Lariat crystal 14" sandwich plate. Charleton Roses decoration, c. 1942-1957. $75-85. *Authors' collection.*

Heisey #1540 Lariat crystal 6" covered candy box, loop and leaf finial. Charleton Roses decoration, c. 1942-1957. $85-90. Scarce. *Authors' collection.*

151

Heisey #1540 Lariat crystal 8" bowl, straight-sided, 2.5" high. Charleton Roses decoration, c. 1942-1957. $140-150. Scarce. *Authors' collection.*

Heisey #1540 Lariat crystal 4.5" cigarette box. Charleton Roses decoration, c. 1942-1957. $75-85. *Authors' collection.*

Heisey #1540 Lariat crystal cologne bottle, 8" tall with stopper. Charleton Roses decoration, c. 1942-1957. $140-150. Scarce. *Authors' collection.*

Heisey #1540 Lariat crystal 4" ashtray or nut dish. Charleton Roses decoration, c. 1942-1957. $25-30. *Authors' collection.*

Heisey #1540 Crystal 8" Lariat hurricane lamp. Charleton Roses decoration, c. 1942-1957. $195-225. Scarce. *Courtesy of Helen & Steve Klemko.*

Heisey #1183 (398) Revere crystal 5" bowl, star ground bottom. Charleton Leaf and Bands decoration, c. 1942-1957. Interior is painted green. AWCO Charleton label #751. Marked with the Heisey diamond logo. $30-35. Scarce. *Authors' collection.*

Heisey #1183 (398) Revere crystal 5" bowl, star ground bottom. Charleton Ebony Whirl decoration, c. 1952. Note the Lacquer Red painted bottom. Marked with the Heisey diamond logo. $30-35. Scarce. *Authors' collection.*

Heisey #1540 Lariat crystal satin finished 7" fan vase. Charleton Floral and Lattice decoration, c. 1942-1957. AWCO Charleton label #4948. $65-75. Rare. *Authors' collection.*

Heisey Crystal 12" Ring Neck Pheasant, size #1. Charleton Naturalistic decoration, c. 1942-1955. AWCO Charleton label #4437. $225-250. Rare. *Courtesy of Barbara Wojcik.*

Kemple Glass Company

It is only recently that several items of Kemple milk glass with Charleton decorations have come to light. Although there are a number of milk glass Charleton decorated items that we suspect to be from Kemple, we have not yet been able to positively attribute these items.

John and Geraldine Kemple were a very successful husband and wife team that produced a wide range of glassware from 1945 to 1970. Most of this glassware was from old moulds that they acquired from defunct glass companies. Although Kemple produced a wide variety of items in a rainbow of colors, their opaque white (milk glass) is what they were best known for, and it is the only color that has been found with Charleton decorations.

Since many of these moulds date from the turn of the twentieth century, you may sometimes find Charleton decorated pieces being touted as Victorian items. These moulds originally came from a variety of older companies, but they were purchased by Kemple Glass in the mid-1940s from the Mannington Art Glass Company in Mannington, West Virginia. These moulds were not produced by Mannington, but were obtained from Gillinder and Ditheridge, glass companies that operated around the turn of the twentieth century.

Many of the items made from these moulds found with Charleton decorations incorporate scrollwork in the pattern which is often traced with gold leaf accents. Only the more traditional floral decorations by AWCO have been found on these Kemple pieces. Due to the limited number of items that have turned up, it is believed that Kemple Glass was not a big supplier to AWCO.

Kemple also decorated their own glassware and some of it is very close to AWCO's style of decorating. Their use of pink roses can be very confusing and only time will help us sort out the subtle differences. Kemple even used a "Hand Painted" black ink stamp similar to the one that AWCO also used, so you must proceed with caution when purchasing these items.

An essential guide in identifying Kemple glass is the book entitled *Kemple Glass 1945-1970* by John R. Burkeholder and D. Thomas O'Connor. The photographs and reprints in this book are very useful and we relied upon them exclusively for the captions on our Kemple items.

Kemple #6 Heavy Scroll 9" Milk Glass decanter. Charleton Roses decoration, c. 1945-1950s. AWCO Charleton label #4671. Green initials "gc" on bottom. $50-60. *Authors' collection.*

Kemple #43 Milk Glass 4.5" heart-shaped pin tray. Charleton Roses decoration, c. 1945-1950s. Made from original Mannington mould. $35-45. *Authors' Collection.*

Kemple #54 Cabbage Rose Milk Glass 6" oval covered jewel box. Charleton Roses decoration, c. 1945-1950s. AWCO Charleton label #4833. $30-35. *Authors' collection.*

Milk Glass Canasta Set ashtrays (Club is missing). Period advertisements show these types of sets offered by Biberthaler, Kemple, and Lornita. Charleton Roses decoration on the Diamond; Charleton Roses and Bows decoration on the Heart; and roses (no gold) decoration on the Spade, probably Lornita decoration, c. 1940s-1950s. AWCO Charleton label #4050 on the Diamond. $15-20 each if Charleton decorated. *Authors' collection.*

Kemple #12 Fleur de Lis Milk Glass 4" powder box. Charleton Roses decoration, c. 1945-1950s. $30-35. Authors' collection.

Two Kemple #204A Maple Leaf Milk Glass 6.5" plates. Embossed Maple Leaf over-painted with Charleton Open Roses decoration, c. 1945-1950s. AWCO Charleton label #4397B. $25-30 each. Scarce. Authors' collection.

Imperial

Very few pieces of Imperial have been found to date with Charleton decorations. This would seem to indicate that AWCO purchased very few blanks from Imperial. However, since this subject has yet to be fully researched, later uncovered facts may prove this to be incorrect.

The Imperial Glass Company was founded in 1901 by Edward Muhleman, an ex-riverboat captain. Muhleman had many years' experience as a director, manager, and investor in glass companies. His aim was to build a very large, modern glass manufacturer close to the river in Bellaire, Ohio. There were so many other glass companies in this area already that Bellaire was known as "Glass City." After three years of planning and building, the Imperial Glass Company opened in 1904. Within a few months the company became a major player in the glass industry in the U.S.

Starting with clear glass in an extensive range of new tableware and imitation cut designs, Imperial moved on to colored glass and carnival glass in 1909. The early Imperial trademarks were Nuart and Nucut.

Along with most other glass companies of the day, Imperial produced great quantities of Milk Glass in the 1940s and 1950s. While only one piece of Imperial made, Charleton decorated Milk Glass has been found to date, it would stand to reason that more does exist.

Perhaps the best known Imperial pattern is their Line #400, Candlewick. Produced from 1936 until 1984, Candlewick pieces can be found in virtually every color that Imperial made. An easy pattern to identify, Candlewick pieces feature beads all along their edges. We have found only one Candlewick item with a Charleton decoration, although certainly more does exist.

Imperial bought the assets of the A. H. Heisey glassworks in 1958, and two years later, those of the Cambridge Glass Company. This brought hundreds of moulds for some very successful lines into Imperial, and they continued to produce them as "Heisey by Imperial" and "Cambridge by Imperial." There is no evidence so far to suggest that any of these Imperial/Heisey or Imperial/Cambridge pieces were bought by AWCO for decoration.

Imperial #1950/486, 8.5" Milk Glass "Masque" vase. Unknown decorator but several design elements point to Charleton, c. 1950s. Originally made by Vallerysthall and called "Mephistopheles." $75-85. Scarce. Authors' Collection.

Imperial #1950/486 Milk Glass 8.5" "Masque" vase. Profile.

Imperial Candlewick #400/51T, 6" crystal center handled wafer tray. Charleton Raspberry decoration, c. 1940s-1950s. $45-55. Scarce. *Authors' Collection.*

Indiana Glass Company of Dunkirk, Indiana

Indiana Glass Crystal 8" salad bowl. Charleton Ivory Bands decoration, c. 1950s. AWCO Charleton label #790. Insufficient data to price. Scarce. *Authors' collection.*

Indiana Glass #158 Flowered Medallion crystal 8" swan. Charleton Roses decoration, c. 1940s-1950s. $100-125. Rare. *Authors' collection.*

Fostoria

Fostoria Colony 13" crystal torte plate. Charleton Roses decoration, enamel paint, c. 1940s-1950s. $40-50. em:*Authors' collection.*

West Virginia Specialty Glass

West Virginia Specialty Glass Company #22, 10" crystal footed compote. Charleton Black Spatter with Gold Bands decoration. AWCO Charleton label #2123. $100-125. Rare. *Authors' Collection.*

U.S. Glass/Tiffin

West Virginia Specialty Glass Company #22, 10" crystal footed compote. Shown for size perspective.

Tiffin #20047, 8 pint, 15" crystal "Dakota" Globe (apothecary) Jar. Charleton Enamel Overlay in Soft Green decoration, c. 1953. AWCO Charleton label #1605. $500-600. Rare. *Authors' Collection*.

Far left: West Virginia Specialty Glass Company #106, 12" crystal footed vase. Charleton Latticed Roses decoration. $50-65. Scarce. *Authors' Collection*.

Left: West Virginia Specialty Glass Company #106, 12" crystal footed vase. Charleton Gold Roses decoration. $50-65. Scarce. *Authors' Collection*.

West Virginia Glass Specialty Company crystal and satin 6" "What Not" server, hand-wrought handle. Charleton Lattice Roses and Circles decoration, c. 1950s. $50-65. Scarce. *Authors' Collection*.

West Virginia Specialty Glass Company #535, 13" crystal footed candy jar. Charleton Enamel Overlay in Soft Green decoration, c. 1953. AWCO Charleton label #1647. $400-500. Rare. *Authors' Collection*.

West Virginia Specialty Glass Company 6.75" crystal vase. Charleton Enamel Overlay in Soft Green decoration, c. 1953. AWCO Charleton label #1644. $60-75. Rare. *Authors' Collection*.

Dunbar Turquoise Milk Glass 8" rectangular vase. Profile. *Authors' collection*.

Dunbar

New Martinsville/Viking

Dunbar Turquoise Milk Glass 8" rectangular vase. Charleton Ivory Fern decoration, c. 1951. AWCO Charleton label #971. $100-125. Rare. *Authors' collection*.

New Martinsville/Viking 9" crystal rooster bookend made from New Martinsville mould #668. Charleton Naturalistic decoration, c. 1942. AWCO Charleton label #4482. $75-100. Rare. *Authors' collection*.

Italian Porcelain and Ceramics

The following Italian pieces were identified through the assistance of Maurizio Burlamacchi (see the AWCO chapter for more about him and his relationship to AWCO). At this point in time we will not elaborate upon these Italian manufacturers. Once we have acquired enough documentation of new Charleton pieces from these firms then we will make it available to readers.

Group shot of three Ceramiche Corte of Bassano del Grappa pieces. Right to left: 7" candy box, AWCO Charleton label #3859; 8" dresser box, AWCO Charleton label #3857; 6" dresser jar AWCO Charleton label #3858. Insufficient data to price. *Authors' Collection.*

Ceramiche Corte dresser jar. Top detail. *Authors' Collection.*

Group shot of two Ceramiche Corte pieces. Right to left: 6" dresser jar, 8" dresser box. Note the Greek Key design around the upper portion of each. *Authors' Collection.*

Ceramiche Corte dresser jar. Bottom detail. Rectangular label is manufacturer's label. Handwritten under glaze is "Made in Italy". *Authors' Collection.*

Ronzan of Bassano del Grappa, Italy, porcelain Dog, 11" high by 13" long. "Italy" stamped in black on the bottom. Facial "fur" and tail are "spaghetti" ware typical of some Italian porcelain. We have named him "Luigi". AWCO Charleton #4200AB, c. 1950s. $150-175. Rare. *Authors' Collection.*

Ars of Sesto Fiorenrtino, Italy, porcelain 8" rectangular dresser box. Charleton Florentine Cherubs decoration. AWCO Charleton label #3442. Handwritten under the glaze is "AWC 3442 Italy". $125-145. Rare. *Authors' collection.*

Ars of Sesto Fiorenrtino, Italy, porcelain 8" rectangular dresser box. Lid. *Authors' collection.*

Ars of Sesto Fiorenrtino, Italy, porcelain 8" rectangular dresser box. Bottom view showing markings. *Authors' collection.*

Limoges

Limoges porcelain is known world-wide for the quality of the porcelain that has come from this region in France over several hundred years. Although we have identified only one factory as a supplier to AWCO, more and more examples of Charleton on Limoges marked porcelains are being found. It is not uncommon for American decorated Limoges to have marks that bear no other symbols than the words "Limoges France."

A detailed explanation of these wares and their respective marks can be found in Mary Frank Gaston's *Collector's Encyclopedia of Limoges Porcelain, Third Edition*. The marks and their numbering system referred to herein are from Ms. Gaston's book.

This dragon handled vase with a Charleton label and Oriental decoration is in the category of American Limoges decorated white ware and has the "Limoges, France" underglaze stamp, identified as Mark #6. The Pouyat firm is one of the oldest names connected with the Limoges porcelain industry. This mark is often found on American hand painted blanks. The earliest production date using this mark would have 1891. The Pouyat Company was famous for its blanks, or white wares, and would therefore have been an able supplier for AWCO.

The Pouyat firm changed hands several times over the years and after World War I, circa 1920, the company, then called Guerin-Pouyat, was purchased by Bawo-Dotter, an American china importer (principally importing Limoges) in New York City. After this final sale the name of the company then became Guerin-Pouyat-Elite. The individual marks of all three companies were used until 1932 when the firm closed its doors for good. This puts the latest production date for this Pouyat vase at 1932 and this time frame would fit nicely with the estimated 1927 start up date of AWCO.

There is a possibility that AWCO may have purchased these Pouyat blanks after the plant had closed, so the actual decoration date could be later. This likelihood will have to await verification pending the surfacing of the AWCO records. However, there has been no evidence uncovered to date that AWCO decorated items for a substantial time after their initial manufacturing date.

An identical picture of this vase is shown on page 404, plate #1032, in Mary Frank Gaston's, *Collector's Encyclopedia of Limoges Porcelain, Third Edition*. This vase is also

Limoges Porcelain 8" tall dragon handled vase. Designed by Jean Pouyat; made by Bawo-Dotter. Charleton Oriental Fisherman decoration, c. 1920-1930 for vase; decoration date is unknown. AWCO Charleton #8262. Marked "Limoges France" in green (Mark 6)[9]. $500-600. Rare. *Authors' Collection.*

marked with the Limoges Mark #6 and in her book there is no mention of a Charleton label. Two other examples of this vase with different decorations are pictured in this book, but they have the Pouyat Mark #5 and are not believed by these authors to be AWCO items.

Limoges Porcelain dresser set consisting of one 4" covered dresser box and two 5" pin trays. Charleton Blue Mist and Roses decoration, c. 1940s-1950s. AWCO Charleton label #8005 on box and #8001 on trays. Each piece is marked "Limoges France" and has the black ink stamp "Hand Painted". Dresser box has "72" embossed on the bottom. $125-150. Scarce. *Authors' Collection.*

Limoges Porcelain dresser box. Detail of bottom. *Authors' Collection.*

Limoges Porcelain 8" tall dragon handled vase. Detail of decoration. *Authors' Collection.*

Limoges 2.25" teacup and saucer. Charleton Ivy decoration. AWCO Charleton label #8023B. Limoges Mark #2 and Mark #6.[9] "Hand Painted" black ink stamp on bottom. Initial "D" in green on both pieces. $45-50 set. Rare. *Authors' Collection.*

Limoges 2.25" teacup and saucer. Detail of decoration on cup.

Limoges 2.25" teacup and saucer. Limoges back stamp on cup.

Castel Limoges Porcelain 8" swan-handled vase. Vase is actually two pieces with the base having been bolted on. Unknown decorator. Note the similarities between this vase and the Limoges swan-handled vase in the AWCO *Gift and Art Buyer* advertisement of September 1947 (see Advertisements section). *Authors' collection.*

Amoges

Not much is known about the Amoges China Company. The manufacturer was located in Trenton, New Jersey, and operated from about 1944 to 1948. Amoges made vases, dishes, candy boxes, jars, perfume bottles, and flowerpots. They also had an in-house decorating department and decorated many of their wares. Amoges has been referred to by some as "fake Limoges," but we do not find this to be a credible statement. If the company were trying to produce counterfeit Limoges Porcelain they would not have put their own company mark on the items they made – they would have utilized some type of Limoges marking. While not all Amoges pieces are marked, many are and there is no evidence to support the theory that the company marked their items with anything other than their own name.

Several decorated porcelain pieces shown in this book are believed to be Amoges. Empirical evidence suggests that AWCO did purchase and decorate Amoges blanks with Charleton decorations. Most notable are the nautically theme cologne bottles. We have found a bottle marked Amoges which is almost identical to the Charleton labeled bottles. A photograph showing these two bottles together follows. The composition of the porcelain from known Amoges pieces is similar, if not identical, to some Charleton labeled pieces, leading us to believe these items to have been made by Amoges as well. This is the basis for our suspected attributions.

Schumann

Amoges Porcelain 5" pin tray. Marked "Amoges Hand Painted". Possible Charleton decoration. NP. *Authors' collection.*

Schumann China 11" plate. Charleton Guinea Hen decoration. AWCO Charleton label #1007A. Marked on bottom "Schumann Bavaria Germany U.S. Zone". Only Charleton decoration on Schumann known to date. Insufficient data to price. *Authors' Collection.*

Schumann China 11" plate. Back detail showing Schumann mark and Charleton label.

marked with the Limoges Mark #6 and in her book there is no mention of a Charleton label. Two other examples of this vase with different decorations are pictured in this book, but they have the Pouyat Mark #5 and are not believed by these authors to be AWCO items.

Limoges Porcelain dresser set consisting of one 4" covered dresser box and two 5" pin trays. Charleton Blue Mist and Roses decoration, c. 1940s-1950s. AWCO Charleton label #8005 on box and #8001 on trays. Each piece is marked "Limoges France" and has the black ink stamp "Hand Painted". Dresser box has "72" embossed on the bottom. $125-150. Scarce. *Authors' Collection*.

Limoges Porcelain dresser box. Detail of bottom. *Authors' Collection*.

Limoges Porcelain 8" tall dragon handled vase. Detail of decoration. *Authors' Collection*.

Limoges 2.25" teacup and saucer. Charleton Ivy decoration. AWCO Charleton label #8023B. Limoges Mark #2 and Mark #6.[9] "Hand Painted" black ink stamp on bottom. Initial "D" in green on both pieces. $45-50 set. Rare. *Authors' Collection*.

Limoges 2.25" teacup and saucer. Detail of decoration on cup.

Limoges 2.25" teacup and saucer. Limoges back stamp on cup.

Castel Limoges Porcelain 8" swan-handled vase. Vase is actually two pieces with the base having been bolted on. Unknown decorator. Note the similarities between this vase and the Limoges swan-handled vase in the AWCO *Gift and Art Buyer* advertisement of September 1947 (see Advertisements section). Authors' collection.

Schumann

Schumann China 11" plate. Charleton Guinea Hen decoration. AWCO Charleton label #1007A. Marked on bottom "Schumann Bavaria Germany U.S. Zone". Only Charleton decoration on Schumann known to date. Insufficient data to price. *Authors' Collection.*

Schumann China 11" plate. Back detail showing Schumann mark and Charleton label.

Amoges

Not much is known about the Amoges China Company. The manufacturer was located in Trenton, New Jersey, and operated from about 1944 to 1948. Amoges made vases, dishes, candy boxes, jars, perfume bottles, and flowerpots. They also had an in-house decorating department and decorated many of their wares. Amoges has been referred to by some as "fake Limoges," but we do not find this to be a credible statement. If the company were trying to produce counterfeit Limoges Porcelain they would not have put their own company mark on the items they made – they would have utilized some type of Limoges marking. While not all Amoges pieces are marked, many are and there is no evidence to support the theory that the company marked their items with anything other than their own name.

Several decorated porcelain pieces shown in this book are believed to be Amoges. Empirical evidence suggests that AWCO did purchase and decorate Amoges blanks with Charleton decorations. Most notable are the nautically theme cologne bottles. We have found a bottle marked Amoges which is almost identical to the Charleton labeled bottles. A photograph showing these two bottles together follows. The composition of the porcelain from known Amoges pieces is similar, if not identical, to some Charleton labeled pieces, leading us to believe these items to have been made by Amoges as well. This is the basis for our suspected attributions.

Amoges Porcelain 5" pin tray. Marked "Amoges Hand Painted". Possible Charleton decoration. NP. *Authors' collection.*

Chapter 8.
Unknown Decorations on Items by Unknown Manufacturers

Porcelain Pig, 15.5" long by 10" high. Suspected to be Wemyss of England??? Suspected Charleton decoration. We have named her "Rosie." NP. *Authors' collection.*

Cased (overlay) glass 10.5" lustre. Unknown manufacturer and decorator. Possibly Bohemian. Decoration is very similar to Charleton. Compare this to the AWCO *Gift and Art Buyer* advertisement of March 1955, shown in the Advertisements section. NP. *Authors' collection.*

Ruby-stained cut crystal thumbprint 12.5" vase. Detail of decoration.

Ruby-stained cut crystal thumbprint 12.5" vase. Unknown manufacturer and decorator. Possibly Bohemian. Decoration is hand painted but probably not AWCO. NP. *Authors' collection.*

Cased (overlay) glass 6" enameled candy box. Made in West Germany, US Zone. Unknown manufacturer and decorator. Decoration is very similar to Charleton. Compare this to the Charleton decorated candy box shown on page 140. NP. *Authors' collection.*

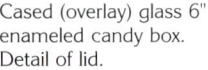

Cased (overlay) glass 6" enameled candy box. Detail of lid.

Emerald Green 7" crystal covered candy box. Unknown manufacturer and decorator but suspected to be Charleton. Gold work on this piece is very similar to Charleton Maze. The overall design is also quite indicative of a Charleton "Modern" decoration. NP. *Authors' collection.*

Colony cased (overlay) glass 6" candy box. Made in Czechoslovakia. Unknown decoration. Decoration is very similar to Charleton. Compare this to the Charleton decorated candy box shown on page 140. NP. *Authors' collection.*

Colony cased (overlay) glass 6" candy box. Top view.

Emerald Green 7" covered candy box. Lid detail.

Crystal and Satin 7.5" wedding bowl. Thought to be Jeanette Glass[10]. Suspected Charleton Decoration. NP. *Authors' collection.*

Crystal and Satin 8.25" amber-stained vase. Side view.

Crystal and Satin 7.5" wedding bowl. Detail.

China 3.5" Wedding Bowl creamer and sugar. Unknown manufacturer – possibly Shenango. Unknown decorator – Beth Weissman suspected. NP. *Authors' collection.*

Crystal and Satin 8.25" amber-stained vase. Possibly Czech. Decoration has some design elements similar to Charleton but a definitive attribution cannot be made at this time. NP. *Authors' collection.*

Crystal 3.75" powder box. Possibly U.S. Glass. Reverse painted with Chinese Yellow, roses, and gold pin stripes on the exterior. Possible Charleton decoration. NP. *Authors' collection.*

Chapter 9.
Similarities and Identification

Labels

The most certain indication of a Charleton item is of course its label. There are three known types of labels that may appear on Charleton items.

The first label mentioned is the standard Navy Blue and Gold foil label. This label will be by far the most commonly found. Some of these labels may be found with the Navy Blue portions considerably lighter in color than is normally seen. It is not known at this time if this lighter coloration is actually a differently inked label or if it is from the ravages of time and moisture.

Sometimes the label number will have faded so badly that it cannot be easily read. However, the foil surface is soft and a pencil lead impression left on the surface will often aid in determining the number. By using low power magnification and tilting the label obliquely under a strong light the number can often be discerned.

There have been times when we have examined pieces that had only a remnant of the original label. If what label remains are not readily identified as a Charleton label then look closer to see if there are the tell-tale signs of what was once the oval shape. Sometimes the adhesive residue will still remain and the oval outline it produces is fairly distinct to AWCO.

AWCO Navy Blue and Gold foil standard label. The most commonly found Charleton label. The Navy Blue portion may sometimes appear much lighter in color.

The second label is made from unbleached paper and is beige in color. As shown in the accompanying pictures there are other differences besides the color and the absence of a foil surface. The paper label has two mustard colored stars on either side of the space for the hand written number. There is also the placement of a mustard color oval border that is quite distinctive. The typeface is the same, but it is slightly smaller in size.

Unfortunately the surface of this label is not well suited for preserving the label number and it will usually be worn to the point of being unreadable.

The beige paper label is very scarce and to date we have only seen a small handful. They will almost always be found on porcelain items that appear to be imports.

The third and final label that we have found is a unique rectangular label that was found on a lamp constructed almost entirely of metal. It was described by the seller as being an Eames lamp, but we have not been able to verify this statement.

The label was very difficult to locate and was finally found inside the metal collar adjacent the socket for the light bulb. The label was almost indecipherable due to its poor condition and awkward placement. With a strong light and magnification we were able to read most of the word "Charleton" and below that the name "Wasserberg".

The label is made of paper, light in color, and is one and one half inches long by one inch wide. This rare label is the only example we have documented to date. That being said, it may be due to the small number of Charleton lamps we have been able to own or examine. Perhaps in time this label will be less scarce as more Charleton lamps are identified and examined.

Ink Stamps

The next best thing to a Charleton label is the black ink stamp that denotes the item as being "Hand Painted". This ink stamp can be found in conjunction with the Charleton label, but often as not it remains intact and the foil label does not. You must become familiar with the size and typeface of this ink stamp to avoid confusion with marks found from other decorators.

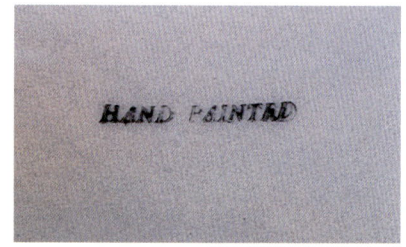

AWCO black ink stamp "Hand Painted". While finding any ink stamp is difficult, this is the more commonly found of the two.

The one we have seen that may cause the most trouble is the mark found on many Kemple milk glass items. Their mark is larger and in block type letters and the AWCO mark is smaller and the block letters are slanted to the right.

This mark will appear on the glass and ceramic items from many different companies. You will most often find it on Cambridge, Consolidated, Fenton, Westmoreland, and Limoges porcelain.

This ink stamp will often be considerably worn and you may only be able to see traces of it left. Avoid rubbing or washing this mark as it is not fired on and can be easily obliterated.

AWCO Beige paper label. Very scarce label. Most often found on porcelain items. Note the mustard color ink and the addition of two stars.

The only other ink mark we have documented is a triangular blue stamp. The outline of the triangle is inverted and the top line is the longest at .75 inches in length. Along this top line appear the words "Hand Painted" that are printed in small block letters and inside the triangle are the abbreviations "A.W.CO." and "U.S.A.". All of this appears in a medium blue about the shade of the ink found in a ballpoint pen.

This stamp is rarely seen and we have documented only two examples to date, both of which were found on Westmoreland rectangular pin trays.

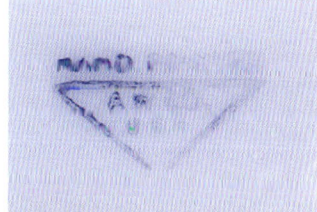

AWCO triangular blue ink stamp. Rarely seen. Only two examples documented with this stamp to date.

Charleton Roses & Bows decoration on Consolidated Regent vase.

Artists' Initials

Sometimes all you will have to rely on for identification besides the decoration is the placement of painted initials. Most often underneath the piece, the initials come in a variety of forms. Found in different colors of paint and in gold leaf, the color of the initials indicates which artist did the china paint and which artist did the gold leaf. Sometimes instead of initials there will be cryptic numbers, one or two digits, and usually in gold leaf.

This type of marking is not unique to AWCO, but in the loosely defined parameters that typify the Charleton candidates, it is distinctive. Although the china paint marks are fired on for permanence the gold leaf is easily removed so exercise caution when cleaning. These initials are most often found on Cambridge items although it is not unusual to find them on Fenton, Consolidated, and others. Very rarely will you find the decorator's initials next to the decoration and we have only documented three items with Charleton labels that appear this way.

Beth Weissman Roses & Bows decoration on Fenton #192 Silver Crest vase. Note the color of the roses, the three gold "teardrops" over the top of the rose, and the straight border on the garland - all unique to BWCO.

Unknown violets decoration on Fenton Hobnail bonbon. Very possibly AWCO but no pieces with labels, decorator marks, or ink stamps have been reported to date. Note the Charleton-like gold "stars".

Charleton Roses & Bows decoration on Fenton #192 cologne.

Charleton Roses & Bows decoration on Fenton #93 puff box (or candy box if not found with cologne bottles).

Fenton in-house decoration "Violet in the Snow", circa 1968. Note the absence of gold leaf.

Chapter 10.
Advertisements

In this chapter we have placed a series of Abels, Wasserberg & Company advertisements. These advertisements cover a period of seventeen years, from 1943 to 1960, and they nicely capture the trends of the giftware market throughout this time period. They are arranged chronologically from the earliest to the latest and most of them appear here in full page layout just as they were found.

None of the advertisements were printed in color and they were all found in trade journals rather than in home furnishing magazines for the consumer. The advertisements are quite revealing in that they portray both domestic items and imports. Most of the imports are from France, Italy, or the Orient.

There are many items and decorations in these advertisements that have never been documented. We felt the need to publish these advertisements not only for their inherent artistic merits, but for collector's research purposes as well. Whatever the purpose you use them for, we hope you enjoy them and that they enhance your appreciation of Charleton.

October 1943, *China and Glass* advertisement. A smorgasbord of items from Fenton, Cambridge, Limoges, Heisey, and other unidentified suppliers. AWCO had only been decorating in their own studio for about a year when this ad came out.

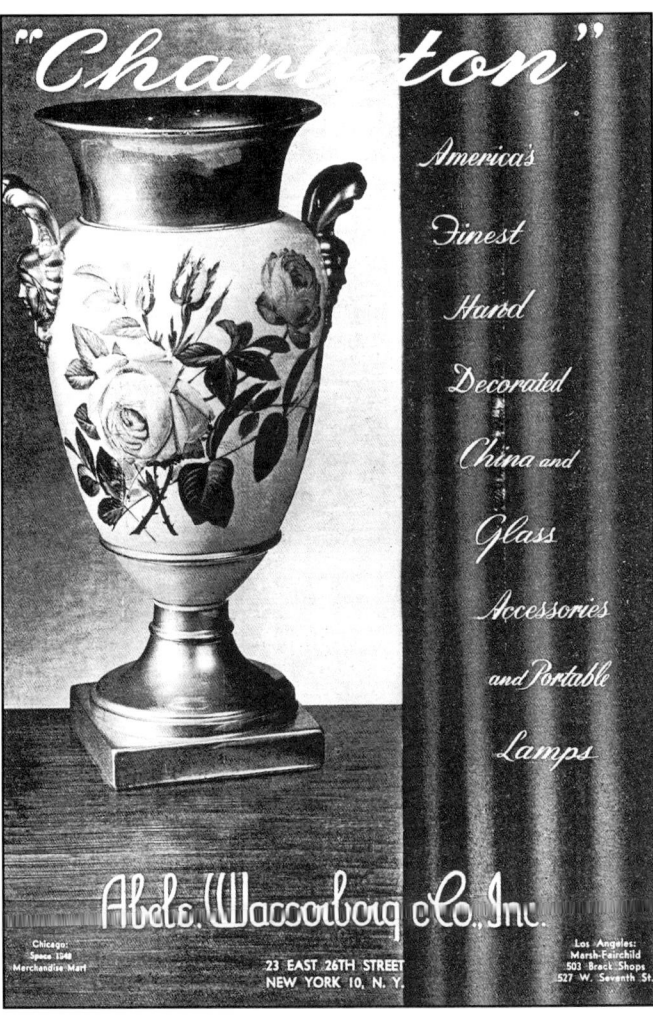

March 1946, *The Gift and Art Buyer*. Note the "face" in the handles. Suspected manufacturer is Limoges.

April 1946, *The Gift and Art Buyer*.

September 1947, *The Gift and Art Buyer*. Thought to be Limoges. See Chapter 7, page 162.

June 1947, *The Gift and Art Buyer*.

January 1948, *The Gift and Art Buyer*.

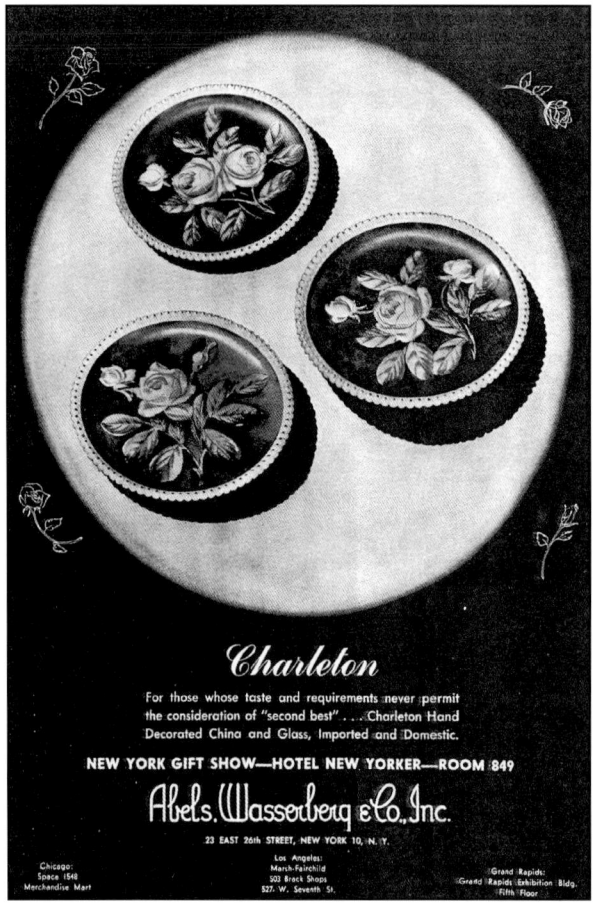

February 1948, *The Gift and Art Buyer.*

November 1948, *The Gift and Art Buyer.*

May 1948, *The Gift and Art Buyer.*

July 1949, *The Gift and Art Buyer.* Manufacturer thought to be Indiana Glass.

January 1950, *The Gift and Art Buyer*. The rectangular dresser boxes are Limoges.

August 1950, *The Gift and Art Buyer*.

June 1950, *The Gift and Art Buyer*. Consolidated cylinder vases.

October 1950, *The Gift and Art Buyer*.

November 1950, *The Gift and Art Buyer*.

August 1951, *The Gift and Art Buyer*.

February 1951, *The Gift and Art Buyer*.

September 1951, *The Gift and Art Buyer*.

January 1952, *The Gift and Art Buyer*.

September 1952, *The Gift and Art Buyer*.

September 1952, *China, Glass and Decorative Accessories*.

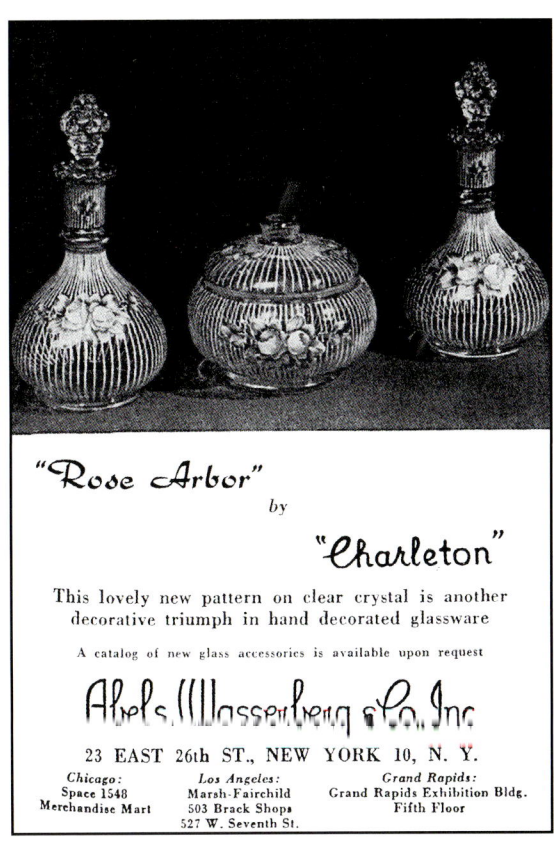
December 1952, *China, Glass and Decorative Accessories*. This decoration has never been reported.

July 1953, *China, Glass and Decorative Accessories*.

March 1954, *The Gift and Art Buyer*.

December 1953, *The Gift and Art Buyer*.

April 1952, *The Crockery & Glass Journal*.

1953, *The Crockery & Glass Journal*.

June 1954, *The Crockery & Glass Journal*.

February 1955, *The Gift and Art Buyer*.

March 1955, *The Gift and Art Buyer*.

October 1955, *The Gift and Art Buyer*.

December 1955, *The Gift and Art Buyer*.

January 1956, *The Gift and Art Buyer*.

May 1956, *The Gift and Art Buyer*.

September 1956, *The Gift and Art Buyer*.

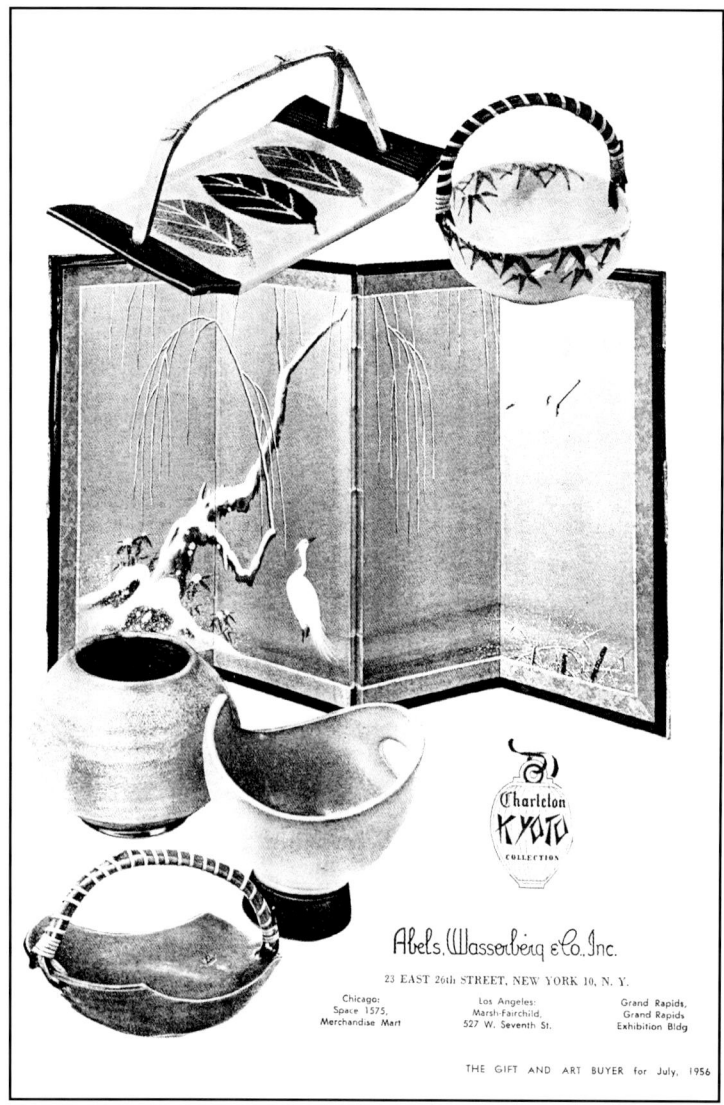

July 1956, *The Gift and Art Buyer*.

December 1956, *The Gift and Art Buyer*.

April 1957, *The Gift and Art Buyer*.

August 1957, *The Gift and Art Buyer*.

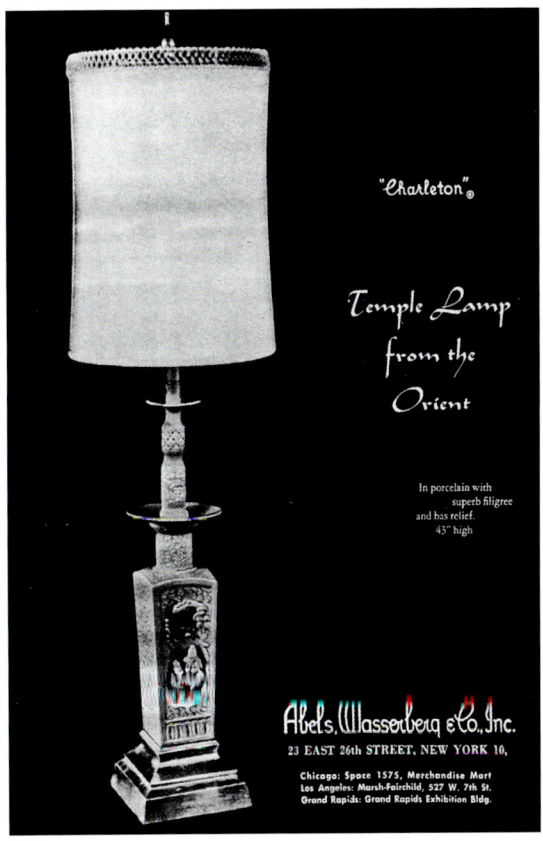

January 1959, *The Gift and Art Buyer*.

April 1959, *The Gift and Art Buyer*.

February 1959, *The Gift and Art Buyer*.

July 1959, *The Gift and Art Buyer*.

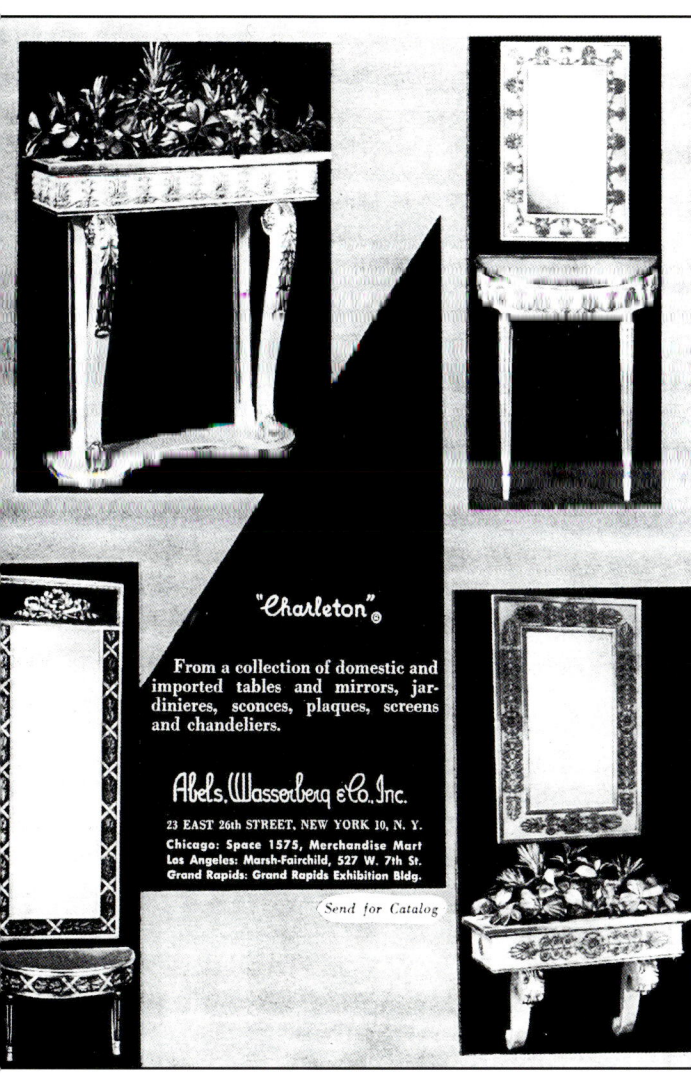

October 1959, *The Gift and Art Buyer*.

December 1959, *The Gift and Art Buyer*.

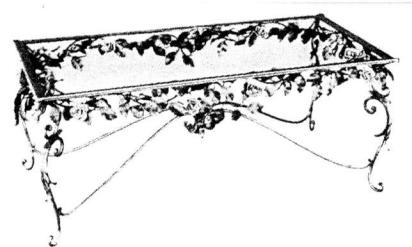

March 1960, *The Gift and Art Buyer.*

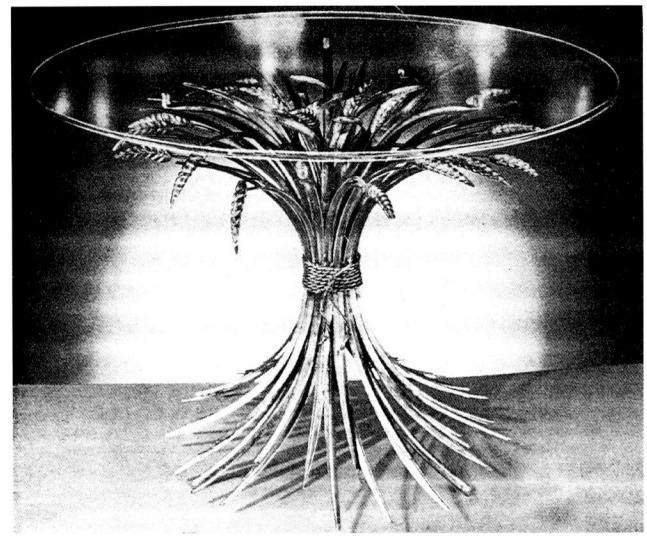

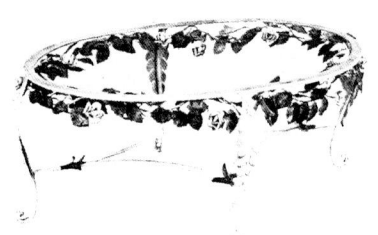

April 1960, *The Gift and Art Buyer.*

Endnotes

Text

1. We have not found any mention of who or what Guthman-Solomon was, but odds are it was a company involved in the same type of business as AWCO.
2. Interestingly enough, Dr. James Measell, noted glass author, informed us that the Michigan Shop was actually operated by J. Stanley Brothers. He sold mostly antiques there but used the store's letterhead to obtain catalogs from various companies in order to advance his research.
3. The trademark for the Charleton name has expired.
4. The labels and ink stamps used are shown and discussed in detail in Chapter Nine – Identification and Similarities.
5. Jade green colored glass with a white opal glass crest.
6. A Ruby Snowcrest Top Hat can be seen on page 104 in the Fenton Art Glass Collectors of America's compilation entitled *Caught In The Butterfly Net*.
7. For those interested, the bottle is pictured on page 140, item number 1382, of Dr. James Measell's book *Fenton Glass The 1990s Decade*.
8. Although signatures of Charleton artists have been found on Consolidated glass, only Charleton artists' initials have been found on Fenton glass.
9. For details on these seventeen decorations, please consult page 158 of Jack Wilson's book *Phoenix & Consolidated Art Glass 1926 – 1980*.
10. See page 155 in *Phoenix & Consolidated Art Glass 1926 – 1980*.

Captions

1. Information on label numbers from Frank Fenton's "black book" detailing AWCO transactions.
2. AWCO occasionally used different label numbers for the same piece in different years. Depending on what year the piece was done, you may find a Charleton label with any of these numbers.
3. Although most collectors refer to this stopper as either "King's Crown" or "Crown," Frank Fenton says the proper name is "Coin Dot" because it was originally issued on Fenton's Coin Dot cologne bottles.
4. This is classified as "unknown" rather than Charleton for two reasons. First, note the different, lighter shade of green used for some of the leaves. Charleton Ivy decorations have only one color of green leaves. Second, and probably most important, is the lack of any gold paint in the decoration. It is highly atypical of a Charleton decoration not to contain gold.
5. Cambridge collectors coined the name "Chocolate Roses" for this decoration based on the coloring of the roses.
6. Since extremely rare items often sell privately with the sales price not reported publicly, determining an accurate market value is virtually impossible.
7. The only example of Charleton Green Mist decoration found on Cambridge to date.
8. Period trade advertisements suggest that DeLuxe was associated with, or a name used by, Rainbow.
9. Mark #6 is commonly found on American decorated Limoges pieces. Factory unknown.
10. See page 311, item 1854 of Measell's and Wiggins' book *Great American Glass of The Roaring 20s & Depression Era, Book 2*.

Selected Bibliography

This bibliography is not intended to be an all-inclusive, comprehensive record of every source consulted in writing this book. All major references have been included and, therefore, this bibliography should prove to be quite useful to those readers who wish additional information.

Books

Bredehoft, Neila and Tom. *Heisey Glass 1896-1957*. Paducah, Kentucky: Collector Books, 2001.

Burkholder, John R. and Thomas D. O'Connor. *Kemple Glass 1945-1970*. Marietta, Ohio: Antique Publications, 1997.

Coe, Debbie and Randy. *Elegant Glass: Early, Depression & Beyond*. Atglen, Pennsylvania: Schiffer Publishing, Ltd., 2001.

The Fenton Art Glass Collectors of America, Inc. *Caught in The Butterfly Net*. Williamston, West Virginia: Fenton Art Glass Collectors of America, Inc., 1991.

Florence, Gene. *Elegant Glassware of the Depression Era*. Paducah, Kentucky: Collector Books, 1999.

Gaston, Mary Frank. *Collector's Encyclopedia of Limoges Porcelain, Third Edition*. Paducah, Kentucky: Collector Books, 2000.

Heacock, William. *Fenton Glass The First Twenty-five Years*. Marietta, Ohio: Antique Publications, 1995.

___. *Fenton Glass The Second Twenty-five Years*. Marietta, Ohio: Antique Publications, 1995.

___. *Fenton Glass The Third Twenty-five Years*. Marietta, Ohio: Antique Publications, 1994.

Kovar, Lorraine. *Westmoreland Glass 1950-84*. Marietta, Ohio: Antique Publications, 1991.

___. *Westmoreland Glass 1950-84 Volume II*. Marietta, Ohio: Antique Publications, 1991.

___. *Westmoreland Glass Volume III 1888-1940*. Marietta, Ohio: Antique Publications, 1997.

Measell, James. *New Martinsville Glass 1900-44*. Marietta, Ohio: Antique Publications 1994.

Measell, James and Berry Wiggins. *Great American Glass Volume 1*. Marietta, Ohio: Antique Publications, 1998.

___. *Great American Glass. Volume 2*. Marietta, Ohio: Antique Publications, 2000.

National Cambridge Collectors, Inc. *Cambridge Glass Co. 1949-53*. Paducah, Kentucky: Collector Books, 1978.

___. *Cambridge Glass Co. 1930-34*. Paducah, Kentucky: Collector Books, 1976.

___. *Colors in Cambridge*. Paducah, Kentucky: Collector Books, 1984.

Newbound, Betty and Bill. *Collector's Encyclopedia of Milk Glass*. Paducah, Kentucky: Collector Books, 1995.

Piña, Leslie. *Depression Era Glass by Duncan*. Atglen, Pennsylvania: Schiffer Publishing, Ltd., 1999.

Walk, John. *The Big Book of Fenton Glass 1940-1970*. Atglen, Pennsylvania: Schiffer Publishing, Ltd., 2000.

___. *Fenton Glass Compendium 1940-1970*. Atglen, Pennsylvania: Schiffer Publishing, Ltd., 2001.

Wetzel-Tomalka, Mary M. *Candle The Jewel of Imperial Book II*. Marceline, Missouri: Walsworth Publishing Company, 1995.

Whitmyer, Kenn & Margaret. *Bedroom & Bathroom Glassware of The Depression Years*. Paducah, Kentucky: Collector Books, 1992.

___. *Fenton Art Glass Patterns 1939-1980*. Paducah, Kentucky: Collector Books, 1999.

___. *Fenton Art Glass Patterns 1907-1939*. Paducah, Kentucky: Collector Books, 1999.

Wilson, Chas. West. *Westmoreland Glass*. Paducah, Kentucky: Collector Books, 1996.

Wilson, Jack. *Phoenix & Consolidated Art Glass 1926-1980*. Marietta, Ohio: Antique Publications, 1989.

Catalogs and Archives

Cambridge Glass Co. *Company Catalogs*. Cambridge, Ohio: Cambridge Glass Company.

Corning Glass Museum. *Archival material and microfiche*. Corning, New York: Corning Glass Museum, 2001.

Fenton Art Glass Company. *Company catalogs*. Williamstown, West Virginia: Fenton Art Glass Co., 1942-1970.

Magazine Articles and Trade Publications

China and Glass, various issues.
China, Glass and Decorative Accessories, various issues.
China, Glass and Lamps, various issues.
China, Glass and Pottery, various issues.
China, Glass and Tablewares, various issues.
Crockery and Glass Journal, various issues.
The Fenton Flyer, various issues.
The Gift and Art Buyer, various issues.
Gift and Tableware Reporter, various issues.

Heacock, William. "Those Confusing Mold Transfers," *The Glass Collector,* Issue Number 2, Spring 1982, 16-17.

___. "Miscellaneous Consolidated and Phoenix Glass," *Collecting Glass, Volume 3*, 1986, 14.

___. "Milk Glass Tableware 1885 to 1955," *Collecting Glass,* Volume 3, 1986, 66-70.